WOMEN WRITERS
IN TWENTIETH-CENTURY
SPAIN AND SPANISH AMERICA

WOMEN WRITERS IN TWENTIETH-CENTURY SPAIN AND SPANISH AMERICA

Edited by

Catherine Davies

The Edwin Mellen Press
Lewiston/Queenston/Lampeter

Library of Congress Cataloging-in-Publication Data

Women writers in twentieth-century Spain and Spanish America / edited
by Catherine Davies.
     p.   cm.
    Includes bibliographical references.
    ISBN 0-88946-423-5
    1. Spanish literature--Women authors--History and criticism.
2. Spanish American literature--Women authors--History and
criticism. 3. Spanish literature--20th century--History and
criticism. 4. Spanish American literature--20th century--History
and criticism. I. Davies, Catherine, 1952- .
PQ6055.W65 1993
860.9'9287--dc20   92-46176
                                                CIP

A CIP catalog record for this book
is available from the British Library.

All rights reserved. For information contact

The Edwin Mellen Press   The Edwin Mellen Press
Box 450   Box 67
Lewiston, New York   Queenston, Ontario
USA 14092   CANADA L0S 1L0

Edwin Mellen Press, Ltd.
Lampeter, Dyfed, Wales
UNITED KINGDOM SA48 7DY

Printed in the United States of America

for Sarah, Ana and Tom

Contents

Acknowledgements   vii

Introduction: Subversive Strategies   1

Jean Andrews: Jane Austen's little "inch of ivory" and Carmen
    Laforet's *Nada*, what else could a woman write about?   13

Catherine Boyle: The Fragile Perfection of the Shrouded Rebellion
    (Re-reading Passivity in María Luisa Bombal)   27

Mercè Clarasó: The Two Worlds of Mercè Rodoreda   43

Catherine Davies: Beastly Women and Underdogs: the short fiction
    of Dora Alonso   55

Jo Evans: Carmen Conde's *Mujer sin Edén*: Controversial notions of 'sin' 71

Catherine Grant: Women or Words? The Indigenous *Nodriza* in the
    work of Rosario Castellanos   85

Stephen M. Hart: The Female Pinup Unpenned: Images of
    Women in Hispanic Art   101

Clara Janés: El ser o no ser de la escritura   115

Jean Mackenzie: Going Places? The Subversion of Linearity in
    Tina Díaz's *Transición*   127

Kathleen March: Engendering the Political Novel: Gioconda Belli's
    La mujer habitada   143

Gustavo San Román: Expression and Silence in the Poetry of
    Juana de Ibarbourou and Idea Vilariño   157

Helen Wing: Julie Sopetrán and Jorge Guillén: Poetry of Harmony? 177
Mirta Yáñez: Poesía femenina en Cuba 195
Montserrat Ordóñez: El oficio de escribir (a modo de conclusión) 209

Illustrations

Eugène Delacroix, *Liberty Guiding the People* (1830) 113
Anonymous, *Allegory of the Departure of Dom Pedro II for Europe after the Declaration of the Republic* (1890) 114

Acknowledgements

This book would not have been possible without the patience and sheer professionalism of Graham Allan who saw it through to its present shape. Special thanks go to him for all his hard work. I should also like to thank the two institutions whose financial support made the conference and the book possible: the University of St. Andrews Committee on Research in Arts and Divinity and the British Academy. They enabled the attendance of Clara Janés, Kathleen March and Mirta Yáñez. Grateful acknowledgement is made to them both for their support. I am particularly indebted to my former colleagues at the Department of Spanish, University of St. Andrews, Professor Alan Paterson, Bernard Bentley and Gustavo San Román, for their years of help and encouragement, and to all the contributors to this volume for paticipating with such enthusiasm. Thanks also go to Richard Fardon for his thoughtfulness.

Grateful acknowledgement is made to the following for permission to reprint copyright material:

Le Directeur du Musée du Louvre for the print of the painting "Liberty guiding the people" by Eugène Delacroix.

The Fundação Maria Luisa e Oscar Americano, São Paulo, for the print of the anonymous painting "Alegoría de la salida de Dom Pedro II para Europa después de la declaración de la República".

Introduction: Subversive Strategies

> Tejamos una gran
> bandera
> para abrazar los
> pueblos.
> (Dulce Ureña, R. Dominicana)

I begin with a poem by the Cuban writer and critic, Mirta Yáñez, one of the contributors to this collection of essays on women writers of twentieth-century Spain and Spanish America:

Recordatorio

Ten presente
siempre
que la posteridad se ha hecho
para que futuros estudiantes
– husmeadores frívolos y pasajeros –
se aprovechen
de la carne viva
que han dejado los pobres poetas
en sus cartas,
en sus sábanas miserables,
en sus miradas suspendidas de un árbol
Pero ten presente

– también –
que los poetas sueñan
con la larga permanencia
y para eso construyen las catedrales
y los poemas.[1]

It engages with the vexed question of the interrelation of texts, hermeneutics and authorial experience; of discourse, poetics and self. Despite the privileging in recent years of the psychoanalytic concept of the subject, the essays in this volume stress, yet again, that in a Spanish and Spanish American context authorship, the female self and the specific experiences of women are important. This is so to the extent that two of the contributions, one by the Colombian writer and critic, Montserrat Ordóñez, and the other by the Spanish novelist and poet, Clara Janés, are reflexions on writing. This book, then, is concerned with the work of women writers, with women as producers of textual meaning, and as such is gynocritical practice, to use Elaine Showalter's (thirteen-year old) term. The approaches taken by individual contributors may or may not conform to what is loosely termed feminist criticism although arguably "Criticism is feminist if it critiques existing disciplines, traditional paradigms about women, nature or social roles, or documents such work by others, from the point of view of women".[2] However, in the view of Elsa Chaney, "the term 'feminist' probably should be avoided [at least] in relation to Latin American women,"[3] which raises again the question of contextualization, even micro-contextualization in the form of autobiography. The inherent dangers of positing a universal female identity or universal feminine writing, of putting what Janet Todd calls "the idea of woman before the experience of women", that is, theory before author and text,[4] have been high on the critical agenda for some years now. Accordingly, while the contributors to this book engage with the social and historical issues prioritized by the Anglo-American schools of feminist theory, and explore the problematic theorizations of the construction of subjectivity, sexuality and language associated particularly with French feminism, they are careful to foreground the Spanish and Spanish American authors and their Spanish or Catalan texts. One of the aims of the book is to participate in the continuing process of widening the feminist canon, of opening up the binary Anglo-America/France into a discourse of difference. Thus, although the book's critical apparatus draws on the work of

Annie Leclerc, Julia Kristeva, Hélène Cixous, Luce Irigaray, Simone de Beauvoir, Toril Moi, Alice Jardine, Catherine Mackinnon and Shoshana Felman, it does so lightly, and at the same time borrows ideas from, among others, Camila Enríquez Ureña and the native American, Starhawk. As Elizabeth Ordóñez asks with reference to Spain, "Is it fair to import willy-nilly theories from abroad and force Spanish texts into their perhaps procrustean beds? Why not Spanish feminist theory?".[5] Contemporary feminist theory and criticism certainly exist in Spanish (for example, with Lidia Falcón in Spain, Magda Portal in Perú, Vilma Espín in Cuba, to name a few) but it has not entered the Western academic market place and despite forceful Spanish American feminist models (such as Tania "la guerillera" and the Amazons) it is marginalized by current metropolitan discourse. The subtle alignment of class and gender politics perhaps poses too many threats. Then again, many female authors feel indifferent or hostile towards feminist literary theory and see it as a "corsé de talla única" into which their work is forced. In a recent interview the Spanish novelist Cristina Fernández Cubas stated, "Literatura y feminismo no tienen nada que ver", and when asked if she felt the absence of feminist theory in Spain replied, "Yo creo que sobra", a sentiment echoed by Soledad Puértolas who added, "No sé si la hay. Pero si no la hay, mejor".[6]

National cultures, ethnicity and third-world status cannot but cut across gender differences. Jean Franco points out in her recent work that in Latin America class and sexual politics are interdependent; women writers cannot avoid involvement with, for example, the objectives of national independence because domination by the metropolis is by tradition cast in sexual terms.[7] The problem is extensive and not limited to feminist theory: "La cultura anglosajona aún teniendo tan pocos puntos de semejanza con la latina, ha ejercido un dominio poderoso en los países latinoamericanos, ejerciendo ese dominio como penetración cultural", writes Jorge Rufinelli. This way foreign values and myths are inculcated into autochthonous cultures which conform and are deformed. He quotes Jaime Mejía Duque, "Se coloniza en la medida en que se bloquea la conciencia del otro. En la medida en que se despoja gradualmente al dominado de las posibilidades de su real aprendizaje, de su propia y real 'originalidad' como pueblo".[8] Of course, such a view would be strongly contested – not unreasonably – by deconstruction theorists who like Gayatri Spivak and Paul Julian Smith, question perceptions of "originality" and "the real". For them, "elite methodology", or feminist theory here, is appropriate and necessary for the study of subaltern texts; to do otherwise would be to conflate identity with knowledge and to marginalize subaltern cultures even further.[9] Although few would argue that the women's liberation movement was imposed by the West onto other parts of the world,[10] few would deny the complexity of contextualization and the theorization of experience. After all, gender still remains a common denominator: "the female subject is always constructed and defined in gender, starting from gender".[11] Yet black North American feminist, bell hooks (Gloria Watkins), warns against adopting "the personal is political" model because, in her view, it has led feminist politics in the United States into depoliticized and uncommitted identity politics. Simply describing personal problems is not to become politicized. But she is equally worried by Jenny Bourne's observation that "Political culture has ceded to cultural politics. The material world has passed into the metaphysical". Hooks advocates the search for a "point of connection" between "material struggle and metaphysical concerns" and adds:

> Even if perceived "authorities" writing about a group to which they do not belong and/or over which they wield power, are progressive, caring, and right-on in every way, as long as their authority is constituted by either the absence of the voices of the individuals whose experience they seek to address, or the dismissal of those voices as unimportant, the subject/object binary is maintained and domination is reinforced.[12]

Hence the importance of including in this volume the "voices" of Clara Janés, Montserrat Ordóñez and Mirta Yáñez and according due significance to the "voices" of the other authors, whose writing – providing a site for critical exploration – is no less "carne viva" for "futuros estudiantes".

If one aim of the book is to expand the feminist canon, another is to continue the recent revision and extension of the hispanic literary canon by introducing little known female authors and/or texts and by bringing to bear new tools of analysis and a fresh critical awareness in rereadings of consecrated works. Some of the writers discussed (Carmen Laforet, Rosario Castellanos, Carmen Conde, Mercè Rodoreda, Juana de Ibarbourou), need no introduction; the work of others (María Luisa Bombal, Gioconda Belli, Dora Alonso, Idea Vilariño), will be less familiar to the reader, and some authors will be quite new (Julie Sopetrán and Tina Díaz). What all the chapters have in common is reference to the subversive strategies practised by the writers in question, writers from Catalonia, Chile, Cuba, Mexico, Nicaragua, Spain and Uruguay, whose strategies tend to be discreetly (rather than radically) subversive and often distinct (discrete) from those used by women writers in other parts of the world.

The essays were first read as papers in the conference "Women Writers in Twentieth-century Spain and Latin America", held at the University of St. Andrews, Scotland, in June 1991. This was not the first meeting of its kind in Britain; Catherine M. Boyle organized the international symposium on "Literatura y crítica literaria de mujer de Latinoamerica" at Strathclyde University, Glasgow, in 1989 and Stephen M. Hart the "Feminism and Hispanic Literature" conference at Westfield College, London, in 1990.[13] Both conferences were extremely successful and served as a necessary and appropriate forum of gynocentric discussion for British hispanists. The approach at the St. Andrews meeting was slightly different inasmuchas the work of solely women, of both Spain and South America, was at issue. No guidelines were set except, where possible, to focus on one author or group of authors. It is interesting, therefore, to note recurrent thematics and tropes. A tentative synthesis accounts for the title of this introduction.

The female authors, selected according to the research interests of the contributors, all partake of the subversive strategy outlined above to some degree; each author seems to deploy in her own way a tactic whereby stereotyped female attributes or culturally defined gender roles are turned against dominant discourses and male supremacy, are turned into a means of resistance by exposing and undermining the soft underbelly of authority. It is subversion through inversion. Domesticity and everyday routine; Catholicism or patriarchal monotheism; silence and passiveness, become sites of resistance, or "shrouded rebellion" in Catherine Boyle's words, a non-violent refusal to cooperate or comply with Hispanic patriarchal ideologies and systems. Women resist through a feminine economy, the family, motherhood and female solidarity, as Jean Andrews and myself show in the work of Carmen Laforet and Dora Alonso respectively; through the appropriation of silence and non-verbal expression to the extent that, Gustavo San Román suggests, in the case of Idea Vilariño it is an inabilty to communicate which is communicated through poetry. Logocentrism is eluded not only through poetry and creative activity, but also through fantasy and horror, as Mercè Clarasó points out when exploring the disturbing narrative of her enigmatic country-woman, Mercè Rodoreda, the paradoxical "mistress of the quotidian"; it is eluded through the demythification of Eve, Mary, the female muse, the male poetic persona and even God the Father, according to Jo Evans and Helen Wing, in the poetry of Carmen Conde and Julie Sopetrán; and, generally, through a canny disregard for dichotomies such as nature/culture, nature/art, subject/object, past/present, present/absent, victim/conqueror, real/ unreal, and human/animal. These Spanish and American authors, untrammelled by linear chronology, manipulating the tenses and aspects of verbal paradigms, as Jean Mackenzie carefully pinpoints in Tina Díaz's *Transición*, itself a paradigm of feminine expression, can override generic categories such as realism and fantasy, autobiographical fiction and fictional autobiography, analytical and creative writing, and other such taxonomies in the search of a female voice. Yet they do this in a way which makes them more subversive in their own cultures than either Cixous or Wollstonecraft, Jean Andrews writes, "because they are the enemy within, the feminist fifth column". The life experience of these authors is crucial for situating and understanding their work, as is indicated in the self-reflexiveness of the "testimonios" of Montserrat Ordóñez and Clara Janés, and the essays of Catherine Boyle, Gustavo San Román, Kathleen March and Mercè Clarasó, among others. But this should not imply slippage from an author's "real" life to the characters delineated in a mimetic text, as Catherine Grant warns apropos of Rosario Castellanos, nor wishful thinking on the part of the Western feminist critic. Rather it involves reading and historicizing the text within Hispanic culture. These authors and their literature are engendered in societies whose configurations hinge on Catholicism, Roman law, a dependent status stemming from colonialism or neocolonialism, late urban and industrial development, repressive militaristic regimes, strong class solidarity, congentital "machismo", clearly defined gender roles, and late, often ineffective, women's liberation movements (national women's suffrage was not introduced in Colombia, for example, until 1957).[14] Stephen Hart's essay, although different from the others as it deals with the representations of women in painting, was included to illustrate a further complication, the problematic interrelation between the female icon and national identity in Spain and Latin America during periods of political crisis and national dissolution. In these societies feminism has come to be, above all, an indirect means of denouncing state violence and repression. The statement "women's history is posited as part of the search for social and political justice for all" could apply just as well to Spain as to any of the Spanish American republics.[15] The scriptural subversive strategies, moreover, reflect what is possibly the most effective and documented feminist strategy, certainly in Spanish America, the "Supermadre". A repressive patriarchy's own legitimized female stereotype, enforced as an oppressive extension of the traditional mothering role to keep women in their "proper" place, and denounced for this reason only a decade ago by Elsa Chaney, has since been used to undo that same authority. The dichotomy public/private is destabilized as the mothers in Argentina, Chile, Central America and Uruguay, leave their domestic space for the streets. By publishing their writing and launching it onto the open market, the authors discussed in this volume do something similar.

However, the need for an "espacio propio" does not diminish, if only to enable "muzzled mouths" to slip the controls of what Virginia Woolf calls the "voluble sex".[16] Both Mirta Yáñez and Montserrat Ordóñez refer to this space. Chaos and the cosmos "sólo se puede[n] plasmar en soledad, con la libertad que da el candado por dentro de la puerta", writes Ordóñez, pointing to woman's urgent "defensa de su mínimo espacio ante la invasión, [que] se convierte en una pelea que la agota más que la misma escritura". Yáñez refers (from personal experience) to the difficulties of writing even in post–revolutionary Cuba; she also reclaims the gender-specific term and category, "poetisa", on behalf of her fellow Cuban women poets whose difference should be recognized and celebrated. The kind of resistance apparent in the narrative and poetry of the authors represented here, the strength, growth, and fruition of woman who shelters and protects and, while firmly rooted in the earth, is expansive in her generosity, is often symbolized by the "polysemic" tree (see, for example, the essays by Catherine Boyle, Helen Wing and Jo Evans). This natural symbol is most central to the indigenous worldview explored by Kathleen March in her study of Gioconda Belli's work. March uses native American myths and traditions in an ecofeminist analysis of engendered armed revolutionary struggle (epitomized by the Amazons) in Belli's novel *La mujer habitada*, and wonders if white Euro-American feminist critics and theorists will feel the novel applies to them. Perhaps foregrounding the tree is a female response to the enforcement of foreign models on colonized or peripheral societies, models which, writes Jean Franco, "they can never perceive as organic or natural".[17] The response avoids language, as in Gioconda Belli's eloquent poem "Sin palabras":

> Yo inventé un árbol grande,
> más grande que un hombre,
> más grande que una casa,
> más grande que una última esperanza.[18]

By means of conclusion, I would like to offer two autobiographical notes. The first concerns Clara Janés whose contribution examines the development, over twenty-four years, of the five versions of her recently published novel *Los caballos del sueño* (1989). Her autobiographical account of the search for a voice and a mode of expression is absorbing and instructive. What proved of particular interest for us both was her previous association with St. Andrews, an association which was purely imaginary yet highly significant in the working out of her narrative and construction of identity since her first visits to Britain. For that reason she accepted the conference invitation. Clara Janés's experience of St. Andrews, which the conference made possible, is already reconstituted and inscribed in the language of narrative fiction, hopefully to be published shortly. To theorize this process of transition from experience to discourse and what it means for a feminist critique will continue to be a central issue in contemporary cultural theory.[19] The second note is a moving poem by Montserrat Ordóñez whose tour of Britain, sponsored by the British Council, was postponed which prevented her from attending the conference. But she too experienced St.

Andrews some months later and rather than just play her role as a critic, she also chose to speak about herself as poet. This poem, in its very writing, is resistance:

Resistencia

Vertical y acosada
    emparedada
sólo los ojos y el largo pelo negro
marcan la voluntad de vida
No hay grito ni mordisco
no hay manos ni papel
Vienen y levantan un listón
le abren un cajoncito
cajoncitos dentro del cajón
por donde se mueve con cuerda sin música
    trabaja fornica saluda
    cumple cumple cumple
    con su pedazo de cartón
Llegan los cómplices a cerrarla
    a guardarla
y los mira inmóvil agradecida
La cubren listones horizontales
    de abajo arriba
yerba y corderos mueren a sus pies.
Gotea el muro. El moho ya corroe la madera.
Diminutas cucarachas prehistóricas le enseñarán a persistir.[20]

Catherine Davies
St. Andrews/London, April 1992

1. Mirta Yáñez , *Las visitas y otras poemas* (La Habana: Letras Cubanas, 1986) p.55

2. Maggie Humm, *Feminist criticism* (Brighton: Harvester, 1986) p.40

3. Elsa A. Chaney, *Supermadre. Women in politics in Latin America* (Austin and London: University of Texas Press, 1979) p.67

4. Janet Todd, *Feminist Literary History: a defence* (Cambridge: Polity, Basil Blackwell, 1988) p.15

5. Elizabeth J. Ordóñez, *Voices of their own. Contemporary Spanish narrative by women* (London and Toronto: Associated University Presses, 1991) p.24

6. "Conversando con Mercedes Abad, Cristina Fernández Cubas y Soledad Puértolas: 'Feminismo y literatura no tienen nada que ver'", *Mester*, 20 (1991) pp.157–65, pp.161–2

7. Jean Franco, *Plotting Women. Gender and Representation in Mexico* (London: Verso, 1989); "Beyond ethnocentrism: gender, power, and the Third-world intelligentsia" in *Marxism and the Interpretation of Culture* ed. Cary Nelson and Lawrence Grossberg (Chicago: Illinois University Press, 1988) pp.503–15

8. Jorge Ruffinelli, *Poesía y descolonización* (Mexico: Oasis, 1985) p.10

9. Paul Julian Smith, *Representing the other. 'Race', text and gender in Spanish and Spanish American Narrative* (Clarendon: Oxford, 1992) p.21

10. See Kumari Jayawardena, *Feminism and nationalism in the Third-world* (London: Zed, 1986) p.2

11. Teresa de Lauretis, "Feminist studies/Critical studies: issues, terms and contexts", Teresa de Lauretis ed., *Feminist studies/Critical studies* (Bloomington: Indiana University Press, 1986) p.14

12. bell hooks, *Talking back. Thinking feminist – thinking black* (London: Sheba, 1989) p.43, pp.105–7

13. See Lisa P. Condé and Stephen M. Hart, *Feminist readings on Spanish and Latin American literature* (Lewiston, Queenston, Lampeter: Edwin Mellen Press, 1991)

14. See The Latin American and Caribbean Women's Collective, *Slaves of slaves. The challenge of Latin American women* (London: Zed, 1980) pp.6–25; Elsa A. Chaney, *Supermadre*, pp.75–81, p.170

15. Francesca Miller, *Latin American women and the search for social justice* (Hanover and London: New England University Press, 1991) p.xv

16. Margorie Agosín, *Women of Smoke. Latin American women in literature and life*, translated by Janice Molloy (Stratford, Ontario: Williams-Wallace publishers, 1989) p.33; Virginia Woolf, *A Room of One's Own. Three Guineas* (London: Chatto and Windus, The Hogarth Press, 1984) p.74

17. Jean Franco, *Plotting Women*, p.xii

18. Gioconda Belli, *De la costilla de Eva* (Managua: Editorial Nueva Nicaragua, 1987) p.31

19. Nancy A. Walker, "Introduction", *Women's autobiographies*, special edition of *Women's studies*, 20, 1 (1991) and Shari Benstock, "The female self engendered: Autobiographical writing and theories of selfhood", ibid, pp.5–14

20. Montserrat Ordóñez, *Ekdysis* (Roldanillo, Colombia: Ediciones Embalaje museo rayo, 1987) p.27

Jane Austen's little "inch of ivory" and Carmen Laforet's *Nada*, what else could a woman write about?

Jane Austen and Carmen Laforet occupy similar canonical positions in the study of women's writing (or, as is still more usually the case, writing which happens to be by women) in universities and at secondary school level. They are what Marilyn Butler terms "syllabus writers". Austen is the earliest woman writer in English to be given this status and she retains a definite pre-eminence over later women novelists. She was recognised by F.R. Leavis, although he would hardly have seen it in exactly these terms, as the mother of his "Great Tradition". In the world of Hispanic letters, Carmen Laforet's first novel, *Nada*, if not her work as a whole, is still the most popular piece of literature by a woman, selected on criteria other than the gender of its author, on university and secondary school reading lists in Britain. Indeed, *Nada* was well and truly canonised as far back as 1958 with the publication of the ubiquitous abridged and annotated schools version.[1] In Spain in that year, it was in its twelfth edition in fourteen years.

Why is it, then, that the work of Jane Austen on the one hand, and Carmen Laforet's *Nada* on the other, should prove so consistently acceptable to university and secondary course designers? There are three obvious areas of coincidence between *Nada* and the work of Jane Austen. Should we be surprised that these are the three most often cited characteristics of novels by female authors: an absence of overt reference to politics, a concentration on female protagonists and domestic situations, and clarity of style? Is it merely that novels which contain no historical references do not date and therefore require no troublesome background reading, that plots which are confined to a relatively restricted domestic world are more likely to be linear and uncomplicated, or that prose which is simply and elegantly written is by default less taxing to the intellect? In other words, is the sort of women's writing which is favoured outside a feminist context selected because, like candy floss, it is perceived to be a delightfully light concoction which boils down to nothing, because it is therefore idiot and boredom proof in the classroom and because it provides some light relief from heavy male syllabus everpresents like Joseph Conrad and Camilo José Cela. Are Jane Austen and Carmen Laforet really past mistresses of this frothy art?

Let us look at the case of Jane Austen first. The veritable industry of academic research and analysis that has grown up around her fiction has for years been convinced that her novels are more restricted in their range of locations, character types and overtly discussed issues than the writing of any other contemporary female novelist in the English language, not to speak of her male contemporaries. There has always been the regret that her talent might have been wasted on such narrow domestic trivia and the suspicion that she could have been much greater had she ventured further afield. In contrast, Roland Barthes remarks of Voltaire, who died only three years after she was born, and about whose life and work nobody would be so smugly condescending, that he was the last happy writer precisely because he ignored contemporary events.[2] Barthes claims that, in fact, Voltaire possessed two great happinesses. The first was the society in which he lived. France under Louis XV gave him material for great writing because he was, in his way, stimulated by the spectacular injustice which surrounded him. His second gift, however, was that of ignoring those historical circumstances completely, allowing him to create fiction in which time stood still, fiction which was free to create a world of the imagination completely apart. Barthes states that in order to be happy Voltaire suspended time and celebrates him for it. Why should these things which make Voltaire great not make Austen great also? Why does vision in Voltaire equal parochialism in Jane Austen? She too lived in and was touched by turbulent times: one of her brothers married his cousin, whose first husband, a French nobleman, fell foul of the Guillotine, another was briefly a soldier and two became admirals, one the friend of Nelson. Scholars such as Marilyn Butler have shown just how much politics and history does impinge on the fiction of Jane Austen.[3] She has shown that Austen was very profoundly politically aware and, more interestingly, that she was, on all moral and political questions, a conservative. Jane Austen's conservatism has always been a blessing to those who would categorise her as merely a woman's writer and has proved a difficulty for feminist critics who would have her both radical and feminist. Yet, although she and Voltaire held opposite political views, their strategies as writers were similar: they both turned their backs on the world. The real difference between them lies in the fact that she has only recently and reluctantly been given credit for having, first of all, any knowledge of contemporary current affairs and, second, the wit to deliberately turn her back on them. Would any critic have dared to point the same finger at a pillar of the male establishment, even a rebellious one like Voltaire?

Nada was written in 1944 and promptly won the first *premio Nadal*. It appeared at a time of astonishing upheaval in world politics and just after the catastrophe of the Civil War in Spain. It was greeted as the first substantial work, apart from Cela's *La familia de Pascual Duarte* (1942), to appear in Spain after the Civil War. It was a broadly realist novel, presenting the hardship and uncertainty of the *posguerra* years in a realist way, and it was not perceived to be politically contentious. This impression was no doubt supported by the very young age, twenty-three, of its female author, who compounded this by appearing to be as shy as Jane Austen's Fanny Price. She was an unlikely successor to the vast bastion of distinguished men of letters Spain had lost during the Civil War but surely infinitely more acceptable because of her perceived shyness and vulnerability. It was followed, to chose some of the more famous landmarks by male writers, by Buero Vallejo's play, *Historia de una escalera*, and by Cela's novel *La colmena*. All three of these works avoided explicit mention of politics and they each presented a cast of poor and impoverished characters about their everyday activities in wartime and post-war urban settings. Yet, the work of Cela and Buero Vallejo is considered to be deeply political while *Nada* is often dismissed as a mere woman's novel, a woman's autobiographical novel at that, despite Laforet's disclaimers. A lot of this is no doubt due to the publicity gained and retained for the political views of the male writers by Cela's *tremendismo* and the censorship of *La colmena* and by Buero Vallejo's famous quarrel with Sastre on the subject of *posibilismo*. While they were thus engaged Carmen Laforet preferred to live a quiet life in Madrid with her husband and five children. Worse, she became converted back to devout Catholicism in December 1951 and wrote about it in *La mujer nueva* (1955). Even the Mulvihill-Sánchez edition, which admits that *Nada* has been variously interpreted as a condemnation of Spain in the forties, an autobiographical *roman-à-clef* or an existentialist-nihilist work, finally denies that it has any real political or philosophical content, quoting Domingo Pérez Minik:

> Se percibe claramente que la autora, cuando escribió su libro, no tenía ningún contenido "ideológico" definido, ningún prejuicio social, ninguna conciencia dirigida o comprometida... Es difícil deducir de *Nada* un mensaje concreto, ni una elaboración intelectual, ni una filosofía de las que andaban por el mundo.[4]

Like Jane Austen therefore she has generally been seen as a narrow woman writer with conservative views who is not particularly concerned with politics, and safely pigeon-holed as such. Her conservatism presents the same difficulty as that of Jane Austen, can she be considered feminist without being radical? Or must she and Jane Austen be considered as "Uncle Tom" female novelists, women's writers as opposed to women writers?

Jane Austen however, was mischievously proud of her unique art, proud of its apparently narrow scope, and its domesticity. Characteristically, her famous pronouncements on her writing are to be found scattered amid the jumble of family matters, gossip and opinions that make up her correspondence. In a letter overflowing with family news and literary advice to her niece Anna Austen, herself an aspiring novelist, Jane Austen makes the brisk, throwaway remark that "3 or 4 Families in a Country Village is the very thing to work on" (Friday 9th

September 1814).[5] Writing to male correspondents she is even more tongue-in-cheek. It is to her brother Edward, another would-be novelist in the family, that she makes the famous inch of ivory observation. He appears to have lost two and a half chapters of his novel in progress and Jane clears herself of having purloined them with the immortal protestation:

> I do not think however that any theft of that sort would be really very useful to me. What would I do with your strong, manly, spirited Sketches, full of Variety and Glow? How could I possibly join them on to the little bit (two Inches wide) of ivory on which I work with so fine a Brush, as produces little effect after much labour?
>
> (Monday, 16th December 1816)[6]

There is surely more than a little gentle leg-pulling here.

In a letter to the Prince Regent's chaplain, James Stanier Clarke, another writer of novels and dispenser of advice, she declares herself incapable of writing a novel about the sort of crusading anti-tithes clergyman hero Clarke recommends to her, (chiefly, it must be said, because that is how he liked to portray himself in life and in fiction):

> A classical education, or at any rate a very extensive acquaintance with English literature, ancient and modern, appears to me quite indispensable for the person who would do any justice to your clergyman; and I think I may boast myself to be, with all possible vanity, the most unlearned and uninformed female who ever dared to be an authoress.
>
> (Monday, 11th December 1815)[7]

Jane Austen's wicked mockery of Stanier Clarke's pretensions should not be mistaken for feminine modesty, nor her more gentle teasing of her brother. If anything it is a supreme confidence in her own achievements which enables her to be so apparently self-deprecating.

Carmen Laforet's approach to her writing is not dissimilar. The following remarks from *Mis páginas mejores*, by virtue of being quoted by Mulvihill and Sánchez, have a similar canonical ring to Jane Austen's famous observations:

> Lo que a mí, como novelista, me preocupa en mis libros, lo que soy capaz de destruir enteramente y volver a hacer de nuevo cuantas veces sea necesario, es su estructura y también su vida. Me preocupa huir del ensayo, huir de explicar mis propias opiniones culturales, que considero poco interesantes, y dar aquello para lo cual me creo dotada, la observación, la creación de la vida.[8]

As for Jane Austen and, in Barthes' reading, Voltaire, turning one's back on the world is a positive attitude. It is truly unlikely that any novelist would consider her own cultural opinions uninteresting, any more than Jane Austen really thought herself ignorant. Perhaps Laforet is implying that philosophy and politics, when not almost a subliminal part of the narrative, as in *Nada*, have no place in her art. Her concentration on "La observación, la creación de la vida" is the equivalent of Jane Austen's delicate work on her little piece of ivory. Both artists claim to be wholly engrossed in their craft; dedicated to the act of writing as opposed to its political and philosophical substance. This is obviously a position which tantalisingly anticipates *écriture féminine*.

Both authors, by opting out of overt political and social comment and constructing plots and characters which revolve around domestic situations, have created literary texts which fulfill the criteria of being well-written and worthy without proving politically contentious or likely to date. That is why *Nada* and Jane Austen are ideal syllabus choices.

This, however, is merely the view from the patriarchal side of the fence. The point about Jane Austen and Carmen Laforet is not that they turned their backs on politics and the wide world because they could not handle it, rather they found it, in Laforet's phrase, *poco interesante*. In *Sense and Sensibility*, Elinor Dashwood sighs over the "fancied necessity" of two men meeting in a duel, from which both return unwounded, over the honour of a lady.[9] Needless to say they did nothing else to restore the lady's position in society; she was sent to live in seclusion with her illegitimate child for the rest of her days, at seventeen, while her seducer married a lady with fifty thousand pounds. In *Nada*, when Andrea listens spellbound to the playing of Román he asks her to tell him what the music says to her. Her answer is very important:

> — A ti se te podría hipnotizar... ¿Qué te dice la música?
>
> Inmediatamente se me cerraban las manos y el alma.
>
> — Nada, no sé, sólo me gusta...
> — No es verdad. Dime lo que te dice. Lo que te dice al final.
> — Nada.
>
> Me miraba, defraudado, un momento. Luego, mientras guardaba el violín:
>
> — No es verdad.[10]

Andrea will not admit to her uncle that he or his music has any power over her. To put her pleasure in the music into words is to betray herself. In fact she may not even be able to find words to express what is for her a pre-linguistic state of *jouissance*. She tells him therefore that the music says nothing to her, *nada*. In saying that she is denying his hold over her, and devaluing his artistry, the one thing that really gives him pleasure in life and power over others. In *Northanger Abbey*, Catherine Morland holds out for a long time against the voice of patriarchal reason represented by Henry Tilney, while she weaves her Gothic tales around his father, the possible mysterious death of his mother and the uncomfortable atmosphere in the Abbey. It is her way of exerting power over an alien environment, of becoming the heroine of her own adventure story, of deferring the marriage which will make her Henry's plaything. His speech, when he discovers her in his mother's room enthralled by her dreadful speculations, appears to reinforce the power of the reasonable patriarchy he represents, but, on the other hand, it does leave itself open to satirical interpretation:

> Dear Miss Morland, consider the dreadful nature of the suspicions you have entertained. What have you been judging from?

Remember the country and the age in which we live. Remember that we are English, that we are Christians. Consult your own understanding, your own sense of the probable, your own observation of what is passing around you. Does our education prepare us for such atrocities? Do our laws connive at them? Could they be perpetrated without being known, in a country like this, where social and literary intercourse is on such a footing; where every man is surrounded by a neighbourhood of voluntary spies, and where roads and newspapers lay everything open? Dearest Miss Morland, what ideas have you been admitting?[11]

Catherine retreats in floods of tears, but of course, the answer to Henry Tilney's disingenuous question, as Charlotte and Emily Brönte were to show almost fifty years later, is very definitely yes. The Gothic is by no means routed at the end of *Northanger Abbey*.

The Gothic is common to *Northanger Abbey* and *Nada*. The atmosphere of foreboding and secrecy that Catherine Morland imagines in the Abbey actually exists in the house on the *calle Aribau*. Catherine is ostensibly influenced by her reading of all those late eighteenth century "horrid novels"; Andrea on the other hand confronts a reality. Her family: the sexually threatening and politically suspect Román, the anguished, frustrated Angustias, the ravaged Gloria and her volatile husband, the sinister Antonia and the almost senile old grandmother are characters whose prototypes could be found in any of Catherine's Gothic romances. Furthermore, the contrast between the inhabitants of the house on the *calle Aribau* and the radiant golden-haired family of Ena and her mother is as blatant as that between the Earnshaw/Heathcliff and Linton families in *Wuthering Heights*, a novel which is surely the epitome of Victorian Gothic.

The Gothic genre is full of hysteria, famously categorised by Freud as a peculiarly female affliction, but useful to women, no doubt, because it is the very antithesis of patriarchal reason. In the "horrid novels", through a display of excessive sensibility: frequent swooning or uncontrollable attacks of weeping, the heroines extract themselves from awkward situations, using ostensible weakness to exert power. In the same way they neutralise male power by forcing the men to behave with a degree of sensibility stipulated by them before they allow themselves to be captured in the bonds of matrimony.

To argue that the deployment of the Gothic in *Nada* and in *Northanger Abbey* is an act of covert rebellion by two apparently conformist female writers is to invoke not Freud but the French feminist theorists, chiefly Kristeva and Cixous, who have used his ideas to preach the supremacy of the hysterical woman. Because Jane Austen and Carmen Laforet are conservative writers, however, it might be more interesting to apply the writing of Annie Leclerc in *Parole de femme* to their work. As soon as it came out, to much acclaim, its feminist credentials were attacked; it was seen to reinforce the patriarchy by extolling the virtues of stay-at-home femininity and childrearing at the cost of addressing the issue of why these roles were really allocated in the first place.[12] Leclerc's position, while full of contradictions, may broadly be described as conservative, within the spectrum of possible feminisms.

She accepts the traditional, culturally defined gender roles without question and goes on to propound a supremacist argument based on the importance of giving birth to and nurturing children. All masculine activity, in the great outside world, is geared towards satisfying the woman at home raising children and therefore of secondary importance. Her arguments imply a society, like that of Jane Austen's novels, where domestic activity is the only sphere open to women. In *Nada*, the domestic is also the only authorised terrain for women. Andrea is an exception only to a limited extent. She may mix with artists but the only artists and intellectuals in her bohemian circle are men and she herself is a hanger-on. Her gallivantings around Barcelona on her own and her unkempt appearance are recognised as eccentric, even, by herself. In the thinking of Leclerc such confinement is an advantage. For her, childbirth is the paradoxical centre of power relations between the sexes:

> In the joy of childbirth I discover what men desire: to give virility the taste of triumph; femininity the taste of humiliation and sacrifice.[13]

While men believe they are subjugating women, the women are in fact at the summit of their powers, as life givers. Leclerc is confirmed by Laforet. It is through childbirth that Ena's mother reconciles herself to her unrequited love for Román and marriage to a husband she does not love:

> Fue Ena la que me hizo querer a su padre, la que me hizo querer más hijos ... quien me hizo, conscientemente, desprenderme de mis morbosidades enfermizas, de mis cerrados egoísmos... Abrirme a los demás y encontrar así horizontes desconocidos. Porque antes de que yo la creara, casi a la fuerza, con mi propia sangre y huesos, con mi propia amarga sustancia, yo era una mujer desequilibrada y mezquina. Insatisfecha y egoísta...[14]

The supposedly bohemian Andrea, on hearing Ena's mother's testimony, privately recognises herself ready for motherhood and renewal also:

> Era fácil entenderlo sabiendo mi propio cuerpo preparado – como cargado de semillas – para este labor de continuación de vida. Aunque todo en mí era entonces ácido e incompleto como la esperanza, yo lo entendía.

Men, in contrast, can only take life away and are therefore fascinated by death:

> Death. Death. Death... For if desire is the only thing on their lips, their hearts harbour only dreams of death... Horror and fascination, death haunts them, these fanatics of desire.[15]

These masculine dreams of death, the horror and fascination would seem to be the stuff of which the Gothic is made. However, the Gothic in the hands of female writers is invariably the tale of how the Gothic nightmare is overcome by the beautiful heroine, who has little in common with the death seeker of later male Romantic poetry. According to Leclerc's theory, Henry Tilney condemns Catherine's Gothic imaginings because they represent his own fear of and desire for death. Women are not afraid of this, of course, so for Catherine there is no danger in her speculations. Similarly, Andrea survives the Gothic nightmare of her starving, cold, unloved existence in the house on the *calle Aribau*, unlike her uncle Román, who cannot take the pressure and finally slits his own throat. Andrea does describe one, almost mystical, encounter she has with death, but, despite her disturbed state, it does not get a hold over her, nor does it frighten her:

> Y me dolió el pecho de hambre y de deseos inconfesables, al respirar. Era como si estuviese oliendo un aroma de muerte y me pareciera bueno por primera vez, después de haberme causado terror... Cuando se levantó una fuerte ráfaga de brisa, yo estaba aún allí, apoyada contra una pared, entontecida y medio estática. Del viejo balcón de una casa ruinosa salió una sábana tendida, que al agitarse me sacó de mi marasmo. Yo no tenía la cabeza buena aquel día.[16]

Andrea survives, but she can only escape the house on the *calle Aribau* through the offices of the golden Ena who calls her to Madrid and a new life, just as hunger and shock are about to drive her mad.

Leclerc's understanding of what it is to be a man is rooted in her biological supremism:

> No, it is no life to be a man...
> For when you are a man, you must be virile without respite, as the least lapse would compromise everything. Forever endeavouring to silence not only women, children, employees and neighbours, but also his own fears and tears, his own lack and longing – even he must feel the pressure, and more than a little...[17]

When Elinor Dashwood sighs at the "fancied necessity" of duelling she is passing a comment on the futility and irrelevance of all male actions which take place, unregulated by women, outside the female world. The fact that this is the only world inhabited by Jane Austen's characters, and that men impinge only as and when their presence is absolutely necessary to the plot, could even be used to imply that protofeminism and conservatism coexist in her work as they do in Leclerc. In *Nada* there is a similar feminine economy at work. Andrea is very likely more in love with Ena than anything or anyone else. Significantly, Ena pays for Andrea when they are out together, she favours her and draws her into a community which is better off and more agreeable than that of the *calle Aribau*, she makes her part of her own family, and she performs the hero's part at the end by taking Andrea away from the horrors of Barcelona to be with her in Madrid. The bonding between Ena, her passionate mother and Andrea overcomes the misunderstandings and petty jealousies their various involvements with Román initially cause. At the end, he has nothing but death and they have their solidarity. Andrea even discovers that she loves Gloria as she leaves the house on the *calle Aribau* for the last time. The irregular lifestyle and Gothic extremes of the house on the *calle Aribau* will cease for Andrea as soon as she finds herself in the bosom of a conventional family in Madrid, leading what it must be presumed will be a more conventional existence. Her friend Ena will marry the dispensable Jaime, Andrea will find a husband, they will both discover the power of childbirth as Ena's mother did before them, and the status quo will appear to be preserved as it is at the end of *Northanger Abbey*.

The *status quo*, however, as in Jane Austen, is anything but the compliant reinforcement of patriarchal values that it seems to be. In fact, theorists like Annie Leclerc, whose work has been much admired by men, and writers like Jane Austen and Carmen Laforet, who are seamlessly integrated into the male canon, are much more subversive than Cixous or Wollstonecraft or Isabel Allende because they are the enemy within, the feminist fifth column gnawing away at the roots of the patriarchy.

Jean Andrews
University of Wales College of Cardiff

1. Edward R. Mulvihill and Roberto G. Sánchez, eds, *Nada*, Carmen Laforet (New York: Oxford University Press, 1958).

2. Roland Barthes, Préface to *Romans et contes*, Voltaire (Paris: Gallimard, 1964) pp.9–17.

3. Marilyn Butler, *Jane Austen and the War of Ideas* (Oxford: Clarendon Press, 1987).

4. op. cit., p.xiv.

5. R.W. Chapman, ed. *Jane Austen: Letters, 1796–1817* (Oxford: Oxford University Press, 1978) p.170.

6. ibid., pp.188–189.

7. ibid., p.185.

8. *Mis páginas mejores* (Madrid: Gredos, 1956) p.8; quoted in Mulvihill and Sánchez, p.xiii.

9. *Sense and Sensibility* (Penguin, 1969) p.220. Colonel Brandon's adopted niece Miss Williams, was seduced and left with child by Willoughby; the two gentlemen fought a duel for the lady's honour from which both returned unharmed. She was sent off to live in retirement in the country with her child, at the tender age of seventeen, while Willoughby continued to move freely in society and make a financially advantageous marriage to Miss Grey and her fifty thousand pounds.

10. *Nada* (Barcelona: Destino, 1963) pp.41–42.

11. *Northanger Abbey* (Penguin, 1972) pp.199–200.

12. See Christine Delphy, "Protofeminism and Antifeminism" in *French Feminist Thought: A Reader*, ed. Toril Moi (Oxford: Basil Blackwell, 1987) pp.81–109.

13. Annie Leclerc, extracts from *Parole de femme*, ibid., pp.73–79, p.73.

14. Laforet, op. cit., p.240

15. Leclerc, op. cit., p.77.

16. Laforet, op. cit., pp.287–288.

17. Leclerc, op. cit., p.73.

The Fragile Perfection of the Shrouded Rebellion (Re-reading Passivity in María Luisa Bombal)

> Ella se había sentado en la cama, dispuesta a insultar. Pero en vano buscó las palabras hirientes que gritarle. No sabía nada, nada. Ni siquiera insultar.
> — ¿Qué te pasa? ¿En qué piensas, Brígida?
> Por primera vez Luis había vuelto sobre sus pasos y se inclinaba sobre ella, inquieto, dejando pasar la hora de llegada a su despacho.
> — Tengo sueño... — había replicado Brígida puerilmente, mientras escondía la cara en las almohadas.
> Por primera vez él la había llamado desde el club a la hora del almuerzo. Pero ella había rehusado salir al teléfono, esgrimiendo rabiosamente el arma aquella que había encontrado sin pensarlo: el silencio.[1]

> ¡Mentira! Eran mentiras su resignación y su serenidad; quería amor, sí, amor, y viajes y locuras, y amor, amor...
> Pero, Brígida, ¿por qué te vas? ¿por qué te quedabas? había preguntado Luis.
> Ahora sabría contestarle:
> — ¡"El árbol, Luis, el árbol! Han derribado el gomero."

A huff. It would seem that the protagonist of María Luisa Bombal's short story, "El árbol" (1939) spends its duration in a huff. Brígida is a young woman characterised by her langour, her silliness (only matched by her beauty) and her

passivity, until she finally discovers the words that will explain her seemingly
sudden abandonment of her husband, words that are meaningless to all but her.
The rubber tree was her protection against the revelation of the truth of her
marriage, without it she is forced to acknowledge that her marriage is worthless,
she is forced to recognise the powerless place she occupies in her household, her
world. The rubber tree gives her the means by which she is able to voice obtusely
what she could not before. Because she did not choose her silence, it was imposed
on her as a weapon, "without thinking", it was part of her total inability to
articulate what she felt: she could not even find the words to insult. Her silence
was pathetic, until words, coherent only in and from her experience, were forced
out of her.

María Luisa Bombal's characters are outwardly silent creatures. It would be all
too easy to say that their silence is a weapon, but it is not. It just is. It may become
a weapon by default, it may be conceived of from outside as a weapon, a
peculiarly easy, energy saving, infuriating, and manipulative weapon, but it is not.
Silence is an imposition that they assume, and within which they nurture a
multitude of lives, as in *La amortajada*:

> Te equivocas. Era engañosa mi indolencia. Si solamente hubieras
> tirado del hilo de mi lana, si hubieras, malla por malla, deshecho
> mi tejido... a cada una se enredaba un borrascoso pensamiento y un
> nombre que no olvidaré.[2]

La amortajada, the shrouded woman, was first published in 1938 in the famous
journal *Sur* (Buenos Aires), whose editor was Victoria Ocampo. It was María
Luisa Bombal's second novel, the first being *La última niebla* (Buenos Aires,
1935). In *La amortajada* a woman lies dead, first on her death bed and then in her
coffin as she is taken to her grave, as relatives and friends come to pay their last
respects. Through her half-shut eyes she can see the procession of people, watch
them without their knowing:

> A la llama de los cirios, cuantos la velaban se inclinaron entonces,
> para observar la limpieza y la transparencia de aquella fanja de

pupila que la muerte no había logrado empañar. Respetuosamente
maravillados se inclinaban, sin saber que Ella los veía.

Porque Ella veía, sentía. (9)

La amortajada is Ana María, wife of Antonio, mother of Anita, Fred and Alberto,
ex-lover in her adolescence of her cousin, Ricardo, teaser of Fernando, her
confidant, sister of Alicia. As these people come to mourn over her death bed, she
watches them with an exhilarating freedom; their presence frees her memories,
and through them she recalls the details of her life. As she observes them, she is
sinking into the oblivion of death, but, every so often, someone, something, takes
her, guides her again to a dubious surface of the living, tempting her with visions
of life. In this process, she becomes another being, objectively observing her own
wasting away, distantly aware of being laid out in all the paraphernalia of death,
whose imagery, made most explicit in the candles that surround her, creeps into
the reality of the day: "El día quema horas, minutos, segundos" (35). In the
structure of the novel, Bombal uses different narrators. One is Ana María herself,
in first person. The second is a third person narrator, a woman of whom María
Luisa Bombal said:

> Es una mujer que contempla a otra mujer y siente compasión por lo
> que le ocurrió en la vida y sólo comprende en la muerte.[3]

Towards the end, in a section added much later on, yet another narrator appears,
the dead woman's confessor. In 1968, at the age of 58 and after not having
published anything in Spanish for over twenty years, María Luisa Bombal
returned to her most famous novel one last time. In this new section she sought to
resolve the religious tension in the novel, and add a passage in which the
protagonist's confessor remembers her deeply personal relationship with
established religion, guided primarily through her sensual reaction to the
recounting of the lives of the saints and Biblical stories. By returning to La
amortajada and adding this final section, María Luisa Bombal intensifies the
peace of the end of the novel; without it Ana María is lowered in body but not in

soul into the earth. María Luisa Bombal returned to this last part as a response to her own need to reconcile religion, living and death:

> Lo juro. No tentó a la amortajada el menor deseo de incorporarse. Sola, podría, al fin, descansar, morir.
>
> Había sufrido la muerte de los vivos. Ahora anhelaba la inmersión total, la segunda muerte: la muerte de los muertos. (107)

In interview the author talked of her feelings about death:

> No creo que existe. Soy religiosa. Creo en una vida en el más allá donde los seres que se han ido tienen influencia sobre los que permanecen en la tierra. ... La muerte me aterra, me da una curiosidad inmensa. Creo que lo peor sería descubrir que detrás de la muerte no hay nada. Sería tan terrible como creer que todo termina con la muerte.[4]

The novel stayed with Bombal all her life, she helped with the translations into English and French, she was involved in the re-editions of the book, and in a project for a film script. She was constantly criticised for and questioned about her small literary output – her last published story was "La historia de María Griselda" (1946) – and about her decision to live outside Chile. Here, I want to tackle a question that, in the light of the novelist's own experience of life, the novel begs. How much of María Luisa Bombal is projected into the novel?

María Luisa Bombal was an extraordinary woman. Born and brought up in the Chilean resort of Viña del Mar, she had a privileged background, an education second to none, studying in Chile and in France, fluent in French and English, writing in both languages, with a real knowledge of Latin. She was attractive, romantic, lively, and given to exalted passions. This was painfully demonstrated in the case of her ill-fated love for Eulogio Sánchez, whom she finally attempted to murder, by shooting at point blank range from a doorway in Santiago. (She was let off when he did not press charges. She then went to New York, in 1941). She lived as a young woman in Buenos Aires, where she joined the vibrant artistic circles of the thirties – Jorge Luis Borges, Victoria Ocampo, Alfonsina Storni, Federico García Lorca, Pablo Neruda, with whom she fought over the kitchen table to write in the house where they both lodged. Pablo Neruda achieved fame, respect, literary prizes in his own country as well as abroad. Like Gabriela Mistral, Bombal's work sat on the edge of oblivion in Chile. But that is another issue. She married the Argentine artist Jorge Larco, but it was a short lived and problematic union; and she published in *Sur*. Everything after moving to New York was silence and dismay. In Chile her writing was new in conception, structure, theme, and in the sex of its author:

> No se ha escrito en Chile prosa semejante y, después de los poetas máximos, sólo buscando mucho en letras universales podría encontrársele paralelo.
> Mezcla singular, fenómeno digno de análisis el don gratuito, la poesía innata, la claridad, el orden y la lógica, unidos a no se sabe qué desdén que la fantasía visionaria siente por los datos concretos, aunque se afirme en ellos paso a paso.
> He aquí a la que inauguró con más derechos que nadie la nueva etapa de nuestra literatura posterior al criollismo, dejándola en pleno dominio estético, hallado y señoreado soberanamente, sin esfuerzo, sin propósito, porque sí.[5]

Yet, built into these declarations of praise are the seeds of her relegation to obscurity – that her writing was somehow intuitive, innate, that she broke literary traditions "porque sí". Not because she was setting out a new writing, or that she thought about the craft of writing. It was the terrain of others to defy consciously the *criollismo* of the previous generations. María Luisa did it because she felt like it, by intuition and osmosis – by dint of being a woman, and not being represented in these traditions in the first place? This attitude plagued her. It put the author into the limbo of the writer who is an attractive, intelligent, lively woman: an anomaly in the Santiago of the thirties. There is a famous quote, in which a writer said, "María Luisa tiene demasiada personalidad para ser mujer".[6] This was not a light observation, but a damning reproach, for it implied a lack of femininity, and succinctly sums up the dilemma that María Luisa Bombal suffered: how to reconcile her reality with her deep, deep desire for conformity to a social role she accepted, romanticised and longed to be able to perform adequately: that of lover, wife and mother. (She finally did marry a French count, Fal de St Phalle, in 1944, and lived in the United States until his death in 1973, after which she returned to Chile, where she died in 1980.)

How relevant is this? It is relevant in that María Luisa Bombal wrote a woman's experience, wrote, for the first time in Chile, works that grew from an experience "peculiar to the female",[7] and in that the knowledge, words and expression grew largely from her own experience, rooted in the unbearably ill defined place she occupied in her society, which she was not able through identification with other women or similar experiences, to define. It is this that she writes into her characters: the fact of being lost in this space. She does not write the attempt to move out of it, nor strategies for defiance, merely the being.

The writing of María Luisa Bombal is coherent in its use of a particular language, a particular syntax. She employs a rather restricted, but tightly connected network of images, made explicit, in the first instance, in the titles of her short stories and novels: *La última niebla, El árbol, Trenzas, Las islas negras*. They are the physical expression of the inner worlds of the protagonists, worlds that find articulation only in this interior identification with natural elements, and seldom through verbal articulation, or action. It is a writing that, accepting notions of the mystery of womanhood, makes this the source of the work of the imagination, in finding the means to express the secrets of this mystery, known only to woman herself. Throughout all her work the same images and themes occur, occupying similar narrative functions: the narrators are led, passively, to places beyond their bounds, yet at the murky edges of their sensual imaginations; boring marriages trap innocent victims; silence becomes a refuge, but terrifying in its immensity, power and autonomous dynamics; time and its passage are threatening, and worlds are in an unstoppable process of decay, a decay finally made most explicit, and resolved in *La amortajada*, where decay becomes decomposition, and finally a union with the complexities of time. And almost every story has a shooting incident: attempted suicides, real suicides, the vengeful murder of a beautiful wife's doves in "La historia de María Griselda". Death as the final and only real solution is never far from this work – shooting is her favourite means. (Before her assault on her lover, María Luisa Bombal had actually shot herself, in the shoulder, in his presence).

On one level *La amortajada* describes a descent into the earth that will harbour the decomposing body, as little by little the protagonist sinks into a consciousness that is not that of the living, but that of the dead. The narrative structure provides the richness of image and experience that characterise the novel. Each narrative level opens a window into another world, onto another personal experience of the world that was Ana María's while alive, and that will leave its traces now that she is dead. Bombal assumes the role of the omniscient narrator, yet without imposing a firm vision of reality, as she once stated:

> el sentimiento de las realidades esenciales, encarnadas en símbolos y descifradas a través del arte son tanto o más verdaderas que las realidades cotidianas.[8]

She achieves control without control by evoking only blurred sketches of both the protagonist and of those who enter into silent dialogues with her:

> Reconsidera y nota que de su vida entera quédanle sólo en el recuerdo, como signos de identificación, la inflexión de una voz o el gesto de una mano que hila en el espacio la oscura voluntad del destino. (*La amortajada*, 74–75)

La amortajada becomes a vehicle for the narration, and for the thoughts, memories, sorrow and relief conveyed by each individual, each one sure that his or her words are protected and rendered silent by the unconsciousness of death. It is this narrative technique that imbues passivity with energy.

La amortajada is the writing of a moment: it is the writing of the dramatically charged moment before total loss of a wordly consciousness, when the world, in all its attractiveness, joy, ugliness, pain and smallness, is still alluring. Ana María is on a journey, and each person that visits her drags her back to a sensibility of a world that, in horrible irony, she is only now beginning to see clearly. If the people that had populated her world bring her back to a former reality, then her own unease with the condition of death does the same, but in a much more oneiric way. At intervals a hand is held out to her, a voice urges her to follow, and transports her to different expanses of this huge, timeless instant between life and death:

> — "Vamos, vamos".
> — "¿Adónde?
> Alguien, algo, la toma de la mano, la obliga a alzarse.
> Como si entrara, de golpe, en un nudo de vientos encontrados,
> danza en un punto fijo, ligera, igual a un copo de nieve.
> — "Vamos".
> — "¿Adónde?"
> — "Más allá". (34)

In journeys that echo the night flights of the protagonist of *La última niebla*, and the transporting qualities of the music in "El árbol", where the imagination of the characters is set free by forces to which they cannot or will not put a name, a force beyond her control guides La amortajada, free, to and fro between different levels of consciousness, and as the mourners pass through her room, this independent force guides her inexorably to the deepest sleep, to which she begins to feel closer and closer:

> Fatigada, anhela, sin embargo, desprenderse de aquella partícula de conciencia que la mantiene atada a la vida, y dejarse llevar hacia atrás, hasta el profundo y muelle abismo que siente allá abajo. (43)

What is it that creates this continuing attachment to life, when she desires sleep and rest after her exhausting illness? The answer is that she is basking in the luxury of that moment, in the glorious freedom of her physical demise, in the final self-indulgent exorcism of her memory, which becomes the final indulgence of her senses, formerly so neatly packed and tied by her adherence to the rules of her role. As she listens to the rain, she "exhausts" the emotion it causes, to the last drop. Yet, it is a cruel, fatal thought, a horrible waste, to live an emotion to the full only in death. It is the ruthless freedom of her remembering. In her memories she can see the way her life was shaped, and it is now she says: "¡Ah Dios mío, Dios mío! ¿Es preciso morir para saber?".

In the final paragraphs of the book Ana María emerges briefly to the surface of life, where she still has the illusion that she can move, open the coffin, return, cold and straight, to the door of her home. But she does not:

> Pero, nacidas de su cuerpo, sentía una infinidad de raíces hundirse
> y esparcirse en la tierra como una pujante telaraña por la que subía
> temblando, hasta ella, la constante palpitación del universo. (106)

With this realisation of the roots that are spreading from her, of the universe that is pulsating beneath her, La amortajada finally establishes a new relationship with her death: she associates it definitively with her life. This is one of the great narrative successes of the novel, linking life and death through threads of central vital images, her hair, the roots of the trees in the earth where she will be buried. Linking it also with her other writing:

> Porque la caballera de la mujer arranca desde lo más profundo y
> misterioso; desde allí donde nace y tiembla la primera burbuja; que
> es desde allí que se desenvuelve, lucha y crece entre muchas y
> enmarañadas fuerzas, hasta la superficie de lo vegetal, del aire y
> hasta las frentes privilegiadas que ella eligiera. ("Las trenzas", 73)

Through her confidant Fernando, who, by her death bed, enters into a silent and, at last, honest dialogue with the woman he had loved for so long and whose only response had been constant humiliation, the reader receives a different appreciation of Ana María's imaginative life, an expression of an experience of the world whose traces are seen to be implanted deep within:

> Te admiraba. Admiraba esa tranquila inteligencia tuya cuyas raíces
> estaban hundidas en lo oscura de tu ser.
> — '¿Sabe lo que hace agradable e íntimo a este cuarto? El reflejo y

la sombra del árbol arrimado a la ventana. Las casa no debieran ser
nunca más altas que los árboles,' decías. (*La amortajada*, 50–51)

As in "El árbol", the tree is sought out as a protector. Again, these images are at
the heart of Bombal's writing; they are the physical elements that delimit the real
experience of a world, extended into the expression of the imagination. Yet,
recounted by Fernando, they have the grating edge of wonder that anything at all
could be imagined inside a pretty little head. The reader becomes acquainted with
layer upon layer of the protagonist's imagination, each layer, though hidden
beneath the weight of subsequent years, reaping its own life. So, while the
protagonists may be able, on one level, to mourn the losses in her life, in her death
every memory, every experience has its own place, a place now awarded in a
ruthless process of equalising. In this way, time loses any accepted meaning, it
passes, it consumes life, but this does not mean that each moment past sinks
inevitably into oblivion. No, life itself is a constant accumulation of time.

Time passes and mounts up hours, seconds, moments, yet somehow, María Luisa
Bombal's characters are outside the experience of time. It is this that lends an
exquisite tension to a novel whose identity must be essentially passive, and it is
this that provides a central dilemma that may never be resolved.

Who is Ana María? She was a member of the land-owning Chilean elite, she was
a woman whose childhood was spent in idyllic comfort, who fell in love with her
cousin during her adolescence, who miscarried his child, and who harboured the
remnants of this love whose end she never quite understood. She was the woman
who married without love the man picked out for her, and she was the woman
who never quite came to terms with the rules of the game according to which she
was to live her life. In many ways, she was just another female product of her
class. In life she had managed to exist behind a veil of conformity, outwardly
accepting her role. She had passed on the values of her class; she had presumed
dead, or as the perverted indulgence of suffering, all the passions and memories
that are now, in her coffin, awakened. She is a woman who has to die to
understand.

Can this construction of a stifling and typical female existence of a certain type be called a social statement? Is it a writing that suggests rebellion, that encourages and calls for rebellion, even a shrouded rebellion? Some critics have seen an implied revolt. And perhaps this is one of the dangers in an analysis of a novel like *La amortajada*: that we, now from the perspectives of the modern female, look for elements of rebellion against a role imposed. Was that not what María Luisa Bombal was suggesting when her protagonist can only find freedom of thought in death? At the roots of this problem is another unresolved tension, that of the identification of the author with her protagonist, into whom she wrote an imagination that sought its own escapes, its own expression, while the external self accepted the social codes into which she had been bred. At the time of writing these works, María Luisa Bombal longed to belong to that society, for it would be a society that would legitimise her existence, actually give her an existence as a person, as a wife, as a mother, and not as a child, an unthinking and irrelevant being, the state allotted to the unmarried woman, who has no social standing, no space where she can yield a certain power, no matter how small that may be. When *La amortajada* was written, women had not yet won the vote in Chile, that was not to happen until 1949. María Luisa Bombal explored the world of the woman complicit in her margination.

When she was in fact asked about the intentions of her work, if she had intended to denounce the role of women in society, she would reply:

> Yo tenía pasión por lo personal, lo interno, el corazón, el arte, la naturaleza. No, yo no perseguía nada...[9]

Yet, it is through this preoccupation with the internal and particular worlds of her protagonists that she finally poses questions that are central to a fundamental misunderstanding between the sexes.

All that the reader learns about Ana María's marriage is negative. It is an arranged marriage, through which she embarks on a route long mapped out for her and now personalised in her husband, Antonio, a good man that she has no legitimate reason, at first, not to love as a good husband. But she, through her marriage, enters a new world – they enter a possible new world. In their first months together Antonio shows her the pond made in the garden, a large, dark blue mirror in which she can comb her long hair, the essence of her vitality and sexuality. Yet all she can see is desolation, and when her husband, showing her how the images break and reform, throws a stone into the water, all she experiences is the violence of the gesture, the destruction of her image, the dis-arming of her self:

> Recuerda. Asiéndose de la balaustrada de hierro forjada, había cerrado los ojos, conmovida por un miedo pueril.
> — "El fin del mundo. Así ha de ser. Lo he visto". (67)

At this stage the language that is used speaks of the passivity of the woman, she allows her life to be lead by her husband, she sinks into a silence that awakes her at night. When her husband, looking to make his wife happy, asks her what she wants, her answer is desperate:

> Se había aferrado al brazo de su marido deseando hablar, explicar, y fue aquí donde su pánico, rebelde, saltó por sobre todo argumento:
> — "Quiero irme". (72)

Again there is no real articulation of the reasons for her unhappiness, there is no consideration of its roots or its solution. There is no consideration for another person, only the panicked whimper ·of an ego trapped, a whimper that could externally be interpreted as rebellion, but that is merely the only words she could find to seek a way out of a state of malaise. Once removed again from the novel, the reader can see another facet of this. It is a reaction against the role she is asked to play, and against the space she is asked to inhabit, and in which physically she cannot be at ease. Her "quiero irme" is her escape to the known and comfortable, a child's world she mistakenly thinks she can return to. Her unwitting rebellion maps out for her an endless married life of jealousy, love and sadness, and the loss of the sexual satisfaction that she had experienced with her husband, who has retreated into his own space, his own "selva negra". When she finally realises that she is no more than one of the passions in her husband's life, she begins to limit herself, she becomes smaller, meaner, she seeks protection in her own withering. It is here that María Luisa Bombal poses the dubious, but in the context relevant, question:

> Pasaron años. Años en que se retrajo y se fue volviendo día a día
> más limitada y mezquina.
> ¿Por qué, por qué la naturaleza de la mujer ha de ser tal que tenga
> que ser siempre un hombre el eje de su vida?
> Los hombres, ellos lograron poner su pasión en otras cosas. Pero el
> destino de las mujeres es remover una pena de amor en una casa
> ordenada, ante una tapicería inconclusa. (78)

Love becomes destructive in this circumstance, the lack of comprehension is almost total, and it is only now, in death, that she indulges in the luxury of attempting to understand how she controlled her love, how she learned the humiliation of giving too much love, learned to ration it, how, now, she understands that little by little she was complicit in the strangling of the most vital part of herself. And how she enjoyed her suffering for love because that was the passion through which she fed the strength to remain where she was.

María Luisa Bombal may not have written a novel that denounced woman's subordinate role in society, but from the depths of one woman's soul comes a chilling portrayal of a role defined by passivity, by an astounding lack of understanding, by the lack of another model of behaviour. It is only in death that Ana María begins to have some notion of the rules of the game by which her life had been governed. It is here that María Luisa Bombal excelled, for in the novel it is through the accumulation and manipulation of details that the identity of the protagonist and her surroundings are created. The most glorious example of this is when Antonio visits his dead wife and kneels by her bed. She finds him repugnant until:

> Repentinamente la hiere un detalle insólito. Muy pegada a la oreja
> advierte una arruga, una sola, muy fina, tan fina como un hilo de
> telaraña, pero una arruga, una verdadera arruga, la primera.
> Dios mío, ¿aquello es posible? Antonio no es inviolable? (83)

It is glorious. She, who now feels herself new, young, beautiful and without wrinkles, is superior. Yet, in the way of María Luisa Bombal, this is not a consolation. The revelation of Antonio's vulnerability, of male weakness, of the human normality of the male, which she had not seen in life, does not come as a consolation. It comes as a surprise that he is not impervious to the passage of time, and she can no longer hate him the way she did, she can no longer feed her relationship on this hate. It is over, the life force between them is destroyed, and with it their present and their past. What would have happened in life if she had understood the weakness, the normality of her husband? How could she have sustained their relationship? Why does she have to discover the awful falsity of their marriage now, when all she wants is peace and reconciliation with the world she had formed around her, not this desire to live again through hate:

> No. No lo odia. Pero tampoco lo ama. Y he aquí que al dejar de amarlo y de odiarlo siente deshacerse el último nudo de su estructura vital. Nada le importa ya. Es como si no tuviera ya razón de ser ni ella ni su pasado. Un gran hastío la cerca, se siente tambalear hacia atrás. ¡Oh esta súbita rebeldía! Este deseo que la atormenta de incorporarse gimiendo: "¡Quiero vivir. Devuélvanme, devuélvanme mi odio!" (85)

All that is hers now is silence and the final descent. For, if she had known this before she could not have sustained the marriage, she hated any mirror of weakness. She despised Fernando for that reason, she denied his love because he wanted to unite their wounded souls, in a mutually manipulative relationship based on a perverse elongating of suffering.

In all of her works, María Luisa Bombal sets her protagonists against an unwelcome other. Most notably the protagonist of *La última niebla*, measured unfavourably against her husband's perfect first wife, enviously looks on as her sister-in-law indulges her sexual desires, which lead ultimately to an attempted suicide. But even that inspires no pity:

> Y siento, de pronto, que odio a Regina, que envidio su dolor, su trágica aventura y hasta su posible muerte. Me acometen furiosos

deseos de acercarme y sacudirla duramente, preguntándole de qué
se queja, ¡ella, que lo ha tenido todo! Amor, vértigo y abandono.
(*La última niebla*, 53)

The protagonist's silence hides a most cruel projection of the ego. And it is in this
way that Bombal most incisively subverts silence, for it is not merely a lyrical
domain of trees, disappearing islands, misty towns. It is, much more than that, a
place for an uninhibited assertion of the self, bound by no moral or social codes.
In this place, the ego is an ego that can envy, hate, lust; in this place, the self –
ignored as frivolous, childish and irrelevant in the social world the possessor
inhabits – is reaffirmed. Sublimely. Immorally. The physical expressions that
María Luisa Bombal creates are not those that relate to the external world, but that
relate to this shameless, hidden self.

This self is shameless. From the literary world of geographic archeology that
criollismo had become, emerged a writer who wrote exclusively and explicitly
about female experience, in which female desire played an important role. Here
was an author who described explicitly female orgasm, discovered, in the most
female of ways, quite by accident: "¡El placer! ¡Con que era eso el placer! Ese
estremecimiento, ese inmenso aletazo y ese recaer unidos en la misma
vergüenza!" (66); an author who, in *La última niebla*, elaborated an intense sexual
fantasy of ideal love, of all-consuming passionate love, narcissistic love, in which
the protagonist's beauty is mirrored in the passion it inspires in her lover. Like the
other protagonists, neither does this one clearly articulate the world into which
she is drawn – for it is a forbidden world, a world that had not been
acknowledged, that had not been given its words, its images, its expression. The
Bombal protagonist is lead by the hand by someone, by a something that is,
finally, sexual longing, that is the lust for the repetition of the once-experienced
orgasm, that is the desire for freedom from a boring marriage, that is the search
for another way of being beautiful beyond the male mind that tortures and
manipulates beauty. In the protagonists these searches may be inarticulate,
unknowing. But in the writing of Bombal, they are given exquisite expression.
From the place of her abandonment in a literary world, María Luisa Bombal gave
a voice to female desire and female loss. The ultimate expression of this is *La*

amortajada, for it is a great artistic leap of the imagination, it is writing that seems to come from behind tightly closed eyes, a writer forcing her way into a deep inner space and squeezing out the means to express it. The fascination that death held for her was not only a fascination with its mystery, but with the mysteries of its literary expression; perhaps it is the fight against the dead woman in literature, woman as muse and inspiration, rather than as producer, creator. Total passivity, in this, the only stage of María Luisa Bombal's writing – for she wrote no more – becomes a goal, because it is the space for the release of the self. The dynamic of death is the dynamic of the space where an experience peculiar to the female meets the word.

Catherine M. Boyle
King's College, London

1. See 'El árbol', in the collection of stories, *La última niebla. El árbol*, (Santiago: Editorial Andrés Bello, 1982) p.74. All further references will be to this edition.

2. See *La amortajada* (Santiago: Editorial Universitaria, 1981) p.65. All further references will be to this edition.

3. In Agata Gligo, *María Luisa (Sobre la vida de María Luisa Bombal)* (Santiago: Editorial Andrés Bello, 1985).

4. See Sara Vial, introduction to *La historia de María Griselda* (Santiago: Ediciones Universitarias de Valparaíso, 1977) pp.17–78.

5. See the introduction to *La amortajada* by the Chilean critic Alone in the edition quoted above.

6. See Agata Gligo, op. cit., p.56.

7. This is a reference to the poem by June Jordan, "A Case in Point".

8. See Agata Gligo, op. cit., pp.20–21.

9. Ibid., p.77.

The Two Worlds of Mercè Rodoreda

Mercè Rodoreda is known first and foremost as the author of *La plaça del Diamant*, a novel that won acclaim from the general public as well as from the critics. Joan Sales states in the preface to the fifth edition that it was the best novel to appear in Europe in many years – "de molts anys ençà". Not only did she give us this book, which the whole Catalan nation took to its heart, but she followed up this success with a series of other novels and four collections of short stories. I shall begin by giving a short sketch of her publications as a background to what I have to say on the two worlds in which she operates.[1]

Born in 1908, Rodoreda had made a more than promising start to her writing career when the Civil War broke out and put an end to her writing for many years to come. She had already published five novels, the first four of which she later disowned. The fifth novel, *Aloma*, published in 1938, she revised and published again in 1969. Between 1938 and 1962, the year *La plaça del Diamant* appeared, she published nothing except for a collection of short stories which appeared in 1958. The first work she wrote after "el gran marasme", the great stagnation, was *Jardí vora el mar*, although it was not published till later. After that she wrote *La plaça del Diamant*, which was published in 1962. Four years later came *El carrer de les Camèlies*, followed by the publication of *Jardí vora el mar* in 1967. Then, in 1974, appeared the book I consider her masterpiece, *Mirall trencat*. Her final novel *Quanta, quanta guerra...* was published in 1980. Parallel with this production was the publication of four volumes of short stories. Although it is as a novelist that she won her greatest acclaim, I should like to stress the fact that the short stories are also outstanding. Had the novels not won her a place in the annals of Catalan literature, I am convinced that the short stories alone would have done so. But the two worlds to which I refer are not the world of the novel and that of the short story. The division is of a far more fundamental nature, and lies not so much in her treatment of a subject, as in the very subject matter itself.

As the author of *La plaça del Diamant*, Rodoreda became known as the undisputed mistress of the narrative of everyday life. But this mistress of the quotidian also betrays an intense interest in the world of fantasy. The harsh reality of the everyday world is counterbalanced by the equally harsh vision of the world of the unseen. For one of the things that these two aspects of her writing have in common is an attitude of total pessimism. Neither the world of everyday fact nor the world of the imagination can offer any hope or comfort. It is almost impossible to find a single happy character in her writing. Even when it would appear that happiness has been achieved, at the last minute, in the last sentence, this is negated, as, for instance, in the story "Felicitat", from the collection *Vint-i-dos Contes*. It describes the agony of a girl who realises that for the first time her lover has got up without first kissing her. She weeps bitterly, imagines herself leaving him and trying to live without him, far away. When he comes back from his shower and finds her crying he kisses and comforts her. In the final sentence Rodoreda tells us that the angry, injured girl has melted away. In her place is "una noia sense espines, sense exabruptes, una noia que es quedarà, ignorant que tirànicament l'empresonen quatre parets i un sostre de tendresa" [a girl without thorns and without agression, a girl who is going to stay, unaware of the tyranny with which she is held prisoner by four walls and a ceiling of tenderness] (*Tots els contes*, 51).

Because I think the short stories are such an important part of Rodoreda's output, I propose to examine two of them, one representative of each of her two modes, before discussing the novels.

The first story is "Fil a l'agulla" from *Vint-i-dos contes* (*Tots els Contes*, 25–31). It tells the story of Maria Lluïsa, a middle aged dressmaker who works at home, sewing for an elegant establishment in France. She thinks about her cousin, an ailing priest who is in hospital. After the operation he is to come to her flat, where she will look after him. He has given her quite a large sum of money to pay for the operation and other expenses. As she sews a glamorous nightdress for another woman's wedding night, she dreams about the future. She dreams of giving him an overdose, so that she will inherit the money and be able to set up her own dressmaking business. Suddenly she realises the folly of her dreams, and decides it's time to go to bed. After she has undressed she tries on the shimmering white nightdress, then goes to bed and cries all night. The story is steeped in the details of daily life – even Maria Lluïsa's little fantasy is totally earth bound.

By contrast, "La salamandra", from *La meva Cristina i altres contes*. (*Tots els contes*, 237) sets a tone of unreality from the start. It tells of a girl arriving at a pond, where the frogs play with her clothes and comb her hair. A salamander, in addition to being a mythical creature that lives in fire, is also a member of a group of tailed amphibians, related to frogs or toads, so we are not too surprised by the action of the frogs in the story. The girl's lover turns up, and while they are making love the man's wife appears, calls the girl a witch, "bruixa", and drags the man away. The lovers continue to meet, and the girl is ostracised and called 'bruixa' wherever she goes. The villagers throw stones at her, and hang dead animals on her door. Eventually her lover begins to avoid her. Then the priest and the villagers tie her onto a pile of firewood and set fire to it. She can see her lover among the spectators, looking on with his wife. As the fire begins to burn her she feels herself being changed into a salamander – of the mythical variety. When the villagers see this they run away shrieking. She manages to escape and goes into hiding. Then she creeps into her lover's house and hides under the bed. She hears her lover telling his wife that he loves only her – the wife, that is. The salamander creeps into the moonlight and lies in the cross formed by the shadow of the crossbars of the window frame, and prays for herself. One day the wife finds her under the bed and chases her out. She escapes to the pond, where she is attacked by two boys who tear off one of her feet. Three eels appear and play with the broken off limb, till they get tired of the game, and "l'ombra" sucks down the broken limb.

Well, nothing very everyday about that scenario! It evokes a nightmare world of cruelty and betrayal and, above all, futility. It is, of course, soaked in symbolism. But it can hardly be less desolating than the theme of "Fil a l'agulla".

In her early novel *Aloma* the same tone of disillusion dominates. "L'amor em fa fàstic" [I find love disgusting] are the very first words of the novel. And this book, like all her earlier novels, is situated unambiguously in the realms of the everyday. It tells the story of Aloma, a girl who lives with her brother and his wife and their little boy. Aloma falls in love (in spite of her opening words) with her sister-in-law's brother when he comes from South America to spend some months with them. At the end of the novel the man leaves. Aloma is pregnant, but is too proud to tell him, aware that he does not love her. In the final scene she leaves the house she has been brought up in, leaving behind all that she has ever cared for. And if it's any consolation to the reader, she doesn't appear to have lost all that much, for she seems to have cared for very little and to have found no joy in life. We are told that "La gent li agradava molt poc i tot la cansava" (30). And again "A l'hora de llevarse no tenia ganes de vestirse i posar – se a viure. Li agradaven tan poques coses." [When it was time to get up she didn't feel like getting dressed and getting on with her life. There were so few things that she liked] (45). There are no dramatic moments in the book. The narrative is taken up entirely by descriptions of the quotidian. Aloma's feeling are described in relation to the all too everyday world that surrounds her. The house, shabby and in poor repair, the garden, Aloma's clothes, the new curtains for the bedroom, the dripping taps, the smell of cooking, the need to iron dry·her only 'enagos' before getting dressed to go out – these things are the subject matter of the story, and from them Rodoreda evokes a nostalgic picture of life in pre-Civil War Barcelona.

More than twenty years later, in the next novel to be published, *La plaça del Diamant*, the setting is almost exactly the same. We may have moved down a rung or two of the social ladder – Colometa lives in the predominantly working-class district of Gràcia instead of the humbler reaches of the more fashionable Sant Gervasi. But her surroundings are evoked with the same minute attention to detail. As this book is so well known I shall say little about its plot – if plot there be in a novel of this type, where the narrative consists of one long, rather rambling reminiscence. The book tells the story of Colometa's marriage to Quimet, of their domestic trials and difficulties, one of them being that Quimet has filled the house full of pigeons, with which he is about to make a great deal of money, which never quite materialises. What does materialise is the mess the pigeons make − and guess who has the job of clearing it up! It is the combination of simple domestic detail and the impact of the Civil War that gives the novel its unforgettable force. One small detail, for instance: Colometa is working as a "dona de fer feines" [cleaning lady] to try to supplement their inadequate income at the beginning of the war. The milkman appears,

> Vaig obrir el reixat i l'home em va donar les dues paperines encerades, i jo les vaig agafar... I l'home de la llet Sila... va dir al senyor si volia fer el favor de pagar-lo, perquè no sabia si l'endemà els podria dur més llet. Va pujar la senyora i ho va sentir i va preguntar què havien fet amb les vaques, i va dir que pensava que les vaques no feien pas la revolució, i l'home de la llet Sila va dir, no senyora, em penso... però tothom va pels carrers i nosaltres tancarem. I com ens ho farem, sense llet? va dir la senyora.

> [I opened the iron gate and the man gave me the two waxed cartons, and I took them... And the man with the Sila milk... asked my master to be good enough to pay him, because he didn't know whether he'd be able to come back the following day with milk. And my mistress came up and heard him, and asked him what had they done with the cows, and she said that she didn't think that the cows were in revolt, and the man with the Sila milk said, no, I think not... but everyone's out on the streets and we're closing. And how will we manage without milk? said my mistress.] (142)

In this one, tiny, everyday incident Rodoreda gives the measure of the shortsightedness and egoism of the Spanish middle class. The Civil War has started, the whole population is on the verge of a catastrophic upheaval, but all they can see is their own tiny routine. "I com ens ho farem, sense llet?"

In one of the short stories, 'Viure al dia' (*Tots els contes*, 291), the same problem is tackled, in a much lengthier and more heavy-handed manner. At a tea-drinking afternoon visit, three ladies give a display of their vacuity and frivolity. When the subject of the incipient Civil War is mentioned they dismiss it as an alarmist rumour. A note at the end of the story gives details of the horrifying fate awaiting all three women as they are caught up in the war. The author makes her point; but how much more elegantly she does it in *La plaça del Diamant*, with the short paragraph about the milk.

The small, everyday detail, in addition to illuminating the state of mind of a whole society, can also be used to add drama to the narrative. Colometa tells us how a stain appears on one of the walls in the dining room of the flat that she, Quimet, and two of his friends are preparing for the young couple to move in to (46–47). After a great deal of fuss and argument with the neighbours, from whose side the offending stain is assumed to be coming, after discussions with the "propietari", the matter ends thus; "I tot plegat, tant anar i verir, tant enraonar i tant enrabiar-se, per res, per una cosa que no valia la pena, per una cosa que va morir posant'hi el bufet al davant." [And in the long run, all that coming and going, all that talking and getting angry, for nothing, for something that wasn't worth the bother, for something that died when we put the sideboard in front of it.]

One of the greatest delights of the book lies in its style. The words are Colometa's; the impression is of a story told by a simple working class girl. The narrative is inextricably mixed up with Colometa's comments, her hopes and fears, her occasional asides to the reader – "no sé si m'explico" [I don't know whether I've made myself clear] – to make sure that she has made her point. The simplicity, of course, is only apparent. By never abandoning the fiction that these are the words of the untutored girl, by never letting her heroine's credibility slip, Rodoreda manages to immerse us totally in Colometa's world. The physical details of the house, her companions, the streets of Gràcia, are the bricks with which she builds a structure that includes so much more than the objects mentioned. We are made aware of Colometa's feelings, of those of the other characters, of the perilous and then disastrous state of the country in the years before, during and after the Civil War. The description of the last days of the war and of the period that followed, limited as it is to Colometa's references to the daily struggle for survival, is as harrowing a document as one could hope to find. So hopeless and weary is Colometa that she is on the point of killing herself and her children. And because Colometa has carried us on so convincingly in her artless account, with such a wealth of documentary detail, we accept this as a possible and reasonable reaction to the circumstances.

Much has been said about the symbolism of the book, especially in connexion with the pigeons and the name Colometa. For me the outstanding symbol is the house in which Colometa goes to work. Many pages are devoted to the description of this puzzling and intricate house, with all its different levels. Colometa never quite seems to get the hang of it. The description ends with these words: "I si parlo tant de la casa, és perquè encara la veig com un trencaclosques, amb les veus d'ells que, quan em cridaven, no sabia mai d'on venien" [And if I've so much to say about the house it's because I still see it as a puzzle, not knowing where their voices were coming from every time they called me] (109). The fact that she feels she is in a "trencaclosques" fits in with what she has already told us about herself earlier on in the book; "però és que a mi em passava que no sabia ben bé per què era al món." [...but the thing is that I didn't really have any idea of what I was doing in this world] (47).

The two novels *El carrer de les Camèlies* and *Jardí vora el mar* are also firmly rooted in the everyday world. *Quanta, quanta guerra...* the last of Rodoreda's novels is the least quotidian and one of the quotations that precede the prologue prepares us for this. It is Goya's "El sueño de la razón engendra monstruos." It tells the story of a young boy who runs away from home to join the soldiers in the Civil War, but soon runs away from the war and leads a wandering purposeless life. The book is, in fact, a version of the picaresque novel – a series of disparate scenes and characters, linked only by the central character. The main difference is that the hero is very far from being a "pícaro" by nature. There are some frankly fantastic episodes in the book; but the really disturbing sense of unreality lies in the assortment of weird people that the hero comes across and the improbable situations he finds himself in. It is true that we are in the middle of a civil war. But one of the tragedies of war is that it affects ordinary, everyday people. And there don't seem to be any of these in this novel. In this it can be said to be the very opposite of *La plaça del Diamant*. There seems to be a certain delight in the unwholesome and abnormal in this book, and in some of the rest of Rodoreda's work, especially the short stories.

And it is in some of the short stories that we find the complete antithesis to the everyday world of the earlier novels. We have already looked at "La salamandra". There are many other examples of the fantastic in the later collections – *La meva Cristina*, *Semblava de seda*, and, most notably, in *Viatges i flors*. This comprises two collections of stories; the *Flors de debò*, written over a long period, and the *Viatges*, written shortly before publication in 1980. Both describe purely imaginary and wholly impossible concepts. Again we are reminded of Goya's "El sueño de la razón engendra monstruos". There would seem to be something especially perverse in the choice of flowers as the subject matter of the second part of the collection. Rodoreda herself frequently tells us how fond she is of flowers, and most of her books bear testimony to this. In *Jardí vora el mar*, for instance, the story is told by an old gardener, and flowers are frequently and lovingly described. But they are normal flowers, beautiful and innocent. Not so in the *Flors de debò* series. Here is the Flor Llaminera; "Se't meja de viu en viu. T'agafa, et plega, se't fica a dins i escup els botons. T'assimila molt lentament perquè es veu que té la digestió difícil. Val més així." [It eats you alive. It takes hold of you, it folds you, it swallows you up, and it spits out the buttons. It assimilates you very slowly, because it seems it has difficulty in digesting. Just as well] (101). There is the Flor Felicitat, which lulls you to sleep till you roll down into the water and are devoured by the "peix forquilla", which bores its way into you and devours you "de dins estant", starting from the inside (80). We can hardly regret the fact that these flowers, despite their name, "flors de debò" [real flowers], are not to be found in the real world. There is, admittedly, a touch of humour in some of the descriptions. But it is a pretty morbid type of humour. And we cannot help wondering at the sort of mental quirk that has produced these descriptions from someone who has a passion for flowers.

The *Viatges* are equally disconcerting. The series recounts the wanderings of the narrator through a collection of villages, each with its own tragic or absurd characteristic. "Viatge al poble de les nenes Perdues", "...dones abandonades", "...de tota la pena", "...les iaies teixidores", "...homes ganduls", "de vidre...", "dels morts..." and "dels penjats" [Journey to the village of the lost little girls, ...abandoned women, ...of all sorrow, ...the weaving grandmothers, ...lazy men, ...made of glass, ...of the dead, ...of the hanged men] (47). In the latter, all the men of the village hang themselves once their wives have given birth to their sixteenth child, all but the last two children having died by then. The narrator has come through a wood full of dead men hanging from the trees, and in the village the wife of the latest victim explains the situation. The horrifying thing is that they all accept this as a perfectly natural thing. As the latest widow says, "...no s'ha adonat quina cara d'estar al cel que fan tots els penjats!" [...haven't you noticed what a blissful expression all the hanged men have?].

Having seen examples of these two extremes in Rodoreda's narrative, we can now study how she has united these two aspects in her second-last novel, *Mirall trencat*.

The book is a family chronicle, and tells the story of Teresa, a poor girl whose beauty enables her to marry a very wealthy old man, who obligingly dies soon after. Her second marriage is to the equally wealthy Salvador Valldaura. They have a daughter, Sofia, who turns out to be rather nasty. Sofia marries Eladi Farriols and they, in addition to having two sons, adopt Maria, Eladi's illegitimate daughter. Sofia's motivation is not altruism, but rather a desire to have power over the girl, and, through her, over Eladi. Maria and the elder boy, Ramon, kill the younger one, and Maria commits suicide when she learns that she is Ramon's half-sister. The family chronicle continues with Teresa's death and the dispersion of the whole family during the Civil War. The house is left in the hands of Armanda, the traditional faithful servant, who really identifies totally with the family. The story is told in the third person, at first mainly from Teresa's point of view, then from that of Armanda, the servant. Both are practical women, and concentrate on the material, everyday aspect of their lives. The luxurious villa in Sant Gervasi, obviously of modernista style, is described meticulously, with special attention paid to the garden, which is, in fact, the scene of two horrifying deaths. The first is that of Teresa's younger grandson, pushed into the pond by his brother Ramon and Maria, and held under the water till he drowns by having a forked bough placed round his neck; the other death is that of Maria, who throws herself from the roof. In this episode too we are given a particularly vivid and distressing description. Not content with letting the girl smash herself to pieces as she falls to the ground. Rodoreda has her land on the pointed trunk of a laurel tree that had been struck by lightning many years earlier. In the morning one of the servants finds blood under the tree, and Maria's disembowelled body is seen impaled on the trunk.

It is in connexion with Maria and her death that the fantastical element enters the book, in the form of the supernatural. Its first appearance is an excellent example of the close link Rodoreda forges between her two worlds. Long after Maria's death her stepmother, Sofia, goes into the dead girl's room, gloating over the fact that she has been freed from the presence of this alien child. She finds everything in perfect order – Armanda has as great a devotion to the dead as to the living of the family, and keeps Maria's bedroom in spotless condition. The room is described in detail, down to the organdie flounces on the bed and the dressing table. As she stands there, on a still, windless day, Sofia sees one of these flounces fluttering gently. There has not been a breath of air to cause the movement. Sofia leaves the room, feeling distinctly uncomfortable. That is our introduction to Maria's ghost. Later there are other manifestations, experienced by a variety of different people. Just on case the reader is tempted to dismiss it all as imagination, Rodoreda dispels all possible doubt by dedicating a whole chapter to the ghost. In "El fantasme de Maria" the ghost itself is the narrator. And we see how well and how purposefully the two worlds have been blended, the natural and the supernatural, in the fact that it is through Maria's ghost that we come to understand her point of view. During her lifetime she was presented as a wilful, rather unsympathetic character. The ghost helps us to feel compassion for her and to see that, however badly she fitted into the family, her place in the novel is central. Rodoreda herself tells us this in her introduction to the book (28).

Nothing in this novel can rival the naive spontaneity of Colometa's narrative in *La plaça del Diamant*. But, through the blending of her two worlds, Rodoreda achieves in *Mirall trencat* a depth that none of the other novels approaches. If not as captivating as *La plaça del Diamant*, the book is perhaps the more satisfying of the two, in the balance it strikes between the two aspects of life that Rodoreda has chosen to highlight. The image of the mirror, very dear to Rodoreda, is the most constantly used symbol to represent the meeting of her two worlds. The mirror reflects reality – or what we take to be the reality of the everyday world. But the reflection is not the same thing as the object it reflects. It is a degree further removed from reality – or, depending on how you look at it, a degree nearer. In a story like "La Salamandra", for instance, the whole action is given to us in the words of the mythical creature that the narrator has become – or perhaps reverted to. Within the terms of the story itself we are not authorised to consider the salamander any less real than the woman it has replaced. Similarly, the question of which is the more authentic, the reflection or the thing reflected, is a teasing puzzle that Rodoreda does not allow us to forget. In *El carrer de les Camèlies*, for instance, the heroine, Cecília, gazing at herself in the mirror, gives us an inversion of the Narcissus myth, for she tells us that the reflection falls in love with the real Cecília; "jo... a fora del mirall era el que enamora i a dintre del mirall era l'enamorat." [Outside the mirror I was the object of love, and inside I was the lover] (50).

A further complication arises when, as in *Mirall Trencat*, the mirror is shattered. Towards the end of the novel, when Armanda is left alone after the rest of the household has fled during the Civil War, she takes up a hand mirror and walks about the house looking at the reflection as she moves about. She falls, and the mirror is shattered, but the broken pieces are left in their place in the frame. What it reflects is now a stage further removed from our everyday world. Rodoreda plays a disquieting game in which the gap between the two worlds is progressively narrowed. It may be, however, that the fragmentary reflection of reality as seen in the broken mirror is as much as we can stand, given Rodoreda's wholly pessimistic view of life. For, to Rodoreda life not only seems cruel but, worse still, futile. "Desencís", disenchantment, is a word that appears again and again. In the introduction to *Tots el contes* Carme Arnau says;– 'Mercè Rodoreda ...tracta, doncs, de desmitificar al vida i mostrar-la tal i cam ella mateixa la veu: dura i desencisada.' [So, Mercè Rodoreda tries to demythify life and show it as she herself sees it: hard and disenchanted] (6). And we are left in no doubt that this is the view taken by all Rodoreda's principal characters – Aloma, joyless and oppressed even in her youth, Colometa penetrated by a nostalgia for a happiness she has never known, Cecília with her sad eyes and her fragmented life, Maria, the tragic child, both murderess and suicide, the bewildered hero of *Quanta, quanta guerra...*, materially and spiritually homeless – all these live in a world of disenchantment and futility. Some of them, like Aloma and Colometa, live entirely in the world of the quotidian; some, like La Salamandra have moved wholly into the world of the fantastic. It is when, as in *Mirall Trencat*, her characters inhabit the dangerous territory between the two worlds, that Rodoreda's vision is at its most compelling, disturbing, and satisfying.[2]

Mercè Clarasó

formerly of the University of St. Andrews

1. All references to Mercè Rodoreda's work will be made to the following editions:
   Mercè Rodoreda, *Aloma* (Barcelona: Edicions 62, 1969)
   La plaça del Diamant (Barcelona: Club Editor, 1968)
   Jardi vora el mar (Barcelona: Club Editor, 1968)
   El carrer de les Camèlies (Barcelona: Club Editor, 1969)
   Tots els contes (Barcelona: Edicions 62, 1979)
   Viatges i flors (Barcelona: Edicions 62, 1980)
   Quanta, quanta guerra (Barcelona: Club Editor, 1981)
   Mirall trencat (Barcelona: Club Editor, 1974)

2. See the interesting article by Ana María Moix, 'Las pasiones secretas de Mercè Rodoreda', *Cambio 16* (6 de mayo, 1991, pp.102–105) which came to my attention after having completed this paper.

Beastly Women and Underdogs: the short fiction of Dora Alonso

This essay engages with some curious paradoxes in Dora Alonso's short fiction, the resolution of which I believe is found in a feminist reading. But first, how to approach stories in which: a frightened, old mare, about to be slaughtered for zoo meat, gives birth to a foal; a caring rat feeds her young on merchandise denied by a profiteer to a hungry human mother and her baby; a cat sees her recently born kittens carried off by her trusted owner to their death; a pampered bitch escapes to find sexual pleasure with a flea-bitten dog, only to be caught and killed by the dog-catcher at the height of her ecstasy; a woman who hates and kills cockroaches dies of shock when one crawls out of the woodwork while she is in her steam bath, stares her in the eye and makes for her neck? These are just some of the eighteen stories, published originally between 1962 and 1987, collected and republished in 1989 in the volume entitled *Juega la dama*.[1] The criterion according to which they were selected, what they all have in common, is the presence of a female protagonist, animal or human. Alonso calls these stories "cuentos de hembra" but insists there is no feminist subtext. Femaleness is a "tema literario nada mas", she says, despite the fact that the original title was *Jaque mate* ("Death to the King") which she thought was too aggressive and therefore dropped.[2] This is the first paradox: a text predicated on femaleness which its author denies is feminist. What is striking, however, is that animality is as prominent a feature as feminality. Even in stories not focussing on animals,

animals are present and in my view this is the most salient characteristic of Alonso's short fiction in general, written both before and after the Revolution.

Dora Alonso has not been canonized; she has not been admitted to the sanctum of Latin American Literature. Yet she is the only female writer of narrative fiction mentioned in any depth, or at all, in the standard surveys of the post-Revolutionary Cuban novel. Seymour Menton lists 78 "novels of the Revolution" of which four are by women. The Cuban critic Luisa Campuzano's figures are equally despairing: between 1959 and 1983, twelve novels were published by women and over 170 by men. Of these twelve, two were by women who subsequently left Cuba and three were "testimonios", leaving seven novels in 24 years of which only two are worthy of attention in Campuzano's view: Mirta Yáñez's *La hora de los mameyes* (1983) and Dora Alonso's *Tierra inerme* (1961). As far as short fiction is concerned, Menton lists only two women (one is Dora Alonso) who contributed more than one story to the twelve anthologies published between 1959 and 1971. 115 volumes of short stories came out in the same period by individual authors; only twelve were written by ten women.[3]

Women writers of adult fiction were seemingly even more affected than their male counterparts by the censorship and persecution of the difficult 1970s when certain genres became more acceptable than others for socio-political advancement. According to Desiderio Navarro, "la poesía, el testimonio y la literatura para niños" were the genres preferred by those who wanted to make a quick name for themselves or earn "simplemente el derecho a presentarse en público como 'escritor'".[4] Dora Alonso could not remain unaffected by this climate and her novel, *Tierra inerme*, was followed by several much acclaimed books for children in the sixties and seventies and two "testimonios" in the early eighties. But she did manage to publish three collections of short stories for adults: *Ponolani* (1966, Gente Nueva); *Once caballos* (1970); *Cuentos* (1976).[5] Like Borges and Rulfo, she excells at short narrative. Alonso belongs to the generation born between 1910 and 1920 which includes Onelio Jorge Cardoso, Virgilio Piñera and José Lezama Lima of the Orígenes group (the latter two estranged from Cuban culture in old age), but unlike the majority of her contemporaries who rejected "criollo" themes for fantastic literature, she kept to the conventions of "realismo criollista". Hence the preponderance of animals.

Tierra inerme was classified a "novela de la tierra" and as such fell outside the main current of Cuban and Latin American narrative of the sixties. It has been judged harshly. For North American critics it was "an anachronistic attempt to justify the agrarian reform" and a failed attempt to apply the novelistic formula of the Venezuelan Rómulo Gallegos (1884–1969, resident in Cuba) to the Cuban landscape.[6] Cuban critics deplored the lack of social realism, the atmosphere of resignation which "no daría a un lector ajeno la versión total de nuestra reciente historia" and the narrative techniques were considered inappropriate for a new socialist state of collectivized farms.[7] Despite winning the prestigious "Casa de las Américas" prize then, the novel was dismissed as an unoriginal "novela de la tierra" on the one hand and too uncritical to be included in the mainstream of Cuban post-revolutionary social realism on the other. But Luisa Campuzano takes a different view: "Dora Alonso se inscribe en la tradición de la 'novela de la tierra', de vieja raigambre latinoamericana, que todavía a principios de este período *tenía algo que decir entre nosotros*" (my italics). Does she imply here "nosotras"?[8] It seems to me that a feminist approach, to *Tierra inerme* and to Alonso's short stories, published over fifty years (between 1936 and 1987), might explain the relative absence of fantasy, experimental techniques, urban guerrilla settings and positive social realism, and the subsequent lack of serious critical coverage. Why did Dora Alonso continue to privilege rural life, animals and women?

Focussing on the short stories, it is clear that the majority exemplify the discourse of the Latin American autochthonous text. The "rhetorical devices" subsuming such narrative, according to Carlos J. Alonso, belong to nineteenth century theories of evolution in which culture is conceived of as an organism with a natural development thwarted by the culprits of history: "the many botanical and biological metaphors that were used throughout the century [in Latin America] ... attest to the organicity that physical and spiritual processes were assumed to have in common; but it is also expressive of the relationship which was presumed to exist between a culture and the physical environment in which it [the culture] obtained".[9] In other words, a national volksgeist was thought to be manifest in the particular way it adapted to an environment. Much of Dora Alonso's short fiction is naturalistic, even Darwinian. Explicit references are made to Darwin and the influence of his *Viaje de un naturalista alrededor del mundo* (Diary of the voyage of HMS Beagle) on the young narrator in two semi-autobiographical stories published in 1969.[10] Her short fiction deals with individuals interacting with a hostile, miserable Cuban environment, usually rural, in which animals – often those associated with human life (dogs, cats, horses, cattle, rats, monkeys) – but many others, including insects (cockroaches, butterflies) and moluscs, abound. Humans are represented as caged wild animals, the passive victims of heredity and other natural forces, their lives meaningless and tragic. Zoo and circus settings are common. From a pre-Revolutionary emphasis on conflict between men ("El lazo", 1937; "Estiba", 1945) or conflict belying profound mutual interdependence between man and beast ("Un filósofo", 1944; "Potrero", 1945; "Negativo", 1947; "Cansancio", 1954), the stories become increasingly woman-centred after 1959. Alonso writes about social injustice experienced (in the past) by poor and black women ("Severina", 1965; "El traje de novia", 1975); the problems older women face, such as physical deterioration, loneliness or sexual frustration ("Una", 1965; "Algodón de azucar", 1969; "Menos veinte", 1972; "Sofía y el angel", 1973; "Ana y los amores", 1979); women whose husbands do no housework and are consequently killed off with poisoned food ("Pollo a la jardinera", 1987) or, worse still, whose husbands emigrate to Miami ("El regreso de Abilio Argüelles", 1987) – these being commentaries on much debated political issues at the time. Particulary interesting are two types of post-Revolutionary short story relating to animals: stories where women clash, fatally, with female animals ("Los gatos", 1964; "La gallina", 1978; "La extraña muerte de Juana Urquiza", 1987) and those in which female animals are personified ("La rata", 1962; "Jaula número uno", 1964); "Once caballos", 1969; "La felicidad", 1983), the plots of some of which have already been described. This brings us to the second paradox in Alonso's narrative fiction. She writes in the naturalist tradition, yet naturalism and determinism are anathema to Marxism and progressive ideology generally. Dora Alonso is no dissident. She publicly stands by Fidel and the achievements of the Revolution. It seems to me that the application of standard categorizations is at fault; the pigeon-holes "naturalism" and "de la tierra" applied to discursive modes, concepts or attitudes from a phallocentric optic are inappropriate, certainly insufficient, when dealing with the work of this (or any?) female author.

A different tack would be to explore further the implications of the narrative sub-genre. It has been suggested that conventional realist narrative techniques, such as those used by Alonso, imply a mastery of outer reality and a coherent viewpoint concomitant with male hegemony. But Alonso also privileges one trope in particular: allegory, where an animal subject-noun is personified, that is, takes on human predicates (verb/adjective). In these allegories the animal subject is almost always female endowed with woman-specific attributes, or constituted as woman through the language of the text, by means of a distinctive lexicon or focalization. Taking examples from *Juega la dama*, "la yegua preñada" is "la parturienta", feeling "pavor de madre" and part of the story ("Once caballos") is told from the point of view of the "potrillo" still in the womb. In "La rata", the rat, "avizora", "azorada", gives birth to "hijuelos" and understands language – but sees only a partial reality, the dehumanized shopkeeper's big feet and arms. Galana the cat in "Los gatos" is also "madre", "parturienta" and later "desconsolada" when Lola – after helping her through labour – takes away her "crías". In "La extraña muerte de Juana de Urquiza" the cockroach is "robusta, lustrosa, resuelta", the implacable "enemiga" of Juana the cockroach-killer. The cosseted bitch of "La felicidad" enjoys perfume, is "melindrosa" (fussy) and "incapaz de reconocer su identidad" except during "el celo ardiente"; she gives up everything, including her life, for sex with her dog. The correspondences sought on the literal and symbolical levels of the allegories pertain to female animals and female humans; the resulting female essence is synonymous with motherhood and oppression, but also resiliance and solidarity, sexual frustration and sexual pleasure. Similarly, the antagonists in the stories are men (not male animals) representing death, violence, victimization and authority ("el matarife"; "el hombre" the storekeeper; "el perrero"). When a woman adopts masculinist attributes in her dealings with female animals (Lola, Juana) there is a tremendous sense of betrayal. Lola, like the "matarife" and the storekeeper, functions as the third term splitting the newly born creature from unity with the mother, representing the law-of-the-father. In

Juana's case, the insect, the female underling, wins out, egged on by a kind of Lamarckian concept of cockroach cultural inheritance.

The effect of these stories is unusually powerful and has to do with the working out of the incongruency inherent in allegory. Samuel Levin suggests that the disparity in allegory (between the literal and the symbolical) can be resolved by dispersonification of either the subject or the predicate "the *mare* (literally, the woman) was inconsolable" or "the mare was *inconsolable*" (literally, nervous or whatever a horse feels). But in addition – and this is significant for my argument – he points to a third "higher level" of meaning which involves readers projecting themselves into non-human life and identifying with it, imagining what a mare feels when sad. The reader thus gains insight into life without the constraints of language and the device expands "our conceptual horizons". It is far easier, argues Levin, to personify the non-human because language is human centred, resulting in a "deficiency in our lexicon".[11]

Feminists would argue that the deficiency in language is its phallocentrism; the resulting view of the world is not simply anthromorphic, but androcentric. The effect of Alonso's use of allegory is an all-encompassing gynomorphic worldview. In it the categories male and female are more important than the categories animal and human. In other words, biological sex differences are privileged over and above class, race or any other sociocultural category, over the nature/culture divide and even anthropomorphism itself. Alonso seems to be attempting to avoid the constraints of the Symbolic in order to put the female, the irrepresentable, "into discourse", engaging in what Alice Jardine terms "gynesis", so that the reader can identify with that which cannot be expressed in language as it stands, that is, female experience and woman as unknowable.[12] Furthermore, if we take into consideration that these are autochthonous texts then the inevitable "mediating analytical construct" described by Carlos Alonso as existing between a nationalist author and his or her subject is, in this case, that of a woman. What bearing does a female mediation have on representations of national culture? The allegories, inherently ambiguous, can certainly be interpreted as national projections exemplifying the subjugation, resistance and revenge of the underdog, which fits in with the emplotment of Cuban history as a trajectory of human freedom, through slavery, imperialism and capitalism. But the projections are cast through the female lens of the author. Similarly, the stories could be said to textualize "what is construed as a collective spiritual essence" (indicated in speech, landscape and human activity) as do the "novelas de la tierra", but again from the female point of view of the protagonists.[13] I have found only one allegory, "Paz al antílope", where the imprisoned personified subject is a young male. The allegories would seem to articulate the female version of a national culture, of a collective spirit.

Does this assertion of the pre-eminence of biological essentialism have much to do with the apparent paradoxes evidenced so far: a female-centred text yet not feminist; naturalistic discourse yet Marxist; an autochthonous culture yet woman-centred? Paradox too thrives on ambiguity. Rather than foreclose apparent inconsistency I would like to explore these cleavages further. The choice of allegory has deeper implications. First, in Cuba the genre is closely associated with the fable, particularly the beast-fable, of West African origins (cf. J. Chandler Harris's "Uncle Remus" stories of 1879). As the living expression of Afro-Cuban popular oral culture the fable was appropriated and rendered fit for the literate by a well-known Cuban woman writer and ethnographer of this century, Lydia Cabrera, who left for the United States after the Revolution. Her 1936 collection of twenty-two Afro-Cuban fables, *Contes nègres de Cuba*, much acclaimed by Carpentier, was published in Paris and gained immediate international recognition; the Spanish version came out in La Habana in 1940. A further collection (*Por qué? Cuentos negros de Cuba*) was published in Cuba in 1948, and two more in the United States: *Ayapá: Cuentos de jicotea*, 1970 and *Yemayá y Ochún*, 1980.[14] The point is that there is no clear distinction in these stories between oral traditions (documentary and ethnographic writing) and creative fiction; "What are these stories?" asks one critic, "the copied stories of a folklorist or artistic creation? They are a bit of both".[15] Cabrera's animals represent human conduct with a moral intention. But her animals (tortoise, rabbit, crab, lizard, goat, snake, duck) are as "criollo" as African; they have a "criollo" mentality, speech and humour and are placed in a Cuban landscape. Alonso's allegories belong not so much to European Naturalism, then, as to a literary tradition which is doubly feminine: Lydia Cabrera incorporated it into the Cuban canon but, more importantly, black women played a key role in its oral transmission. Like Cabrera, Dora Alonso collected and reworked Afro-Cuban legends, many first-hand accounts from her nursemaid Emilia and other black women on her father's estate. [16] Several were published in the volume *Panolani* (1966) by 'Gente Nueva' as "literatura infantil". *Panolani* contains conventional beast-fables where anthropomorphized animals, male and female, exemplify a moral ("El cuento de jicotea", "Cuento del perro", "El que no pudo entrar", "Condioco"). Other fables humanize animals to a greater degree to comment on human family relationships, for example, in "Toro padre" a father (bull) is jealous of his male child who is protected by the mother (vaca) until he grows up. But more moving and personal are the first six stories or lyrical "viñetas", which pay tribute to the genealogy of black women story tellers, from the "abuela" in Africa, to her daughter Panolani captured as a child and brought to Cuban slavery, and her grand-daughter Emilia who nurses the anonymous white child, the female narrator (a "desdoblamiento" of Dora Alonso) who passes on the tale:

> Quizás por la secreta sangre que había bebido del pezón oscuro, amó [the narrator] el ánima del pozo... ya la siembra estaba hecha y en la sangre andaban, a través de Emilia Trías Carol, la fuerza del río donde se asomaba Panolani en busca de mariposas que vuelan en el fondo del agua, del fuego de los loros rojos y del redondo espejo del ojo de la leona. [17]

What Alonso added to her later allegories was this extra dimension: feminality. Her discourse is rooted in that of black women's culture inextricably bound to African traditions, the institution of slavery and, eventually, to the formation of an indigenous, Afro-Cuban syncretic culture. Black feminist commentary is relevant in this respect. As it points out, women slaves were not considered human but "simultaneously racially and sexually – as marked female (animal, sexualized and without rights)", excluded from culture, so that "white women inherited black women [and men]". [18] In Caribbean culture such as this, indeed, in the whole of Latin America, motherhood, mothering and the family is exceptionally important. Because of it, according to Pat Ellis, women "have considerable influence and authority and respect". [19] Cuba is no different and this attitude has survived the

Revolution intact. But, of course, sex roles considered innate are a double-edged blade.

This was nowhere more obvious than in the Cuban policies towards women of the two decades following the Revolution, which, like Alonso's short fiction, smack of biological essentialism. Cuba made exceptional advances with regards to women's material conditions, the erradication of sexual discrimination, health, education and childcare on a scale unequalled in Latin America or even in parts of the developed West. An example is the Family Code (1975) which stipulates shared-parenting and shared-domestic labour. By the 1960s a third of the workforce was female. And yet in 1968 women were prohibited from taking up 500 posts (another 500 were reserved for them) on the basis that they were physically weaker and more vulnerable than men. Referring to interviews carried out in 1970 Margaret Randall writes "the consensus still seemed to be that, in Cuba, differences between men's and women's roles were thought to be biological as well as social in origin".[20] The turning point came in the late seventies. Before then a deep-seated paternalism seeps through official communications despite the sweeping reforms.

The President of the "Federación de Mujeres Cubanas", Vilma Espín, explained (in 1960) the need for collective action "debido a la inferioridad fisiológica que por naturaleza procreadora tiene la mujer". In 1975, Fidel declared that freedom for women was liberation from domestic chores and active participation in social production, but then qualified his statement, "con las solas limitaciones que le imponen su papel en la reproducción del ser humano, su augusto papel de madre y las peculiaridades de su constitución física".[21] Throughout the sixties and seventies the stress fell on: woman as "supermadre", heterosexual marriage and the nuclear family as social norm, echoing Marx's view that heterosexuality was the "most natural relation of human being to human being".[22] Marx did not historicize sex or nature. For Fidel woman was "nature's workshop where life is formed"; while scorn was poured on "falsos intelectuales que pretenden convertir el esnobismo, la extravagancia, el homosexualismo y demás aberraciones sociales en expresiones del arte revolucionario" (1971).[23] So although well-meaning towards women's liberation, recommendations such as the following (in Fidel's 1974 speech) constantly undermine the project:

> There must be certain small privileges and certain small inequalities in favour of women. And I say this clearly and frankly, because there are some men who feel they are not obliged to give their seat on a bus to a pregnant woman [Applause] or to an old woman, or to a little girl, or to a woman of any age ... [Applause]. Just as I understand it to be the obligation of any youth to give his seat on the bus to an old man [Applause]. Because it would be very sad if, with the revolution, there wasn't even the recollection of what certain men in bourgeois society did out of bourgeois or feudal chivalry, there must exist proletarian manners ... [Applause]. And I say this with the certainty... that every mother and every father would like their son to be a chivalrous proletarian.[24]

Castro was not alone, of course; similar supremacist remarks were constantly made by political leaders, a case in point being the Mexican president Luis Echeverría.[25] Despite the view, nevertheless, that in Cuba "today there is no capitalist ruling class which seeks to profit from racism and sexism" it would seem that, as Johnetta Cole states, "the Cuban case underlines the necessity of on-going attacks on the level of the superstructure even after socialist transformation is in process".[26] The corollary is that sex differences are more pernicious, more ingrained than class division.

Biological explanations of sexual differences such as those found in Alonso's allegories and predominant Cuban ideology, originated – like naturalism and cultural evolutionism – in the natural sciences, in the work of Herbert Spencer and Darwin, and were developed by modern evolutionists such as Edward Wilson in the 1970s (sex roles are determined; male dominance is innate). As mentioned earlier, essentialism (ie, biology gives women an essential feminine nature, for example, special maternal instincts) is a double-edged weapon and has been used traditionally to bolster anti-feminist positions regarding women's status and agency.[27] Is Dora Alonso's position then profoundly conservative in as much as it is inscribed in the parameters of predominant ideology, as she implies when remarking that the stories in *Juega la dama* are non-feminist "cuentos de hembra"?

The allegories, however, could be read equally from the radical or cultural feminist standpoint which also upholds essentialism in an effort to avoid phallocentric explanations of feminine sexuality. So female biology (pregnancy, mothering, parturition) and "virtues" (support, care, nurturance, relatedness, self-reliance), all attributes associated with femininity in Alonso's stories, should be exalted, celebrated as different yet equal to masculine values. For radical feminists women constitute a class and it is the biological division by sex not the relation to the means of production (but rather to that of reproduction) that forms the first class division in society. More recently, proponents of "feminité" have put forward ideas in which women's bodies are contrasted to the Symbolic in Western thought, the maternal body thus subverting the law-of-the-father. Femininity for Luce Irigaray is constituted by biology and women have a specific female desire.[28] They should assert their femininity from which they have been alienated in a patriarchal society and which they are unable to express in phallocentric language. Cixous too, states that "in women there is always more or less of the mother who makes everything alright, who nourishes and who stands up against separation; a force that will not be cut off...".[29]

I believe, however, that Alonso's animal allegories express the constructionist view that women are subjected because culture is valued over nature. By persuading the reader to identify with the animal "hembra" she revalorizes a concept of natural femaleness and if human consciousness indicates culture then by endowing animals with such consciousness the nature/culture binary is straddled. Woman is somewhere in the space between the female body (invoking biology) and the language of the narrator, in the space between the literal and symbolical readings of allegory. The body is a given and female sexuality is constituted through the language in which it is expressed. Furthermore, Alonso's interest in the experiences of black women in Cuba and her anti-racist concern (she is white) would point to the affirmation of "the primacy of family life" as resistance, stressed by black feminists, "because we know that family ties are the only sustained support system for exploited and oppressed peoples".[30]

Above all, I believe Alonso in questioning the Western nature/culture divide itelf, challenges the sex/gender distinction, expressing the Marxist-humanist idea that "neither our personal bodies nor our social bodies may be seen as natural, in the sense of outside the self-creating process called labor... Therefore culture does not dominate nature nor is nature an enemy".[31] Through the ambiguity of allegory, often masquerading as fiction for children or folklore, using the well-worn paradigms of the "novela de la tierra", she deconstructs false paradoxes from a position of alterity, located within a particular writing practice and autochthonous tradition – itself "sprung from the land". By reaffirming the female body detached from the defining limits of culture, nature becomes all-encompassing; it is life itself. The implications of this remain open to interpretation.

Catherine Davies
University of St. Andrews

1. Dora Alonso, *Juega la dama* (La Habana: Letras cubanas, 1989).

2. In an interview with Catherine Davies at the author's home, La Habana, 24th July, 1990.

3. Dora Alonso is mentioned briefly in Raimundo Lazo, *La literatura cubana* (México: UNAM, 1965); Remos y Rubio, *Historia de la literatura cubana*, vol. III (Miami: Mnemosyne, 1969); Salvador Arias, "Literatura cubana (1959–75)" *Casa de las Américas*, 113, (1979) pp.14–26; and more fully in Ernesto Méndez y Soto, *Panorama de la novela cubana de la revolución (1959–70)* (Miami: Ediciones Universal, 1977), pp.68–74; Seymour Menton, *Prose Fiction of the Cuban Revolution* (Austin: Texas U.P., 1975) pp.34–35; *¿Quiénes escriben en Cuba?*, eds. J. L. Bernard and J.A. Pola (La Habana: Letras cubanas, 1985) interviews Dora Alonso, Mirta Yáñez and Nersys Felipe; Luisa Campuzano, "La mujer en la narrativa de la Revolución: ponencia de una carencia", *Letras cubanas* 7 (enero, marzo) 1988: 132–149. See also Seymour Menton, "El cuento de la revolución cubana: una visión antológica y algo más" in *El cuento hispanoamericano ante la crítica*, ed. E. Pupo-Walker (Madrid: Castalia, 1973) pp.338–355.

4. Quoted in Roberto González Echevarría, "Cuban criticism and literature: a reply to Smith", *Cuban Studies* 16 (1989) pp.101–106, p.103. See also Verity

A. Smith, "Recent trends in Cuban criticism and literature", *Cuban Studies* 16 (1989) pp.81–99.

5. Alonso published two novels, *Tierra adentro*, 1944, originally for radio, and *Tierra inerme*, 1961; testimonial narrative, *El año 61*, 1981, and *Agua pasada*, 1981; poetry, plays and narrative for children: *Aventuras de Guille*, 1964; *El cochero azul*, 1966; *La flauta de chocolate*, 1980; *El grillo caminante*, 1981; *El valle de la pájara pinta*, 1984, among others. The edition used in this study is *Dora Alonso. Letras*, ed. Imeldo Alvarez García (La Habana: Letras cubanas, 1980).

6. Seymour Menton, op. cit., p.34.

7. E. Méndez y Soto, op. cit., p.73.

8. L. Campuzano, op. cit., p.136.

9. Carlos J. Alonso, *The Spanish American regional novel: modernity and autochthony* (Cambridge: Cambridge University Press, 1990) pp.8–9, p.59. Interesting too is the following comment by Doris Sommer, "...positivists tended to favour biology as the hegemonic discourse for predicting and directing social growth. They became the doctors who diagnosed social ills and prescribed remedies... One result was that national history in Latin America often read as if it were the inevitable story of organic development", "Irresistible romances: the foundational fictions of Latin America" in *Nation and Narration*, ed. Homi K. Bhaba, London (Routledge, 1990) pp.71–98, p.72.

10. "La lluvia y el puma" and "Un gato siamés".

11. Samuel R. Levin, "Allegorical language" in *Allegory, Myth and Symbol*, ed. Morton W. Bloomfield (Harvard University Press, 1981) pp.23–38, p.34.

12. Alice A. Jardine, *Gynesis: configurations of woman and modernity* (London and Ithaca: Cornell University Press, 1985) p.25. See Ann R. Jones, "Writing the body: toward an understanding of 'l'écriture feminine'" in *Feminist criticism and social change*, eds Judith Newton and Deborah Rosenfelt (New York: Methuen, 1985) pp.86–101.

13. Carlos J. Alonso, op. cit., p.5, p.61.

14. See Susana A. Montero, *La narrativa femenina cubana 1923–58* (La Habana: Academia, 1989) p.34. Estelle Irizarry, "Lydia Cabrera, fabuladora surrealista" in *The Contemporary Latin American Short Story*, ed. Rose Minc (New York: Senda Nueva de ediciones, 1979) pp.35–43.

15. R. S. Boggs, "Testimonio", *Homenaje a Lydia Cabrera*, eds Reinaldo Sánchez, José Antonio Madrigal (Miami: Ediciones Universal, 1977) p.15.

16. See Dora Alonso, "Yo vi besar las metralletas" in *¿Quiénes escriben en Cuba?*, op. cit., pp.15–30, p.16, p.26.

17. *Letras*, op. cit., p.181.

18. See Donna J. Haraway, *Simians, Cyborgs and Women. The reinvention of nature* (London: Free Asscociation Books, 1991) p.145.

19. *Women of the Caribbean*, ed. Pat Ellis (New York: Zed Books, 1986) p.6. See also Cheryl Williams, "The role of women in Caribbean culture", ibid., pp.109–114, p.110.

20. Margaret Randall, *Women in Cuba: twenty years later* (New York: Smyrna Press, 1981) p.29. According to the *Statistical Abstract of Latin America*, vol. 28, ed. James W. Wilkie (UCLA Latin American Center Publications, 1990) 31% of the economically active population in Cuba is female. The life expectance percentages for babies under one year old were higher than those of the United States; similarly, for the population over eighty years old. Like the United States, Cuba also has the highest divorce rates of the Americas.

21. Laurette Sejourné, *La mujer cubana en el quehacer de la historia* (Mexico: Siglo XXl, 1980) p.x, p.xi.

22. See Donna J. Haraway, op. cit., p.132.

23. *Women and the Cuban Revolution*, ed. Elizabeth Stone (London: Pathfinder Press, 1981) p.68, and Salvador Arias, "Literatura cubana (1959–75)", *Casa de las Américas*, 113 (1979) p.24.

24. *Women and the Cuban Revolution*, op. cit, p.68–69.

25. "Being interested in world and community affairs, women complemented their natural roles as mothers" (1975), quoted in Asunción Lavrín, *Female, feminine and feminist: key concepts in understanding women's history in twentieth-century Latin America* (Bristol: Department of Hispanic, Portuguese and Latin American Studies, 1988) p.3.

26. Johnetta B. Cole, "Women in Cuba: The Revolution within the Revolution" in *Anthropology for the nineties: introductory readings*, ed. Johnetta B. Cole (New York and London: Free Press-Macmillan, 1988) p.545.

27. Janet Sayers, *Biological politics: feminist and anti-feminist perspectives* (London and New York: Tavistock, 1982) p.29, pp.108–109, pp.130–136,

p.150. Sandra Harding, "The instability of the analytical categories of feminist theory", *Signs*, 11, 4 (1986) pp.645–664.

28. Luce Irigaray, "When our lips speak together", *Signs*, 6 (1980): 69–79.

29. Helene Cixous, "The laugh of the Medusa" in *The Signs Reader. Women, gender and scholarship*, eds Elizabeth Abel and Emily K. Abel (Chicago University Press, 1983) pp.279–297, p.286. But see Gayatri C. Spivak, "French feminism in an international frame", *Yale French Studies*, 62 (1981) pp.154–184; Jean Franco, "Beyond ethnocentrism: gender, power, and the Third-world intelligentsia" in *Marxism and the Interpretation of Culture*, eds Cary Nelson and Lawrence Grossberg (Illinois University Press, 1988) pp.503–515, and "Trends and priorities for research on Latin American literature", *Ideologies and Literature*, 4, 16 (1983) pp.107–120, and "Apuntes sobre la crítica feminista y la cultura hispanoamericana", *Hispamérica*, 45 (1986) pp.31–43. See also Gloria Joseph, "The incompatible ménage à trois: marxism, feminism and racism" in *Women and revolution: a discussion of the unhappy marriage of marxism and feminism* (London: Pluto Press, 1981) pp.91–107. Judith Butler argues in *Gender Trouble: Feminism and the Subversion of Identity* (New York, Routledge, 1990) pp.79–93, that the law-of-the-father simply creates the maternal body through discourse.

30. bell hooks, *Feminist theory: from margin to center* (Boston: South End Press, 1984) p.37. The following lines from *Cinco estudios sobre la situación de la mujer en América Latina: estudios e informes de la CEPAL* (Santiago de Chile: Naciones Unidas, 1982) p.70, are significant in this respect: "En este contexto [la abolición de la esclavitud] se comprende que la tierra tenga un valor más social y mítico que económico. Durante la esclavitud, la tierra significó valorización social y status. Durante la emanicpación, la tierra fue un símbolo y una concreción de la libertad".

31. Donna J. Haraway, "Animal sociology and a natural economy of the body politic, part 1: a political physiology of dominance" in *The Signs Reader*, op. cit., pp.123–138, p.127.

Carmen Conde's *Mujer sin Edén*: Controversial notions of 'sin'

Carmen Conde has published prolifically throughout this century and in 1979 she became the first woman to join the Real Academia in Spain. So she is not, then, a particularly marginalised figure on the Spanish literary scene. And yet, even for a woman who has published so easily in twentieth-century Spain, the sex war is an issue. Here I am looking in particular at the conflict which arises between religious faith and sex in *Mujer sin Edén* (1947).[1]

Before exploring religious faith, I am going to look at literary faith, in order to sketch the paradoxical nature of Conde's writing position. Conde has claimed that one of the strongest faiths in her life is the faith in writing, the faith in what she calls the "blanquísimo papel de la literatura".[2] This deification of the act of writing; the accentuated symbolism of "whiteness", (with its connotations of purity, abstraction and virginity), reveals an attitude to writing which can only be described as privileged – privileged in that it involves the abstraction of the act of writing from the fact of being able to write. All of which would suggest that she has very little in common with the average feminist who would, at the very least, begin by engendering the "papel". This stress (on the "blanquísimo papel") gestures towards Jiménez and notions of "poesía pura". Jiménez, himself, has been known to define poetry not only as beyond the boundaries of human reason, but moreover as Woman, a fact which might leave Conde in an awkward position.

Looking back, for a moment, at Jiménez's infamous comment, "Yo tengo escondida en mi casa, por su gusto y por el mío, a la Poesía, como una mujer hermosa; y nuestra relación es de los apasionados", the objectification of the female body in these lines is seen to give tangible form to poetry.[3] Jiménez's fantasy appropriation of poetry is envisaged in the, equally fantastical, vision of the "mujer hermosa, escondida", both poetry and Woman, being moulded, in this fantasy, to the dictates of Jiménez's intellect and desire. Conde has acknowledged that her work is influenced by Jiménez but she has also acknowledged that it is difficult for a woman writer (and here she may be referring to her own experience), to find an authentic, rather than imitative, voice, claiming that "La mujer, al ingresar en el mundo de la creación, obedecía a un total mimetismo; impostaba su voz en tono ajeno, y por ajeno falso."[4] So where, then, does Conde situate herself? Among the patriarchs of "poesía pura" or among the matriarchs of modernity? And does the ungendered "blanquísimo papel" struggle with the specifically gendered writing of *Mujer Sin Edén*? Because, in many ways, *Mujer Sin Edén* voices a need which is summed up in Irigaray's question, "How can we speak to escape their compartments, their schemas, their distinctions and oppositions: virginal/deflowered, innocent/experienced... How can we shake off the chain of these terms, free ourselves from their categories, rid ourselves of their names? Disengage ourselves, *alive*, from their concepts? Without reserve, without the immaculate whiteness that shores up their systems." [5]

Mujer Sin Edén focusses on the women of Catholic myth, and in particular, on Eve. In the work, the female voice moves chronologically through various biblical stories, questioning the validity of the role allocated to women. A cursory glance at any *Feminist Reader* will show that there is nothing surprising in this itself, but it is interesting to examine the depth of Conde's quarrel with the patriarchal model bearing in mind its context, the Spain of the 1940s, to look at whether she is making a significantly transgressive attack on Catholic myth.

One of the problems with myths is that they are not true, and another problem is that their power comes largely from their anonymity. This anonymity has been extensively examined in the course of the sex war, and the revealing of the anonymous, but patriarchal hand has provoked much more, and less, serious analysis of the female role. Irigaray has analysed women according to three essentially mythical categories, those of mother, virgin and prostitute, and (to cut her ruthlessly short) she concludes that "Neither as mother nor as virgin nor as prostitute has woman any right to her own pleasure." This separation of the female body from its own desires, Irigaray says "has as its founding operation the appropriation of woman's body by the father or his substitutes" [6] and it this position that Conde attempts to adopt in *Mujer Sin Edén.*

However, moving from the radical to the traditional, here is an example of the kind of biblical misogyny which provokes Conde's ambivalent response to the story of Eden:

> Let the woman learn in silence with all subjugation. But I suffer not a woman to teach, not to usurp authority over the man, but to be in silence. For Adam was first formed, then Eve. And Adam was not deceived, but the woman being deceived was in the transgression...
> Not withstanding she shall be saved in childbearing, (1, Tim 2: 11–15)

It may be worth noting that the message behind this can be compared to that behind any ideology which assumes male supremacy. But the biblical rhetoric offers additional damnation for women in that it justifies this system with the assumption of a female transgression, which can only be atoned for by the further subservience of the female to her man and offspring. *Mujer sin Edén* is deeply confused by such mythology. The title contains two meanings. The first possible meaning is situational and places the work in the context of woman post-Fall, and the second is controversial, or even radical, in that it poses the question as to whether woman ever had a place in the world of the Father, and was therefore always "without" Eden. In the opening sections of the work, the female voice challenges God:

> Si es que soy tu mal que me retornen
> a tu espalda castigada por mi fuego.
> ¡Vuélveme a la Nada, Tú, señor!

> Y haz que el hombre te refleje absorto
> en su extática admiración sin lucha... (40–41)

From this it might be assumed that the female is the source of evil ("tu mal"). She is to be punished for her "fuego", presumably the fires of her passion for Adam, which have distracted Father and son from their ecstatic shared gaze. The desire to be returned to "la Nada" is a desire for self-annihilation, caused by the acknowledgement of female guilt and female weakness. But the words, "si es que..." throw this reading into some doubt. Moving on, post-Fall Eve offers consolation to Adam:

> ...Ven a mi pecho
> que yo seré tu tierno prado tibio
> y seguro soñarás en mi corteza...
> Toma el paraíso de mi cuerpo (46)

The image of the woman here is that of nurturing lover, offering herself to the abandoned male as solace in his isolation. The words "tierno prado" echo and complement the old earth/woman association, symbolic of the kind of soft, fertile malleable, passivity which is said to have caused the female to fall prey so easily to the temptations of the serpent. Eve here echoes the assumptions about femininity behind the dogma which condemns her. The offering up of the female body for the consolation of man, "toma el paraíso de mi cuerpo", becomes the offering of but a poor copy of the true and godly paradise. The female body is but a substitute to assuage the loss of the irrecoverable.

And yet can the "paraíso" of the female body be taken to be merely a poor substitute, or is there behind this image a hint of the heretical? Heretical, in the sense that it may be conferring divine status on the fatally flawed female body. So to continue with the possibly heretical opening lines of the first "Canto":

> La rama de lumbre de la espada
> segó los tallos de todas las hierbas.

> Me empujó violenta y fúlgida
> precipitándome del Jardín Edénico. (33)

This opening links the banishment with violence and focuses this violence on Eve. The use of "me" foregrounds the female protagonist. The male figure in the myth is absent, and the figure of the Father is absorbed into one abstract image of violence "La rama de lumbre de la espada". Through the use of "me", author, reader and female protagonist (Eve) all take part temporarily in the characterisation of the damned woman of the Fall. The woman Diane Kelsey has described as "The mother of mankind in art and verse" who "is weak, vain, useless, mindless, trifling, grasping, vacillating, wanton, obstinate, presumptuous and (nonetheless) fatally seductive".[7] The literary and visual, image of Eve holding out the apple has been fixed eternally at a point between the states of innocence and of damnation. Its significance as an image depends upon this uneasy equilibrium between two mutually exclusive states (pre-Fall and post-Fall). Here that stasis is to become movement forward.

The female speaker, Eve, rejects the popular image of silent and submissive femininity personified in the ideal of the Virgin Mary. For the female figure, not only to utter, but to express displeasure with the symbolic order which places her in a secondary position is an attack on patriarchal monotheism, which Kristeva suggests has depended for its functioning on the silence of women.[8] From the opening sections, doubt is cast upon the notion of female guilt for the Fall:

> ¿Quién era de nosotros el culpable:
> la bestia que indujo a mi inocencia;
> Aquel que me sacó sin ser yo nadie
> del cuerpo que busqué, mi patria única. (33)

By focussing the debate on God and serpent, ("la bestia" and "Aquel") Conde removes the male image of female seductress fron the dynamics of the Fall. The silent temptress is now vocal subject, fixing the male protagonists with her gaze. The figure of Eve holding out the apple is absent.

This kind of questioning expands into a direct attack upon the supposed omnipotence of the Father:

> ¿Hice yo la bestia o los árboles serpientes
> de espasmos ajenos a tu poderío? (41)

The sexual imagery of the tree of "espasmos ajenos", is placed firmly outside the spheres of Eve's control. The female voices her struggle with the limited degree of autonomy her status as other, allows, placing responsibility with the Creator, "¿Cómo dejaste nacer a tus contrarios?" (41) And she looks back at the Creation with the fear of having been unloved by her own creator:

> ¿Qué es el tiempo ante Tí, que son los truenos
> que blandes contra mi cuando me nombras...?
>
> ...Tú no me quieres. (58)

It is this assumption, that the Father was incapable of loving the female child of his creation, which explains female damnation. The inconsistency of the damnation, or idealisation of the female is brought into relief by the figure of Mary in the work who laments the impotence of her maternal role as well as her inability to comprehend the irrelevance of maternal love to the structure of the relationship between Father, son and Holy Ghost, a triad in relation to which she must be no more than a symbol of unquestioning purity.

This challenge to the authority of the Father continues into the final section of the work (120–122) reaching a peak of violence in the accusatory repetions of "¿Tú no perdonas?" ...which lead into:

> Pues soy vieja Señor. ¿No escuchas cuánto lloro
> cuando el hombre, dormido, me vuelca su simiente
> porque Tú se lo ordenas sin piedad de mi duelo?
> ¿No ves mi carne seca, mi vientre desgarrado;
> no escuchas que te llamo por bocas estalladas

> por los abiertos pechos de niños, de mujeres?
> ¡En nada te ofendieron, sino en nacer! (121)

In this final climax, the hysteria ("bocas estalladas") of the female voice vigourously attacks a model of femininity which forces the female into a prostitutional role; man has become an unconcious ("dormido") agressor, the Father, however, is conscious but ruthless, ("sin piedad"). Both woman and child are condemned, in this image, by the mere fact of their existence. And the conclusion reached, that the female sex is damned at birth by the Father allows debate to arise as to whether or not there ever was a place for woman in Eden.

> No soy yo sustancia de Dios pura.
> Hízome El del hombre con su carne... (33)

> ¡Amor de mi Jardín, Edén primero
> creado para Dios y para el Hombre! (37)

From her re-reading of the Fall the female voice comes to understand that the garden is Man-made for man. Woman is created as the other, the necessary reflection required to bring man (unwhole) closer in his relationship to God (whole) Man is created in god's image, "Tú, réplica de Dios, hombre callado" (40), but woman is the difference which causes strife. The images of deity and male creation are reflected one in the other. The birth of Eve ripples the waters of the timeless reflection of their narcissistic gaze. If man is the perfect object of the divine gaze, then the image of woman must be disruptive, discordant. Only by the dissolving of the image which does not correspond, ("Devuélveme a la Nada"), can the "extática admiración sin lucha" of prelapsarian bliss recommence. If these, then, are the premises for Edenic bliss then woman has no place in Eden.

Although the female sex may have motivated the alleged crime, the crime itself lies with the creation, "en nada te ofendieron sino en nacer". It is this notion of an arbitrary condemnation of the female which allows the poetic voice to move freely through the figures of Eve, Lot's wife and Mary, and it is a voice driven by the fear of divine indifference ("Tú no me quieres"), towards suggesting that

Original Sin is the sin of the Father. The question of the Father's jealousy, "¿Por qué tuviste celos..?" illustrates the motivating impulse behind her reappraisal of the virtues of female sexuality as against the traditional system of Catholic thought which reveres female virginity above all other female virtues. If God and man mirror one another in an "Extática admiración sin lucha". Man and Eve on the contrary, find in one another a mirroring of the two halves which together make the whole. Thus their mirroring stimulates desire. The narcissistic gaze of the initial relationship, God/man has only one dynamic the eternal mirroring of one likeness. In this relationship there can be no communication of meaning. In this way the Fall brings about both the dynamics of desire and of discourse:

> Hermosos caminantes son los ángeles
> que vienen y acompañan nuestro exilio.
> Aquellos de la espada son hostiles,
> severos e implacables; y no duermen.
> Mas éstos, no; son instrumentos
> de elocuencia en el brío de sus alas. (171)

The angels of God's vengeance are absolutely removed from human experience ("no duermen") whereas the path into exile, as the violent agents of the revenge are left behind, is watched over by "Hermosos... instrumentos de elocuencia..." The association of these angels with eloquence, language, suggests that from Eve's creation arises discourse.

Before Eve, Adam was no more than a silent dream of humanity "réplica de Dios, hombre callado", an existence without consciousness and without speech, therefore without power and without experience. In this way the patriarchal interpretation of the biblical myth which gives man precedence over woman according to the bibilical hierarchy of birth is subverted. Man in Conde's work owes his existence to woman. Male and female desire come into existence simultaneously, there is no separation of the sexes. Refusing the traditional split male/female, spiritual/sensual, both the sexes are sensual. Post Fall, Eve plays the creator, and the new world is characterised by the fluctuating union of difference. And female sexuality is not only a vital and potent element of the new world, but is, more importantly, innocent:

> También yo fui cual ellos inocente;
> después de amarle a él seguía siéndolo.
> El Angel y su antorcha me acusaron... (36)

The insistence ("Después de amarle a él seguía siéndolo") on the coexistence of female innocence and female sexual awareness marks the fusion of the oppostion of virginal saint with non-virginal sinner By removing Eve as catalyst for the Fall and replacing her with "El Angel y su antorcha", the figure of the angel becomes guilty of transgression, the transgression then comes to signify the punishment of the innocent instead of the actions of the guilty. In this way the female body becomes the paradise of the new world and from this that the "paraíso de mi cuerpo" may justifiably be read as significantly more than a poor substitute for the "paradise lost":

> Toma el paraíso de mi cuerpo.
> Mis labios son de ascua, mis hogueras
> serán lo único vivo de la noche. (46)

Desire in the New World of *Mujer Sin Edén* is free-flowing and self-generataing, thus evasive of the patriarchal law. The "Original Curse"of the Fall, according to this reading of *Mujer Sin Edén* entails the perversion of this course of desire through the harnessing of female desire to male demand. So the Eve-created world of the Fall is tainted, not by human corruption, but by the fear of the Father. It is this fear of divine retribution, the fear of the infinite power of divine irrationality which precludes the return to the state of innocence and disturbs the harmonious pleasure of the world of woman's creation:

> Cólera rugiente entre tus barbas
> miraste mi creación junto a la tuya.
> Los seres se fundían unos en otros... (35)

The fusion of passion with fear, and pleasure with guilt, marks the legacy of the divine father's violation of the daughter, as Conde's positive, decriminalised

evaluation of female sexuality finally removes the pedestal which places the
Virgin Mary above all other examples of femininity:

> A Ella la llama *Ave*, saludándola.
> A mí me llamaste *Eva*, que es lo mismo.
> El Ave de María es terrenal morada tuya,
> y yo fui lanzada de tu Huerto, acá a la tierra. (97)

And yet, if this is a reasonable reading of Conde's work, if *Mujer Sin Edén* does
attack Catholic myth and misogyny so overtly, how, then, does this publication fit
into its context? What redeems a work which seems to provide such an intense
and emotive attack upon the patriarchal myths of the Catholic Church? According
to Leopoldo de Luis, *Mujer Sin Edén* is "un gran símbolo, o quizá mejor decir,
una gran parábola, de la condición de la mujer... la fórmula es sumamente válida
– también conmovedora – para alzar un gran canto de queja y dolor – añademos,
de protesta..." ("Prólogo", 27) and *Mujer sin Edén* is certainly concerned with the
inconsistencies of Divine favour, expressing confusion over the arbitrary
dichotomy Virgin/Whore (which was, as Martín Gaite has explored, encouraged
in popularised visions of feminity in the 1940's).[9] And she is also aware that this
dichotomy, as if it weren't enough on its own, is further exacerbated by the
impossible ideal of the maternal, but virginal, figure of Mary. The conflict which
arises between this projection of the ideal woman as untouchable (being both
mother and virgin) and the nature of desire (in this case male desire, since we are
dealing with a male myth) forces into existence the myth of the whore. The
essentially touchable and, indeed, touched woman. These two images of
femininity exist simultaneously, one giving meaning to the other. *Mujer Sin Edén*
fuses the two, giving both temptress and silent idol a voice. The questioning
female voice rejects the distinction between sexual and asexual models of
femininity and replaces these with one image of the nurturing female who is also
capable of taking pleasure; thus questioning the value of the unknowing bliss of
the Edenic garden, "¿Fue tan bella en su inocencia la mansa ignorancia de los
seres?" (36) – and from this, on to the suggestion that the prelapsarian world was
an ideal from which woman was alienated, and for which, therefore she can feel
no profound sense of nostalgia.

However, looking again at one of the more vehement attacks on paternal
authority:

> ...¿No escuchas cuánto lloro
> cuando el hombre, dormido, me vuelca su simiente
> porque Tú se lo ordenas sin piedad de mi duelo? (121)

Is this really an explicit depiction of the sexual slavery of the female under the
authority of the Father, or is it merely reinforcing an image of woman as subject
to male demand? In the final analysis the reason the text remains essentially
unthreatening to the system it appears to attack lies precisely with the Father.
Ultimately, each attack Conde's female voice makes on the patriarchal myth is
undermined by the object of its attack – the Father. Even the powerful evaluation
of female sexuality (radical as it may have been during these years) falls victim to
the traditional sexual stereotyping of the biblical story of the Fall.

From its opening lines the work fluctuates uneasily between accepting and
rejecting a myth which is transparently unjust in its narration of the female role:

> Si soy Sarah perdonas. Si soy Agar ayudas
> si la hembra de Lot, no perdonas que mire.
> Y me dejas que yazga con un padre embriagado
> y ni escuchas mi voz que es un cardo sin flores. (89)

This uneasy stance, combined with the inability to reject the idea of the Father,
causes the work to acquiesce, in its final lines, to a stereotypically female form of
inarticulacy:

> ¿Quién si Tú eres Todo, de no ser Tú podría
> darte un Paraíso por el perdón que te pido? (122)

These lines of capitulation articulate only the omnipotent presence of the Father.
The strident voice of Eve has succumbed to an image of the omniscient deity,
before which it can raise no more than an inarticulate babble of submission.[10]

With these final lines the female voice becomes the "cardo sin flores" of its own fears. The fluctuating debate over the two possible notions of "sin", finally comes to rest with the Father and the return of the idea of the paradise lost.

Aleixandre speaks of Conde's, "...Visión llena de majestad dolorosa que hace una voz única, la voz de la antigua Eva, voz de la *intemporal mitad* de la especie..." (my stress) and Conde's work, although controversial in many aspects of its treatment of the female role in Catholic myth, does indeed move full circle within the closed boundaries of an essentially static myth of femininity.[11] The female voice, in the closing lines of the work fails to escape its own "blanquísimo papel", becoming lost in the babbling of the myth of subservience, the myth which relegates women to the realms of the timeless, (so innocently reproduced by Aleixandre) that woman is the "*intemporal mitad* de la especie."

Jo Evans
University of Edinburgh

1. All page numbers refer to the 1985 edition published by Torremozas. The book was first published in 1947 by Ediciones Jura, Madrid. Geraldine Scanlon cites the two official institutions which retarded the evolution of feminism in nineteenth-century Spain as Religion and Science. She goes on to illustrate this with the figure of Eve who,"representa todo lo malo de la mujer; su debilidad justifica que el hombre la tenga bajo su dominio, y sus artimañas justifican la propia debilidad del hombre." concluding, "No cabe duda de que la aplastante influencia de la religión católica en España, especialmente sobre las mujeres, desempeñó un importante papel en el retraso del nacimiento del movimiento feminista." *La polémica feminista en la España contemporánea (1868–1974)*, (Madrid: Akal, 1986) p.159.

2. *Cartas a Katherine Mansfield*, (Zaragoza: Doncel, 1948) p.11.

3. *Tercera Antología Poética* (Madrid: Editorial Biblioteca Nueva, 1970).

4. Carmen Conde, *Brocal y Poemas a María*, ed. Rosario Hiriart (Madrid: Biblioteca nueva, 1984) p.45.

5. Luce Irigaray, *This Sex Which Is Not One*, translated by Catherine Porter with Carolyne Burke (Ithica, New York: Cornell University Press, 1985) p.212. Originally published in French as *Ce Sexe qui n'en est pas un*, Editions de Minuit (1977).

6. "Women on the market" ibid. pp.185–191, p.187, p.189.

7. Diane McColley Kelsey, *Milton's Eve*, (University of Illinois Press, 1983) pp.1–2.

8. "The economy of this system requires that women be excluded from the single true and legislating principle, namely the Word, as well as from the (always paternal) element that gives procreation·a social value: they are excluded from knowledge and power." – "About Chinese Women", first published 1974 (Paris: des femmes) reprinted in *The Kristeva Reader*, ed.Toril Moi (London: Blackwell 1986) p.143.

9. Carmen Martín Gaite, *Usos amorosos de la postguerra española* (Barcelona: Editorial Anagrama, 1987).

10. This "babble of submission" has much in common with the mythically female art of "nagging", described by Meaghan Morris as the, "unsuccessful repetition of the same statements. It is unsuccessful, because it blocks change; nagging is a mode of repetition which fails to produce the desired effect of *difference* that might allow the complaint to end." (my stress). *The Pirate's Fiancé*, (London: Verso, 1988) p.15.
María Zambrano makes a contradictory, and provocative, comment about successful (here, male) expression and female language, "La expresión nace en la queja – una independencia y una afirmación de existencia... Puede ser esta la razón de por que el hombre ha alcanzado la más alta cima de expresión, mientras que la mujer normalmente apenas balbucea." *Pensamiento y poesía en la vida española*, (México: La casa de España, 1939) p.73.

11. Vicente Aleixandre, "Carta a Carmen Conde" in Leopoldo de Luis, *Carmen Conde* (Madrid: Ministerio de cultura, 1982) p.131.

Women or Words? The Indigenous *Nodriza* in the work of Rosario Castellanos

Much of the feminist criticism of the work of the Mexican author, Rosario Castellanos (1925–1974), has sought to examine the female characters in her prose fiction, poetry and drama, in order to draw certain conclusions, first, about the feminist orientation of the author and then, about the position of women in the Mexico of the 1950s, 1960s and 1970s.[1] This project has, in general, been undertaken without any prior discussion about the tenability of such an approach at a time when developments in literary theory have rendered what has come to be known as "Images of Women" criticism naive, impressionistic and ahistorical.

When Beth Miller, one of the foremost feminist critics of Castellanos' work, writes of the Mexican author's poetry that "Castellanos' women suffer, but often ironically. In her own case, suffering was learned"[2] and that "Castellanos' identification with other women, whether illiterate Indian peasants, or nineteenth century noblewomen, fictional heroines or historical villains, may be ascribed to her radical feminism",[3] an all too easy elision is made between what the critic regards as the authenticity of the author's life and the "real message" of the text. Literary doubles or feminist role models are being sought in fictional characters, and we are meant to be left in no doubt as to the fact that Castellanos' literary work "proves" just what a good feminist she was.

It is all too easy to lampoon this style of criticism at this point in the 1990s when Castellanos' work is read and studied almost solely – in European and North-American academic circles at least – for its feminist interest. When Beth Miller wrote the words I have quoted, and when other critics were engaged in similar studies in the early 1980s, it was in the entirely different context of an ongoing ideological battle: should Castellanos' 1950s and early 1960s texts be regarded as of interest from an *indigenista* viewpoint, and then subsequently dismissed as second rate literature, superceded by the texts of the "Boom"? Or, of feminist interest, where the author could be portrayed as one of many neglected Latin American women writers, of subversive potential, whose work could then be rescued by academic publications, and afforded places on university syllabuses?[4]

In the present context, then, in which Rosario Castellanos' feminist credentials are not really in doubt, is there any point in examining the characters, female or otherwise, which appear in her work? Is it, in fact, possible to do so in an approach, informed by post-structuralist criticism, which is more concerned with the discourses and ideologies of texts than with studying characters as rounded, whole beings, or as projections of an author's personality?

I believe this is a very good point at which to begin going over "old ground" with the work of authors such as Castellanos. It is becoming clear that, even, or, perhaps, principally among feminist critics there is a growing unease with teaching and writing about texts which, whilst clearly feminist – in other words, which exhibit a concern with women's rights or oppression – can hardly be considered subversive now, even if they were rather more so at the time of their publication. With Castellanos' work, this unease has begun to be examined recently in two studies by Chloe Furnival and Jean Franco, where attempts have been made, in the light of developments in contemporary critical theory to "situate" the politics of texts by Castellanos, rather than simply to proclaim or praise them.[5]

What I propose to do in this discussion, is to undertake a case-study examination of specific women characters – all of them indigenous *nodrizas* – in three texts by the Mexican author, first, to see if anything useful can come out of a reformed approach at "Images of Women" criticism which is aware of some of the pitfalls of this exercise, and second, in order to take up the project of situating Castellanos' work where it is left off by Furnival and Franco.

I would like to begin by outlining some of the major problems afflicting "Images of Women" criticism, in particular, and character analysis, in general. Toril Moi has described how, when feminist critics go hunting for fictional sexist images or positive role models, they usually look in texts of the realist variety, and invariably fail to recognise the "literariness" of literature.[6] Moi also writes that those who adopt this simplistic form of content analysis, based on ideas about what is "true to life", "simply cannot accommodate notions of formal and generic constraints on textual production, since to acknowledge such constraints is equivalent to accepting the inherent impossibility of ever achieving a total reproduction of reality in fiction".[7]

Toril Moi does not, at least in *Sexual/Textual Politics*, go on to outline a non-mimetic theory of character. But neither does she put forward the theory at the other extreme, that of semiotic or structuralist criticism:

> Under the aegis of semiotic criticism, characters lose their privilege, their central status, and their definition. This does not mean that they are metamorphosed into inanimate things (á la Robbe-Grillet) or reduced to actants (á la Todorov) but that they are textualized. As segments of a closed text, characters at most are patterns of recurrence, motifs which are continually retextualized in other motifs. In semiotic criticism, characters dissolve.[8]

Shlomith Rimmon-Kenan writes in *Narrative Fiction: Contemporary Poetics* that these two approaches to character – mimetic and semiotic – do not have to be seen as cancelling each other out,

> provided one realizes that the two extreme positions can be thought of as relating to different aspects of narrative fiction. In the text characters are nodes in the verbal design; in the story they are – by definition – non (or pre-) verbal abstractions, constructs. Although

these constructs are by no means human beings in the literal sense
of the word, they are partly modelled on the reader's conception of
people and in this they are person-like.[9]

Rimmon-Kenan's approach acknowledges that literary characters are, in the first
instance, just words on the page, but it also allows for an explanation of what
generally goes on in the reading process: that characters, like stories, may be
extracted from their purely textual existence, and be remembered and discussed
separately. This can take place because the words on the page are not raw and
undifferentiated textual material but structured, "made of separable components,
and hence having the potential of forming networks of internal relations".[10]

This understanding of separable and structured "character-indicators" which the
reader may imbue with "life" – or as I would put it, anthropomorphize – returns
us to Toril Moi's point about the formal and generic constraints on textual
production. It is these constraints which partly manifest themselves in the
different conventions of characterization which are possible for individual
authors, writing from specific cultural backgrounds at particular moments in
history. Analysing these conventions and their cultural contexts, can not only help
us to situate individual texts politically and historically, but, as I hope to show in
the case of the texts by Rosario Castellanos, might also lead us to draw different
and rather more complex conclusions about the ideologies which inform her
writing than those drawn by earlier feminist critics.

The first indigenous wet-nurse character I have chosen to analyse is one of the
most celebrated female characters from Castellanos' work, and especially beloved
of feminist critics: the anonymous *nana* from the Mexican author's first novel,
Balún-Canán (1957).[11] This character appears in the first of the three parts of the
novel, and briefly at the beginning of the final part. Her role as a plot device is
very simple: rejected by her own community because she works for a white
family and despised by the whites because she is a Tzeltal Indian, she is the
"embodiment" of the complexities of racial oppression for the little girl who is the
protagonist and narrator of the first and last parts of the novel. The little girl loves
her as a human being who responds to her needs, and only comes to view her as

just another Indian – under the constant bombardment of racial hostility – after the *nana* has been dismissed by her family and removed from her immediate sphere of concern. She is also the surrogate mother figure for the little girl, whose own mother has effectively rejected her in favour of the younger son and heir. Finally, in her role as the foreteller of the death of the son, the nana precipitates the demise of the Argüello family for whose children she has cared.

Most critics have concurred about the didactic and nurturing roles that the *nana* plays in *Balún-Canán*, but feminist critics have tended to concentrate instead on praising the realism of the character. For these critics, the *nana* is realistic because she is "complex": she clearly loves the little girl and her brother, but is torn between them and her own sense of identity as an alienated Tzeltal; she is effectively a slave to the Argüello family, but this does not stop her from standing up to them as in the case of her unwelcome prophesy. For one critic, the *nana* is not only realistic and three-dimensional, she is also drawn directly from the author's real childhood and her experiences with her own wet nurse, Rufina.[12]

Whilst *Balún-Canán* is clearly an autobiographical novel of sorts, the claim that the *nana* is entirely a realistic character is faintly ridiculous, if based on an understanding of the conventions of literary realism. When the illiterate and uneducated *nana* opens the novel telling a story which exactly mimics the style and tone of the quotation from the Maya-Quiché text, *Popol-Vuh*, which serves as the epigraph to the novel as a whole, and which directly precedes the *nana*'s intervention, I, for one, am reminded of a comment made by Rosario Castellanos about her prose fiction in general:

> Muchos de mis personajes eran indios. Para hacerlos recurrí a los modelos literarios que crearon sus antepasados, imité deliberadamente el estilo del *Libro del consejo*, de los *Chilam Balam*, de los *Anales de los Xahil*...
> ¿Qué esto no es real ni verosímil? No. Es una convención que es lícita si el lector la acepta la recibe.[13]

I do not quote this because it reveals Castellanos' "authentic" authorial intentions (although clearly it does) but simply because it should serve to remind us that

Castellanos was not writing texts informed solely by the conventions of a 1950s
literary feminism, but also by the generic conventions of 1950s Mexican
indigenismo. The *nana* of this genre, rather like some of the Maya characters in
the Guatemalan author, Miguel Angel Asturias' work, serves as the anonymous
voice of an ancient people, warning of the cyclical nature of time and history, and
the inevitable rise and fall of civilisations:

> Y entonces, coléricos, nos despoyeron, nos arrebataron lo que
> habíamos atesorado: la palabra, que es el arca de la memoria.
> Desde aquellos días arden y se consumen con el leño de la
> hoguera. Sube el humo y se deshace. Queda la ceniza sin rostro.
> Para que puedas venir tú y él que es menor que tú y les baste un
> soplo, solamente un soplo. (*B.C.* 9)

The *nana* in *Balún-Canán* is there partly, as Martin Lienhard writes of several of
the Tzeltal characters in the text, to provide "una ascendencia *Popol-Vuh*".[14] Yet
this does not mean that the *nana* is nothing more than a stock character of
indigenista fiction, and this is where I must turn to the question of specific
conventions of characterisation that I raised earlier.

It is significant that the *nana* only appears in the first and last sections of the
novel. These are the parts narrated in the first-person by the little girl who, as
many critics have noted, could well have been intended as a self-portrait of the
author as a child. This again may very well be so, but I would prefer to dismiss
the idea of an intentionality reliant on the details of the author's life, and focus
instead on the generic expectations that the text itself raises, expectations that the
narrative is to be read at least as "fictional autobiography", if not as
"autobiographical fiction".

The first of the textual conventions to raise these expectations is, of course, the
first-person narrative voice, which leads the reader to presume that the first and
last parts of the novel are to be read as a realist fictional autobiography, that of the
little girl. The first indication that the text could be read as autobiographical
fiction comes with the disruption of this realist first-person voice by the
introduction of complex syntactical and lexical elements untypical, in terms of

literary realism, of the register of a seven-year-old child. This might lead the reader to assume that the story is being "secretly" related by an adult narrator, using a retrospective judgmental voice characteristic of the conventions of autobiographical narratives.

The way that this functions in *Balún-Canán* is extremely complex, because the little girl's story is ostensibly presented as if it were instantaneously narrated. One episode from Chapter Four of the first part of the novel will serve as an example of the conventions at work here, and incidentally concerns one of the text's most important themes: the girl's awareness of the way in the which the racism which surrounds her operates. As the Indians from the family ranch at Chactajal are arriving in Comitán for a fiesta, the girl is made aware that her *nana* fears them. When she asks why, the *nana* shows her some scars and tells her that she was attacked because "he sido crianza de tu casa. Porque quiero a Mario y a ti" (*B.C.* 16). The girl asks:

> — ¿Es malo querernos?
> — Es malo querer a los que mandan, a los que poseen. Así dice la
> ley.

As the litle girl leaves her *nana*'s side temporarily after this conversation, she reflects on what she has been told, and in a rare moment of psychological maturity, she relates a discovery:

> Yo salgo, triste por lo que acabo de saber. Mi padre despide a los
> indios con un ademán y se queda recostado en la hamaca, leyendo.
> Ahora lo miro por primera vez. Es el que manda, el que posee. Y
> no puedo soportar su rostro y corro a refugiarme en la cocina... [Mi
> nana] como siempre desde que nací, me arrima a su regazo. Es
> caliente y amoroso. Pero tendrá una llaga. Una llaga que nosotros
> le habremos enconado. (*B.C.* 16–17)

Although this short passage is essential for what it reveals about the plot and the wider themes of the novel, it is perhaps even more fascinating from the point of view of the narrative techniques it employs. For despite the fact that this incident is relayed in the present tense, it has a curiously retrospective and considered ring to it. In fact, there is nothing curious about how this works. None of the chapters narrated by the little girl employ the stream of consciousness technique that Castellanos favours, for interiorisation purposes, in certain parts of the mainly omnisciently-narrated middle section of the novel. This means that while most of the child's narrative is in the present tense it nonetheless reveals its traditional retrospective organising structure. Frequently this is done, as it is in this episode, by means first of recounting a significant event and then relating the conclusions to be drawn from it, in the manner of a physical stimulus followed by a psychological effect. The use of the present tense mainly serves to underline the "simplicity" of the narrative style for the purposes of realism, as if it really were the work of a seven-year old, while in no way altering the retrospective signals it simultaneously sends out.

Even if the reader is not forearmed with information that many of the episodes in the book run parallel to real events from the author's childhood in Chiapas (a detail which is in any case announced on the cover of the first edition), the particular literary devices used plant more than a suspicion that the novel, or large parts of it, is to be read as an autobiographical fiction, written by an adult narrator remembering her childhood days. With no clues furnished as to the adult identity of the anonymous girl narrator, other than the name on the front cover of the novel, most readers, and certainly most critics, conflate the narrator's identity with that of the author.

What does this mean in terms of the character of the *nana*? The fact that her story is told by the little girl, and told only, as in the episode recounted above, from the point of view of revealing her role in the socialisation of the girl and the formation of the latter's sense of identity, helps to explain why the figure of the *nana* is in fact so "one dimensional", in conventional literary terms. Her own motives, her physical appearance, and so on, are not described; they are irrelevant to this other story. The *nana* is hazily invoked as a surrogate maternal icon, then removed before the little girl has learned her complete lesson of racial tolerance, allowing the more important story to take over: the little girl's testimony of her own struggle for self-affirmation and survival, and the cyclical decline of her family into superstition and relative poverty. It is this story which provides the only available narrative closure to the novel, as the *nana* along with the other Tzeltales and the story of their revolt, disappears from view in the final chapters.

Thus even with its powerful *indigenista* elements *Balún-Canán* relies more heavily on the conventions of the European autobiographical family chronicle, adapted here for the purposes of a modern feminist *bildungsroman* narrative: a typical confessional tale where the female protagonist's quest for self-identity through writing both mirrors and prefigures similar narratives by other twentieth-century feminist authors. With the indigenous *nana* – the usual pole of cultural authenticity in many *indigenista* texts – removed from the d enoument, the whole issue of National Identity (generally central in such texts) is articulated not only in the sole terms of the white *ladino* community, but is in fact completely submerged in this other plot about individual identity and personal liberation. In this plot, the anonymous *nana* can only ever be a feminist character *manquée*.

My discussion of the next indigenous *nodriza* from the work of Rosario Castellanos will be briefer and less complicated than that of the nana in *Balún-Canán*, mainly because this second character comes not from a novel but from a dramatic poem, *Salomé* (1959).[15] This poem is frequently quoted by feminist critics as a cipher for Castellanos' attitudes to mother/daughter relationships, but has rarely received any detailed analysis.

In the poem, the biblical story of Salomé is transferred to Castellanos' familiar terrain, San Cristóbal in rural Chiapas, at the time of a Chamula Indian uprising. Germaine Calderón neatly summarises the issue of how the institution of motherhood passes on female oppression across generations which most feminist critics have seen as central to a reading of this poem:

> Salomé, la Madre, la Nodriza, están unidas por la antigua y pesada cadena de las convenciones que va apretando, poco a poco, las manos y la conciencia hasta obligarlas a sentarse en un sillón que tiene ya la forma de su cuerpo: la obediencia.[16]

Unlike in Balún-Canán, where the interventions of the *nana* are fictionally
mediated by the little girl's narration, in *Salomé* the *nodriza* (like Salomé and her
mother) speaks "directly" to the reader, apparently telling her own story this time:

> Niña, olvidé su lengua, no aprendí sus costumbres
> Y nunca usé su ropa
>
> Pues soy como una malva trasplantada
> en un solar que no es de mi abuelo
> He de morir hasta una muerte ajena
> puesto que amamanté hijos que no eran míos
> y me crié en el patio de las huérfanas.
>
> Yo no menosprecié a los de mi raza
> Pero entre ellos y entre todos soy
> la despreciada. (*S.128*)

The *nodriza*'s story is very similar to that of the *nana* from the first novel, and
this section of the poem might well remind us of the "he sido crianza de tu casa"
episode examined above. However, her story is told not only without the
mediation of a fictional character, but neither does she seem to be telling it solely
in order to punctuate and back up Salomé's story. In fact, the stories told by all
three female characters seem to be relatively independent from one another, even
when the dramatic requirements of the poem stipulate that they must be talking to
each other. The female voices in this poem are like individual contributions to a
strange feminist consciousness-raising session, where the participants learn not
from each other but only from themselves. There is the testimony of the stifled
daughter, who longs for freedom:

> Madre quiero vivir y el amor tuyo
> no me deja. (*S.126*)

Then there is the account of the long-suffering wife and mother, in one of the
most frequently-quoted stanzas from Castellanos' poetry:

Y fui educada para obedecer
y sufrir en silencio.

Mi madre en vez de leche
me dio el sometimiento. (*S.127*)

The *dialogue des sourdes* which develops in this dramatic poem provides
characters which are a far more felicitous object for "Images of Women" criticism
than the *nana* in the first novel. The characters here are more obviously
"motivated" and communicate this to the reader, if not to each other, because they
are more self-aware. In this, these three female voices prefigure later poems by
Castellanos, such as "Kinsey Report", where monologues from different female
characters explain how they feel and how they came to be the way they are.

Fictional self-expression is again the key here, although this time the *nodriza* is
seemingly allowed to "speak for herself" and exist in her own right, not just as a
character in someone else's story.

Finally, I wish to examine the only named *nodriza* in Castellanos' work who
appears in the Mexican author's second and final published novel, *Oficio de
tinieblas* (1962).[17] I have examined elsewhere my belief that *Oficio de tinieblas* is
effectively a rewriting of *Balún-Canán*.[18] In this second novel, we have the same
story with a slightly different, perhaps more historically accurate ending in which
a far more severe critique of neo-Cardenista ideals, such as national integration,
land redistribution and literacy campaigns, is played out than that which appears
in the first novel. This time, the defeat of the Tzotzil Indian community is
alllowed to provide the narrative closure, as an omnisciently-narrated text
replaces the different perspectives offered up in *Balún-Canán* with its different
concerns.

The *nana* in this story is given a name, Teresa Entzín López, as is her charge,
Idolina; together they form a parallel relationship to the *niña* and the *nana* from
the first novel, even entering the narrative in the same way as the first pair, with
Teresa telling a story and Idolina telling her to be quiet. There are other
similarities between the characters, too. Idolina is a lonely and unloved child

rejected by her mother. Teresa makes prophesies. But they are a degraded version of the couple in *Balún-Canán*. This time, although Teresa serves the same purpose of providing "una ascendencia *Popol-Vuh*" with her stories and prophetic visions, we learn that her role as a storyteller is separately *motivated*. She is not the only surrogate mother figure in the novel. She has a rival for the the affections and attentions of Idolina in Julia Acevedo, the mistress of Idolina's stepfather, Leonardo Cifuentes. So her storytelling is shown as a calculated effort to regain her privileged position with her mistress. We also learn of the reasons which prompted her to stay to care for Idolina, long after her role as wet-nurse had finished. Her own child had died when she was forcibly taken to look after Idolina, and so she had nothing to return to her community for.

It is clear thus far that Teresa Entzín López is a far more "rounded" character than the hazily-traced nana from the first novel. What should be of interest here is how this "filling out" process operates on this character in the second novel. Whilst the *nana* of the first novel appears in sections narrated by the little girl, Teresa appears in passages of third-person narration, with its techniques of direct speech, . and, to a lesser extent, free indirect discourse. What we do not learn about her motivations and her personal history from her speech is explained by the omniscient narrator in the zones which surround her interventions in the novel, though these passages are frequently focalised through Teresa's own speech style, as in the following example:

> — ¿Qué estoy haciendo aquí?·se preguntó de pronto Teresa con un disgusto que husmeaba, para cebarse, el olor de los cuerpos apiñados, de las flores marchitas, de la cera en combustión.
> — ¿Qué estoy haciendo aquí? Y repentinamente la invadió una nostalgia de gentes blancas, de palabras españolas, de espacios libres. Si esta mujer que nos reclama deberes, razonaba Teresa, fuera verdaderamente capaz de hacer algo, yo no estaría aquí sino con Idolina.
> (*O* 256)

Like the *nodriza* in the poem *Salomé*, Teresa seems to "exist" separately from the mediation of another character in the text. Yet, unlike the *nodriza* she is not the only – albeit fictional – author of her story, for in *Oficio de tinieblas* her character is partly presented through the "all-seeing eye" of an omniscient narrator, who explains what she does not. It is through these traditional novelistic devices of omniscience and interiorization that Teresa is shown to be following at all times the imperatives of intense personal experience and history.

Several critics have praised this as a step forward in the poetics of *indigenista* fiction that an indigenous character can be traced in this way, usually reserved for the white characters in the novels. But this "equal opportunities characterisation", in which indigenous characters are seen as having experiences in the same way as white people hardly disrupts the discursive format of the Novel, whose rise coincided with the birth of European industrial capitalism and the growth of bourgeois individualism. As Catherine Belsey writes,

> Classic realism presents individuals whose traits of character, understood as essential and predominantly given, constrain the choices they make, and whose potential for development depends on what is given. Human nature is thus seen as a system of character-differences existing in the world, but one which nonetheless permits the reader to share the hopes and fears of a wide range of kinds of characters.[19]

This is the tradition from which the character of Teresa Entzín López derives its intelligibility. The interior monologues and free indirect speech ensure that there are few characters in this second novel with whom we cannot have some sense of shared humanity. And just as Castellanos gives authority to her characters as individuals, she authorises herself and her readers as subjects. Even in the "higher form" of realism of the first and last parts of *Balún-Canán*, in the first person-narrated text, the same practices are at work.

These practices, here adapted by the discourses of egalitarian politics, are based, as indeed are Castellanos' views on feminism and the national integration of Mexico's indigenous peoples, on the idea of the experiential individual who lies at the heart of Western society, and on the belief that experience is "real", in other words pre-linguistic, and can be represented in writing. This view, which sees the establishment of the subjectivity of women and other oppressed peoples as an unquestioned good, together with the discourses of realism which convey it, situate the Mexican author firmly in the historical moment of liberal feminism. Or rather, they help to situate her work of the late 1950s in this way, for the career of Rosario Castellanos continued for a period of twelve more years, after *Oficio de tinieblas* – with poetry, short stories, articles and plays – which saw these discourses of feminism change.

In this analysis of the three indigenous *nodriza* characters from the work of Castellanos, an examination which under the usual processes of "Images of Women" criticism would have served to homogenise the objects under investigation, many differences between the presentations of the characters have been addressed. If we return to Shlomith Rimmon-Kenan's discussion of the whole endeavour of character analysis we can see why these two approaches are not entirely incompatible. For in each case the story of the *nodriza* is the same: an oppressed indigenous woman, taken out of her own community and forced to care for the child of a white family, whom she eventually comes to love. What differs each time are details of writing strategies, or, in Rimmon-Kenan's words, the *text*: the anonymous *nanas* and the named *nana*; the character who only exists in order to illustrate someone else's story and the characters who seem to exist in their own right, whose actions and decisions appear to have a cause or origin.

These then are not "Images of Women" cast in timeless stone, but cast in historically and culturally situated *writing*. It is this recognition which may provide a response to those forms of criticism which, in seeking to champion the work and the author against the grain of prevailing sexist attitudes, have provided only very generalised readings which have revealed more about the political priorities of the critic than about the texts themselves. Clearly, however, this last censure can be extended to most forms of critical activity. At this point in time, though, it must surely be the task of the committed feminist critic to recognise that there have been, and still are, many different forms of feminism, and that one way of writing about and teaching texts, like these by Rosario Castellanos, which do not really seem all that radical with the passage of time is, as Gayatri Spivak puts it, "to situate feminist individualism in its historical determination rather than simply to canonise it as feminism as such".[20]

Catherine Grant
University of Strathclyde

1. Some examples of such criticism include the following: Phyllis Rodríguez-Peralta, "Images of Women in Rosario 'Castellanos' Prose", *Latin American Literary Review*, 6, 11 (1977) pp.68–80; María Rosa Fiscal, "La mujer en la narrativa de Rosario Castellano", *Texto crítico*, 5, 15, (1979) pp.133–53; Martha Oehmke Loustanau, "Rosario Castellanos: The Humanization of the Female Character", in "Mexico's Contemporary Women Novelists" (Unpublished dissertation, University of New Mexico, 1973) pp.48–74.

2. Beth Miller, "Women and Feminism in the Works of Rosario Castellanos", *Feminist Criticism: Essays on Theory, Poetry and Prose*, ed. Cheryl Brown and Karen Olson (London: The Scarecrow Press, 1978) pp.198–210, p.202.

3. ibid. p.206.

4. I have outlined this ideological struggle in my unpublished PhD dissertation (Leeds University, 1991) "Authorship and Authority in the Novels of Rosario Castellanos", from which some other elements of this discussion are also drawn.

5. Jean Franco, "On the Impossibility of Antigone and the Inevitability of La Malinche: Rewriting the National Allegory", *Plotting Women: Gender and Representation in Mexico* (London: Verso, 1989) pp.129–46; Chloe Furnival, "Confronting Myths of Oppression: The Short Stories of Rosario Castellanos", *Knives and Angels: Women Writers in Latin America*, ed. Susan Bassnett (London: Zed Press, 1990) pp.52–73.

6. Toril Moi, *Sexual/Textual Politics* (London: Methuen, 1985) p.49.

7. ibid. p.46.

8. Joel Weinsheimer, "Theory of Character: *Emma*", *Poetics Today*, 1, 1–2, (1979) pp.185–211, p.195.

9. Shlomith Rimmon-Kenan, *Narrative Fiction: Contemporary Poetics* (London:

Methuen, 1983) p.33.

10. ibid. p.6.

11. Rosario Castellanos, *Balún-Canán* (Mexico: Fondo de Cultura Económica, 1957). All future references to this edition will be made in the text between brackets, eg. (*B.C.* 9).

12. María Estela Franco, *Rosario Castellanos: una semblanza psicoanalítica* (Mexico: Plaza y Janes, 1985) p.40.

13. Rosario Castellanos, "Rosario Castellanos habla de Rosario Castellanos", *Mujeres (suplemento cultural)*, mayo (1969) p.22.

14. Martin Lienhard, "La legitimación indígena en dos novelas centroamericanas", *Cuadernos Hispanoamericanos*, 138, no. 414 (1984) pp.110–20, p.115.

15. Rosario Castellanos, "Salomé y Judith", *Poesía no eres tú (Obra poética: 1948–1971)* (Mexico: Fondo de Cultura Económica, 1972). All future references to this edition will be made in the text between brackets, eg. (*S.*9).

16. Germaine Calderón, *El universo poético de Rosario Castellanos* (Mexico: UNAM, 1979) p.50.

17. Rosario Castellanos, *Oficio de tinieblas* (Mexico: Joaquín Mortiz, 1962). All future references to this edition will be made in the text between brackets, eg. (*O.*9).

18. I have examined this point in detail in Chapter Four of my unpublished dissertation.

19. Catherine Belsey, *Critical Practice* (London: Methuen, 1980) p.74.

20. Gayatri Chackravorty Spivak, "Three Women's Texts and a Critique of Imperialism", *Critical Inquiry*, 12 (1985) pp.242–61, p.244.

The Female Pinup Unpenned: Images of Women in Hispanic Art

ː

The aim of this paper is to evaluate the interconnection between womanhood and nationhood in specific examples of modern Spanish and Latin–American art. I shall be using the term nationhood to refer to a cluster of ideologies projected by an individual or a class of individuals to create what Benedict Anderson calls an "imagined community" whose totality can never be experienced concretely but which is no less real for that.[1] Its imaginary quality suggests a comparison might be made with Lacanian knowledge, and specifically its contention that the creation of personal identity is predicated on the reflection, or projection, of the self via the mirrorstage.[2] I am therefore taking the symbolic entry into nationhood as parallel to and sustained by the entry of the individual into the Symbolic Order, as presided over by the Law– and the Name–of–the–Father. Nationhood, therefore, like human identity, can only exist in a gendered form. The question I will be addressing in this paper can be formulated as follows: is entry into the Symbolic Order of nationhood, projected in the figure of a woman, a subversion of the phallocentric version of human/national development, or merely a confirmation of its strategies? As we shall see, there is no simple answer to this question. This is due, primarily, to the epistemological problematics incumbent upon the projection of the woman as a grand abstraction (i.e. as Truth or Beauty, etc.) within a patriarchal economy. In addressing this problem Lacan adopted a radical approach; to emphasize the dangers inherent in a universalist projection of womanhood, he set his sights not on the "woman" but the indefinite article which precedes her, which he strikes through with a bar, to produce "La femme".[3] According to the Lacanian model, thus, woman occupies a space within the discursive economy which is in effect a nonspace, and might be compared to what the discursive practice of science calls a "black hole". If we transfer this notion of womanhood to the sphere of nationhood, dissonance and resistance are produced. Rather than a clean, sharp image of nationhood, what typically emerges is what Sara Castro–Klarén has called in a different but related context the "undulating surface of a mirror" which distorts "epochal, national or gender differences".[4] Bearing this model of nationhood/womanhood in mind, I want now to turn to a discussion of a small number of works of art which focus on the Wars of Independence in Latin American (1808–1824) and the Spanish Civil War (1936–1939). I have chosen these particular works since, during these two periods, the Hispanic world was gripped by a paranoiac frenzy caused by the dismemberment of national identity which expressed itself (like all paranoia) in a gendered form. But before reviewing some examples of Hispanic art, some elucidation of the backdrop in nineteenth-century art will be necessary.

In her important study, "Daughters of the Century", Isabelle Julia points to the French Revolution of 1789 as a watershed for the depiction of women in the visual arts. Before that time, she argues, society was aristocratic, the Academy of Painting with its codification of artistic genres ruled supreme, and the female figure had a conformist, idealist role to play. "Women were goddesses and nymphs (or Virgins and Saints) in history painting; queens or princesses in portrait painting; embodiments of handicrafts or peasant life in genre painting."[5] As a result of the French Revolution, however, a new sensibility emerged which led, firstly, to a boom in portrait painting by the newly wealthy middle classes, and, secondly, greater realism in the depiction of women. But the most important change for our purposes was the re-historicization of a traditional theme, namely, the personification of the nation, *la patrie*, as a woman. There were, of course, still traces of the old sensibility; the depiction of female saints such as Joan of Arc increased dramatically in the nineteenth century, aided by the dogma of the Immaculate Conception (1854). But, as Julia concludes, evidence for the changing attitude towards the image of woman is unmistakable: "The Revolution saw Woman as wife, a mother and a patriot; Romanticism made her a sentimentalised victim and a patriot; Realism saw her as the glorified or sacrificial symbol of the new society" (95). While offering different perspectives on the same phenomenon, these artistic movements were united in their desire to project the nation within the frame of womanhood.

The central painting in any discussion of the image of woman and the idea of nation is, of course, Eugène Delacroix's *Liberty Guiding the People* (1830) which celebrates the three glorious July days in the Revolution of 1830 (Illustration 1).[6] *Liberty Guiding the People* clearly fits into the Revolution genre identified by Julia since the female protagonist of the painting is nothing if not a patriot, bearing the three-coloured flag and thus emblematizing French nationalism. But her status as a female is more problematic. Is she a wife or a mother, which were the two versions of motherhood stipulated by the Revolution genre? The audience of the time seemed to concur that she was neither. To quote a sample of contemporary critics: "A woman of dubious reputation." "Shameless and filthy." One of the most outspoken critics spoke of her as the basest whore from the filthiest streets of Paris, as evidenced by "la pelosité de ses aiselles". By the 1830s, as Martha Kapos points out, images of women with body hair were in circulation in pornographic photographs, and her hairy armpits therefore gave her away.[7] But the problem with seeing Delacroix's woman as merely a whore lies in the fact that the painting gave every indication that she was not to be taken as a real women but rather as an allegory. She is, after all, named as an abstraction; her figure, compared with the others in the painting, is considerably larger than life; she is placed at the peak of a compositional triangle which pushes upwards towards an ideal represented by the tricolour flag and as if in transcendence of the death/corruption signified by the corpses along the bottom of the painting. The Phrygian cap she is wearing is also to be read as a symbol of the Revolution rather than actual head gear. In the final analysis, thus, Delacroix's painting is allegorical, but the exposed breasts of his heroine embody a sexual latency which introduces a note of dissonance into the frame.

When passing to Hispanic art which projects nationhood as a woman, one encounters the immediate problem of cultural transference centring on the issue of nudity. While in France by the 1860s there was an established vogue of painting nude courtesans surrounded, in Kitsch-like manner, by the accoutrements of Greek culture, Spanish and Latin–American art circles still shunned nudity.[8] Semidraped nudes shocked the Mexican audience of a special exhibition held in Mexico in 1864. In Venezuela drawing of the nude female model was still forbidden in the Academy as late as 1904.[9] Artistic circles in Latin America clearly took literally Maxime Du Camp's 1863 axiom that "l'art ne doit pas avoir plus de sexe que les mathématiques".[10] Thus, when we do find the use of the female body in LatinAmerican nineteenth-century art as an image of nationhood, the body is normally clothed.

A typical example of this genre is Juan Manuel Blanes's *Paraguay: Image of your Desolate Country* (c.1880), which is clearly inscribed within the Delacroix tradition. Blanes's work closely parallels the latter's *Greece Expiring on the Ruins of Missolonghi* (1827) which shows a women standing on the ruins of the Greek town. The two paintings depict national conflicts which are similar in terms of the scale of devastation involved. Missolonghi was besiged by the Turks in 1821 and buried under its own ruins in 1826; Paraguay was destroyed in the War of the Triple Alliance (1865–1870) in which Brazil, Argentina and Uruguay ganged up on their tiny neighbour in order to oust its dictador, Francisco Solano López. Both paintings focus on a lost nationshood which is not that of the painter.[11] Blanes's painting, like Delacroix's, focusses on the woman as representing the consciousness of defeat. There are other explicit parallels: both paintings, for example, depict a woman who is mourning the death of a man. Delacroix's version has the man lying under the rocks (we see his arm sticking out), while Blanes wraps the dead man's body in a flag which serves as his shroud.[12] Blanes's work has individual features. In a touch which is more allegorical than realistic the flag closely hugs the countours of the dead man's face. The existential loneliness of the women is echoed firstly by the bird on the gun on the left and, secondly, by the man and animal on the cliff face in the distance on the right. Perhaps most allegorical of all, in the book lying open at her feet can be read the two words, "Historia" and "Patria". In what is essentially a visual simile the body of the man is covered partially by the earth, just as the word "Patria" is covered by a clod of earth. *Paraguay: Image of your Desolate Country*, therefore, despite having a woman in the centre of the frame, takes for granted that nationhood is co-substantial with manhood.[13] The woman becomes by default the token observer, merely the consciousness of defeat; she experiences power through the man in whose (dead) body the (absent) power of the nation resides. At this point it is clear that Blanes's canvas echoes the political strategy of Delacroix's *Greece Expiring*. In *Paraguay* the woman is as much a victim as the man, but she is represented as mourning the loss of nationhood rather than embodying its power. In terms of the national allegory, therefore, she is no more than a "surrogate wife".

It is important to differentiate clearly between the different categories of the nation-as-suffering-woman trope. Similar images to those typified by Blanes's *Paraguay* would recur with some insistence a century later, specifically in art inspired by the Spanish Civil War. But there is a difference and this concerns the degree of victimhood involved; the women who figure as victims in Spanish Civil War art are depicted as "sentimentalised victims", to use Julia's term (see above), who experience victimhood physically. A stock precedent for this topos was the *Massacre of the Innocents*, and a striking example of its remanipulation is Picasso's *Guernica* (1937).[14] The one woman to appear in *Guernica* (she is on the lefthand side of the canvas) is clearly a reworking of this classical source. In an early sketch of the woman, entitled *Study for Screaming Woman* and dated 9 May 1937, the gesture of the head thrown back in despair is highly stylized and reminiscent of Ingres's depiction of Thetis's head in his *Jupiter and Thetis* (1811).[15] In Picasso's painting the woman takes on a classical suppliant pose in order to underline the destruction of innocence and political freedom. We find a similar allusion to the *Massacre of the Innocents* topos in the Civil War work of one of Picasso's contemporaries, Julio González, particularly his sequence of works on the Screaming Montserrat theme. His sketch *Imploring Woman on her Knees* (1939) and the three sculptures *Mask of the Screaming Montserrat* (1938–39), *Small Frightened Montserrat* (1941–42), and *Head of Screaming Montserrat* (1942), all express a raw, gendered agony not evident in Picasso's work.[16] Given the name of the woman depicted, and it is noteworthy that she *does* have a name which contravenes the convention of anonymity, it is clear that González's work has a *catalanista* dimension which may well explain its political urgency. In the politically-charged 1930s, as might be expected, images of this kind were not restricted to Spain. Similar woman-as-victim tropes appear in the work of the Mexican muralist, Diego Rivera, notably his *Police Breaking Strike* (1935) and *Class Struggles* (1935). The work of Picasso, González and, to some extent, Rivera represents womanhood as victims on account of the power they embody. Indeed, in some cases, particularly González's work, the woman is figured as the gender which most adequately embodies (lost) nationhood. There is evidently a difference, though, between González's Screaming Montserrat sequence and Blanes's heroine who is represented as only possessing surrogate power through the absent male.

It could be argued that the work considered so far, whether it takes the form of Blanes's projection of woman as the consciousness of lost nationhood or González's prioritization of the female experience, is ultimately subject to the woman-as-victim image institutionalized by phallocracy. To quote Gilbert and Gubar's metaphor, even when they are admired for their beauty, women cannot escape the cage of phallocracy for they are "penned-in" when "penned".[17] The archetypal example of the woman who is penned-in by the forces of patriarchy in the Latin–American context is La Malinche. The most celebrated version of this idea is that crystallized by the Mexican poet and essayist, Octavio Paz, who argues in *El laberinto de la soledad* (1950) that every Mexican is born of the rape of La Malinche by Cortés. The work of many writers/artists casts the primal scene of Latin America in similar terms. Diego Rivera's *Priests and Exploiters*, for example, by disclosing *male* priests as exploiting *female* Indians, (re)presents a gendered reading of the Conquest. La Malinche becomes, by definition, a second politicized version of Eve who is responsible for the original sin of capitalism.[18] Antonio Ruiz's work, however, diverges from this orthodox version of Latin–American history. Rather than bearing the blame of colonialism, La Malinche becomes in *The Dream of Malinche* (1939) a prime mover of the creation of the New World. Far from succumbing to the invader's desire, La Malinche is presented as dreaming the New World into existence *through* her body since, as Ruiz's reading suggests, her body becomes the space in which the new civilisation took root and now flourishes. It could be argued that Ruiz's canvas denies this female creativity even as it ostensibly gives birth to it but, however one reads *The Dream of Malinche*, it evokes dissonance within the established *machista* version of the primal scene of Latin America since cultural creativity is shown to be feminocentric.

A similar dissonance is evident in some depictions of another prime mover of Latin–American history, namely, Simón Bolívar. There are countless paintings of Bolívar in existence, which comes as no surprise, and most of them cast him in the role of father to the Latin–American nation, a view he himself helped to foster as his *Carta de Jamaica* (1815) makes clear. In Fernando Leal's *The Epic of Bolívar* (1930), to give but one example, Bolívar is presented as a Godlike figure, and, revealingly, his subjects are in the main female (*Art in Latin America*, 152). Pedro José Figueroa's *Simón Bolívar, Liberator and Father of the Nation* (1819) provides a rather curious re-writing of this trope. It was presented to Bolívar in the main square of Bogotá during the victory celebrations after the Battle of Boyacá on 18 September 1819. The painting alludes to the tradition, common since Colonial times, of representing America as an indigenous woman (*Art in Latin America*, 16). The young Republic is shown as an Indian woman wearing the upright feather dress, carrying bows and arrows and seated on the head of a mythical cayman. The catalogue entry notes that "she stands in relation to Bolívar as daughter" (*Art in Latin America*, 17), but we might question whether this is the whole story, for the young Republic is a hybrid being. In racial terms, for example, she wears the pearls and jewels of a European, but her features are unmistakably "mestizo". Not only is she racially and culturally hybrid, she is a sexual hybrid to boot; she has the body of a minor but the face and indeed the crown of a queen. This makes it impossible to dismiss the painting as paying lip-service to patriarchy. *Simón Bolívar, Liberator and Father of the Nation* might more usefully be discussed in terms of what Judith Butler has defined as "gender trouble", namely a state of play in which generic and sexual divisions which traverse the space of the individual are elided, thereby unsettling the spurious symmetrical balance inscribed by gender.[19] In particular, Figueroa's painting problematizes the boundary between girl and woman, or what might be called the "puberty-line". In its curious mix of the realist (Bolívar) and the allegorical (the woman), this painting traces a radically anti-phallogocentric gesture since the woman is a hybrid mixture of mother and daughter, and of the allegorical and the real. She is, in conclusion, irremediably Other, untrapped by the patriarchal frame epitomised by Bolívar's fatherly arm.

A similar dissonance emerges when we evaluate the political allegory inscribed in the body of the woman in an anonymous painting depicting the emancipation of Brazil, *Allegory of the Departure of Dom Pedro II for Europe after the Declaration of the Republic* (1890) (Illustration 2). This canvas, held at the Fundação Maria Luisa e Oscar Americano in São Paolo, depicts the tantalizing moment just before the power of Dom Pedro II's monarchy is entrusted to the new Republic. The boat is in the background, ready to take Dom Pedro II and his family back to the Old World of Europe (an event which took place on 15 November 1889). The picture has realistic elements, such as the dress of the Emperor's men (which is so formal that it justifies Dom Pedro II's nickname as "Queen Victoria in trousers"), the steamers in the distance, and the black women in the foreground who are whispering to each other.[20] Even the realistic details bear the imprint of allegory, as a study of the role that Dom Pedro II's daughter plays in the canvas reveals. On the right of the picture, Princess Isabel can be seen crying amidst the family group who are preparing to move back to Europe. This is an overtly realistic detail, yet, as Vera Waller de Oliveira points out, the woman representing the Republic also bears the face of Princess Isabel.[21] *Allegory of the Departure*, therefore, deftly combines the real (Princess Isabel left Brazil on 15 November 1889) with the allegorical (Princess Isabel remained in Brazil, becoming the embodiment of the New Republic).

Other details help to stress the painting's allegorical nature. The hand appearing above Princess Isabel's head to crown here with a Phrygian hat (which here, as in Delacroix's *Liberty Guiding the People*, is a stock symbol of Republicanism) belies this apparent realism, and gives the painting an Italian Renaissance allusiveness; one is reminded of the dove which appears over Christ's head in paintings of His baptism by John.[22] The transferral of power is, indeed, played out symbolically in the language of the hats. Just as the men of the Ancien Régime take off their hats, the woman of the New Republic puts on hers. This transferral of power inevitably makes the female the focus of political power in the canvas, which is suggested by the detail of the scroll (of the new constitution?) which she is *already* holding in her hands, and of which the emperor's men seem to be holding reduced versions. One curious element about this canvas is the dress of the woman who stands for the New Republic; her attire is classical, if not actually regal, a detail which undermines her Republican status. Pointing in a similar direction is the fact that the symbol of power which Dom Pedro II is passing on to her is a transparently regal one: the crown he holds in his right hand. For this reason *Allegory of the Departure of Dom Pedro II for Europe* can probably be read in (at least) two mutually exclusive ways; firstly, as an example of the survival of male patriarchal values despite its female mystique (Princess Isabel is, after all, her father's daughter and could be seen as promoting her father's values in a gender-displaced form); or, secondly, as a projection of the new utopian political order via the image of womanhood. The most fruitful reading may well be somewhere in between, but the fact that the woman who stands for the Republic is physically larger than the men (similar in this to Delacroix's *Liberty Guiding the People*), and certainly more imposing in terms of attire and scroll, suggests that the latter reading is more valid. This anonymous allegory implies that, in Brazil as much as in France, the new order embodied by Republicanism is encoded in an intrinsic sense within femininity.

We have seen in this brief discussion that national identity is projected in Latin America and Spain in times of historical turmoil in the figure of a woman and that although in some cases this presupposes a confirmation of the Law-of-the-Father, in other cases, particulalry Ruiz's *The Dream of Malinche*, Figueroa's *Simón Bolívar* and the anonymous *Allegory of the Departure of Dom Pedro II for Europe*, an epistemological dissonance emerges which casts the power of phallocracy into doubt. In certain cases, thus, the female pinup was unpenned and, we might add, unpinned.

Stephen M. Hart

Queen Mary and Westfield College, London / University of Kentucky

1. Benedict Anderson, *Imagined Communities: Reflections on the Origin and Spread of Nationalism* (London: Verso, 1983).

2. "Le stade du miroir comme formateur de la fonction du Je", *Ecrits* (Paris: Seuil, 1966) pp.93–100.

3. For a lucid discussion, see Paul Julian Smith, *Representing the Other: "Race", Text, and Gender in Spanish and Spanish–American Narrative* (Oxford: Oxford University Press, 1992) p.100.

4. "Introduction", in *Women's Writing in Latin America: An Anthology*, edited by Sara Castro-Klarén, Sylvia Molloy and Beatriz Sarlo (Boulder–San Francisco–Oxford: Westview Press, 1991) pp.3–26, p.6.

5. "Daughters of the Century", in *La France: Images of Woman and Ideas of Nation 1789–1989* (London: South Bank Centre, 1989) pp.87–96, p.87.

6. Another is Honoré Daumier's painting *La République* (1848), which depicts the French Republic as a woman holding a flag and on whose breasts two infants are suckling; see *La France: Images of Woman and Ideas of Nation 1789–1989*, p.21.

7. *International Dictionary of Art and Artists*, with a foreword by Cecil Gould, edited by James Vinson (Chicago and London: St James Press, 1990) p.631.

8. For a discussion of the use of courtesans as nude models in classical art, see T.J. Clarke, *The Painting of Modern Life: Paris in the Art of Manet and his Followers* (London: Thames and Hudson, 1985), pp.79–146. Pradier was an example. According to Du Pays in 1865: "on a dit de Pradier qu'il partair le matin pour Athènes et arrivait le soir à la rue de Bréda [a well-known red-light district]. Aujourd'hui, un certain nombre d'artistes vont à la rue de Bréda directement"; quoted by Clarke, pp.86–87; p.285.

9. Dawn Ades, *Art in Latin America. The Modern Era, 1820–1980. The Hayward Gallery, London. 18 May to 6 August 1989* (London: South Bank Centre, 1989) p. 30. Subsequent references are to *Art in Latin America*.

10. Quoted by Clark, *The Painting of Modern Life*, p.128; p.295.

11. René Huyghe, *Delacroix* (London: Thames and Hudson, 1963) p.73.

12. Delacroix is a Frenchman witnessing the destruction of Greek sovereignty, and thus is Romantically involved in the Greek issue in a way similar to Lord Byron. Blanes, on the other hand, is a Uruguayan (he had an Argentinian mother) witnessing the aftermath of the destruction which his own country

carried out on a neighbouring state; it is likely that his sympathy would have been diminished for this reason.

13. Mary Louise Pratt's research into the related field of nineteenth-century Latin–American literature leads her to a similar conclusion: "women inhabitants of nations were neither imagined as or invited to imagine themselves as part of the horizontal brotherhood"; see "Women, Literature, and National Brotherhood", in *Women, Culture and Politics in Latin America*, ed. Emilie Bergmann et al. (Berkeley–Los Angeles–Oxford: University of California, 1990) pp.48–73, p.51.

14. Anthony Blunt goes as far as to suggest that Picasso's masterpiece is "the *Massacre of the Innocents* of the Spanish Civil War"; see his *Picasso's "Guernica"* (London: O.U.P., 1969) p.44.

15. For background, see Blunt, *Picasso's "Guernica"*, pp.44–53. Ingres's painting recreates the scene from the Iliad in which Thetis is pleading with Jupiter for divine aid for her son Achilles, fighting in the earthbound war below. Picasso consciously used Ingres as a model according to Robert Rosenblum, *Jean-Auguste-Dominique Ingres* (London: Thames and Hudson, 1967), pp.23–24. There is a later version of Picasso's drawing of the woman with dead child entitled *Study for Head of Screaming Woman*, dated 13 May 1937; see Blunt, p.48. For further discussion of Picasso's painting, see Nigel Glendinning, "Art and the Spanish Civil War", in *¡No pasarán! Art, Literature and the Spanish Civil War*, edited by Stephen M. Hart (London: Tamesis, 1988) pp.20–45.

16. Julio González. *Sculpture and Drawings* (London: Whitechapel Art Gallery, 1990).

17. See Sandra M. Gilbert and Susan Gubar, *The Madwoman in the Attic: The Woman Writer and the Nineteenth-Century Literary Imagination* (New Haven: Yale University Press, 1979) p.13.

18. Rosario Castellanos, from a feminist Mexican perspective, offers a different version of La Malinche's role; see her poem "Malinche", *Meditation on the Threshold* (Ypsilanti, Michigan: Bilingual Press, 1988) pp.134–35. For further discussion of this theme, see Sandra Messinger Cypess, *La Malinche in Mexican Literature: From History to Myth* (Austin: University of Texas Press, 1991), and Stephen M. Hart, *The Other Scene: Psychoanalytic Readings in Modern Spanish and Latin–American Literature* (Boulder, Colorado: SSASS, 1992) pp.29–37. For Peruvian examples, see Mary Louise Pratt, "Woman, Literature, and National Brotherhood", *Women, Culture and*

Politics in Latin America, pp.59–66; see also Francine Masiello, "Women, State, and Family in Latin American Literature", *ib.*, pp.27–47.

19. Judith Butler, "Gender Trouble", in *Feminism/Postmodernism*, edited and with an introduction by Linda J. Nicholson (New York and London: Routledge, 1990) pp.324–40.

20. Pedro II's nickname was coined by Gilberto Freyre; Eugenio Chang-Rodríguez, *Latinoamérica: su civilización y su cultura* (Rowley, Massachusetts: Newbury, 1983) p.125.

21. Waller de Oliveira is the Curator of the Fundação Maria Luisa e Oscar Americano and pointed out this fact in a letter to Catherine Davies dated 2 March 1992; I am grateful to Cathy for passing this information on to me.

22. For an example of this topos, see Giotto's *The Baptism of Jesus*, in Cesare Gnudi, *Giotto* (London: Willilam Heinemann, 1959), illustration 94. To emphasise the visual parallel, one might note that the Phrygian cap in *Allegory of the Departure of Dom Pedro for Europe* is vaguely dove-shaped.

1. Eugène Delacroix, *Liberty Guiding the People* (1830).

2. Anonymous, *Allegory of the Departure of Dom Pedro II for Europe after the Declaration of the Republic* (1890).

El ser o no ser de la escritura

Publiqué mi primer libro en 1964, es decir hace 27 años, y desde esta perspectiva lo que a mí más me seduce es ver las fluctuaciones de la escritura, las apariciones y desapariciones de temas, los trasvases de estilo, los motivos permanentes que subyacen con frecuencia más que en los textos en la mente, y son móviles y desencadenantes, no sólo de escritura sino de vida. En este ir y venir, en este oscilar, se detecta el tanteo o pulular inicial – verdadero ser o no ser – de las ideas que encierra ya el germen de lo que será después el mismo texto.

Ya he dicho la frase "ser o no ser". ¿Quiero decir con ello que considere que en la escritura haya algo de experiencia hamletiana? No sé si se puede generalizar, pero la gestación de algunas obras sí lo resulta. En mi caso, además, al decir "ser o no ser" refiriéndome a mis textos, no puedo limitarme a hablar del modo de producirse éstos, sino que tengo que hablar también del tema de Hamlet, puesto que estuvo rondándolos casi desde un principio, es decir desde 1964, año en que escribí la primera versión de la que sería 24 años después la novela *Los caballos del sueño*, aparecida en 1989.[1]

Aunque he publicado fundamentalmente poesía, once libros en total: *Las estrellas vencidas*, *Límite humano*, *En busca de Cordelia y poemas rumanos*, *Libro de alienaciones*, *Eros*, *Vivir*, *Kampa*, *Lapidario*, *Fósiles*, *Creciente fértil*, y *Emblemas*, mi vocación inicial se dirigía tanto a la poesía como a la prosa, y de hecho ya en 1969 apareció mi primera novela, *Desintegración* (que ahora estoy

revisando y reeditaré en breve con el título de *Espejismos*), y aunque tardé 20
años en publicar la siguiente eso no quiere decir que no escribiera prosa mientras
tanto.[2] Sucedía que si tenía claro qué era y qué quería lograr con la poesía, ante la
prosa me sentía en una gran confusión, y realizaba tanteos que no me parecían
satisfactorios, así llegué a escribir cinco versiones de *Los caballos del sueño*.

Desde que llevé a cabo mi primer libro de poesía supe que ésta nacía
fundamentalmente de un ritmo – unión del ritmo interno del ser y del externo del
propio cuerpo – que se traducía en palabras. Ese libro está hecho prácticamente en
la calle, brota del mismo ritmo de los pasos al andar. Ritmo, melodía y palabra
formaban una unidad, y el poema era ante todo aspiración a la música. Años más
tarde esta aspiración se hizo realidad en la segunda parte del libro *Kampa* cuyos
poemas son cantados.

La poesía, además, y eso estaba también muy claro en mí, tenía un carácter
ontológico, por utilizar las palabras de Heidegger, de "desocultación del ente".
Ser y existir (existir en el tiempo, algo que el ritmo delimita) son los dos polos
entre los que oscilan mis primeros libros de poemas, de carácter tanto esencialista
como existencialista. Se trata de una pugna que culmina en *Libro de alienaciones*
y se resuelve en *Vivir*.

Por las fechas de edición se ve un lapso de seis años entre mi primer libro *Las
estrellas vencidas*, de 1964, y el segundo, *Límite humano*, de 1971. De hecho a
finales de 1964 había acabado ya el segundo pero por entonces una oleada de
escepticismo me hizo dejar de escribir poesía y por lo tanto no pensé en
publicarlo. Con el mismo escepticismo me puse a escribir en prosa sobre una
historia vivida, una pelea que me parecía shakespeariana y por ello me
obsesionaba. Se trataba de la primera versión, ya mencionada, de *Los caballos del
sueño* que concebí como ejercicio. No era este mi primer texto en prosa, el
primero que luego consideré válido y publiqué, un relato titulado "Tentativa de
encuentro", lo había escrito, no por azar, en Oxford durante el verano de aquel
mismo año, 1964.[3] Ese impulso de lo shakespeariano en mi se halla vinculado a
mi adolescencia, pues a través de la lectura ritual de Shakespeare, que yo durante
un período llevé a cabo diariamente y de madrugada, me fui creando la imagen

ideal del mundo. Esto lo explico en mi libro de memorias de infancia y adolescencia, *Jardín y laberinto* (1990):

> La noche..., el sueño de aquellos años, y las charlas interminables previas a él... Luego yo colocaba debajo de mi almohada el despertador, quería amortiguar su timbre, aunque era muy débil, para que Nona no lo oyera. A las tres me ponía en pie y me acercaba a la ventana, miraba por un instante la masa de sombras con algunas luces que era Barcelona y las sombras más próximas del jardín del monasterio; luego volvía a la cama y abría el libro, y durante una hora seguía los pasos de Julieta o de Ofelia, de Perdita o de Porcia, para disponer las regiones más hondas de mi espíritu cara a un destino trágico o heroico que tal vez había de cumplirse sólo en mi mente. Pero ¿qué importaba? La comunión con lo invisible era lo que estaba a mi alcance, otorgada por el nexo enigmático de la oscuridad. (16–17)

Eso hacía, y como lo hacía medio dormida no me enteraba del todo bien de lo que leía, pero sí penetraba en mí la atmósfera, situaciones, caracteres, personajes. Entre todos destacó pronto el de Hamlet y yo románticamente – no me explico por qué – me identifiqué con Ofelia. Sucedía esto ya a final de los años cincuenta y pronto un chico inglés que conocí me desengañó: "Tú no eres Ofelia, eres Cordelia", me dijo. De ahí que el libro que supone mi reencuentro con la poesía y conmigo misma se titule *En busca de Cordelia*.

Aquella primera versión de *Los caballos del sueño* estaba escrita en forma de diálogo dramático entre tres personajes, una mujer y dos hombres, y en ella pretendía sólo reproducir la pelea que me obsesionaba. Sabía que tenía carácter de borrador para un texto futuro en el que pensaba ya buscando procedimientos literarios. El primero que encontré fue la identificación de mi protagonista con Hamlet, y me puse a investigar en el tema. De todos modos la labor quedó interrumpida por mi escepticismo de siempre. Escribí entoncos *Desintegración*, que era una historia que tenía muy clara, la publiqué, y, siempre sin convicción en lo que hacía, escribí la segunda versión de *Los caballos del sueño* (he de decir que estas dos primeras versiones no tenían título y que la obra tuvo su título definitivo en el año 1988, una vez terminada). Una vez más deseché el texto, guardándolo sólo por si volvía a intentarlo.

Así llegó el año 1971, un año clave en mi vida y mi escritura. Siempre dándole vueltas al tema de Hamlet, alguien me regaló un libro del que no sabía nada pero cuyo título le hacía pensar que me interesaría, se llamaba *Una noche con Hamlet*, y era de un autor completamente desconocido, un poeta checo, Vladimír Holan. Pues bien, la lectura de ese libro se convirtió para mí en algo definitivo. El impacto que me produjeron los poemas de Holan me arrancó del escepticismo y me llevó a la convicción de que por un solo lector que reaccionara con la intensidad con la que había reaccionado yo ante ellos merecía la pena escribir, de modo que volví a la poesía, escribí entonces *En busca de Cordelia*, *Poemas rumanos* y los primeros poemas de *Libro de alienaciones*. Mi interés por Holan rebasó la mera lectura de *Una noche con Hamlet*, me hizo entrar en contacto con él, conocerlo y aprender el checo para poder hablar con él y traducir su obra. Como consecuencia de todo esto escribí mi primer libro de poesía amorosa con el título de *Kampa*, el nombre de la isla del río Moldava, situada en medio de Praga, donde él vivió en aislamiento total, por motivos políticos, y sin querer recibir a nadie.

Mi primer viaje a Praga para conocerlo lo realicé en 1975 y fue en este mismo año cuando empecé a ver los motivos que desde un principio me empujaron a escribir aquella novela cuyo protagonista se identificaba con Hamlet, y de la que mientras tanto había redactado ya una tercera versión con el título de *Fuga* que, como las anteriores, deseché. Vi claramente que aquella pelea de la que partía representaba la confluencia entre la realidad y la imaginación, y que yo fracasaba siempre porque el estilo no respondía a ello. Vi tambén que mi propósito era estudiar, a lo largo de una historia, dos tipos de amor, el eros y el ágape, y que por lo tanto los elementos simbólicos y alegóricos debían cobrar en ella una importancia. Así empecé a profundizar en todo aquello que intuitivamente había utilizado pero sin darle el relieve necesario, como por ejemplo el tema de la herida y más tarde el de la unión de imágenes entre los dos protagonistas.

Convendría ahora apuntar por lo menos en dos palabras las sucesiones argumentales de *Los caballos del sueño*. Los dos personajes masculinos Lobo y Raúl polarizan respectivamente el eros y el ágape, siendo el enlace la protagonista femenina Alma. Habiéndose conocido de estudiantes en la ciudad de Pamplona y tras surgir el amor de Alma por Lobo, se casa, sin embargo, con Raúl. Poco después del matrimonio aparece Lobo e instiga a Raúl a la pelea. Derrotado Lobo se desvanece si bien en la mente de Alma sigue representando siempre la imagen del eros.

Cuando en 1975 me enfrenté de nuevo con la escritura del texto sabía ya varias cosas, por ejemplo que sólo soportaba el relato en primera persona pero quería ofrecer los tres puntos de vista, por lo tanto decidí que cada personaje hiciera su propio relato de los hechos, Sabía además que quería hacer una breve presentación simbólica de los relatos y que esta se escribiría en tercera persona. No sabía, en cambio, exactamente si la historia acabaría con la pelea o no. Con mucha más seguridad que al hacerlo anteriormente me puse e escribir pero a las veinte páginas abandoné una vez más el proyecto. Me impedía continuar el hecho de no saber cuál podía ser el final y esto no lo vi hasta cinco años después, en 1980, cuando a raíz de un viaje a un pueblo de Cádiz, Grazalema, pensé que aquella historia sólo podía acabar con un elogio del amor platónico de la protagonista situado en el pinsapar de aquel pueblo. Escribí entonces otras veinte páginas y lo dejé de nuevo.

Creo que fue a principios de 1985 cuando me di cuenta de cuáles podían ser los pasos intermedios que de la pelea condujeran al elogio del amor platónico: se necesitaba una etapa de derrumbamiento total de todos los presupuestos de los personajes. Así que por de pronto seguí adelante con la parte ya iniciada de relatos paralelos, de hecho serían tres partes, con sus introducciones simbólicas y llegué hasta el punto de la pelea. Esto es lo que considero cuarta versión de la novela, que se titulaba entonces *Elsinor*, y que utilicé casi en su totalidad en la quinta y definitiva.

Al enfrentarme con la etapa posterior a la pelea – y fue eso ya en el año 1987 – comprendí que necesitaba un estilo más rápido que me permitiera avanzar en los acontecimientos y pensé en la forma de diario. No tardé mucho en comprender que la complejidad de todo aquello requería escribir también unos enlaces entre las partes y modificar el orden para dar mayor fuerza al relato. Y estando en esto, en enero de 1988, me vino la iluminación final: el relato de la escritura de la novela formaría parte de ella, el paseo por el pinsapar de Grazalema no sería casual, sino que la protagonista se habría ido allí precisamente para escribir la novela, una novela que, de hecho, era una carta al personaje amado, es decir a Lobo, el que representaba el eros. La obra, que estilísticamente se aproximaba al teatro, a la poesía y al ensayo filosófico, contenía diálogos, relatos, partes simbólicas, enlaces y diarios, estaría sustentada, pues, en una red epistolar. El trabajo a partir de aquel momento fue apasionado y apasionante.

En todos estos ires y venires, en todas estas versiones y facetas incorporadas o desechadas, en todas estas construcciones y derribos se iban produciendo recuperaciones fragmentarias de textos o de ideas. Así el hilo del diálogo de la primera versión subyace en lo que va motivado los relatos paralelos de la cuarta, lo mismo sucede con algunos flashes de Pamplona de la segunda y con mínimos detalles retratísticos de la tercera. De igual modo a medida que escribía me iba atreviendo más a utilizar la poesía. La cuarta versión de la novela empezaba con un verso de los *Cuatro Cuartetos* de Eliot: "A través de la desconocida recordada puerta", y aunque esto se perdió en la última, versos de Eliot surgen de vez en cuando en el texto, y en momentos concretos todo un episodio gira en torno a ellos, como en el que se habla de la danza:

> ...plenamente entregados al ritmo y a la melodía, prescindimos de todo excepto de aquel intenso goce de la danza, danza sacra, danza de integración a la naturaleza, a los movimientos internos de la tierra, de los árboles, los animales en celo; danza genésica, corporeización del devenir; danza cósmica – como la de Siva, que representa la unión de espacio y tiempo en evolución –; danza simbólica del acto creador; que encarna la energía eterna; y por ello también forma de la magia – el arte del amor.

> Así fue aquel 14 de julio. Antonio al despedirse me dijo: «Te llamaré una mañana. Me gusta la mañana.» Cuando me senté en el saliente del muro y recibí el primer sol, no eran estas palabras las

que ondeaban por mi cabeza, sino otras muy distintas: «*En el inmóvil punto del mundo que gira... /... /Excepto por ese punto, el inmóvil punto./ No habría danza, y allí solamente hay danza*»... Estos versos de Burnt Norton se resolvían mas adelante así: «*El tiempo pasado y el tiempo futuro/ No permiten sino una escasa conciencia./ Ser consciente no es estar en el tiempo/ Pero sólo en el tiempo el momento en el jardín de rosas./ El momento en la arboleda donde batió la lluvia./ El momento en la iglesia cruzada al anochecer por la niebla/ Pueden ser recordados; envueltos en pasado y futuro./ Sólo a través del tiempo se conquista el tiempo.*» Tal vez era, pues, eso, aquella calma, aquella serenidad naciente, del frugal desayuno, del cuerpo por fin quieto, integrado al velo rosado del alba – jardín de rosas en la cúpula celeste – hasta el momento de la definitiva claridad, para entonces levantarse, subir las escaleras, acostarse y dormir una hora, y empezar el día con extraña plenitud. (*Los caballos del sueño*, 160)

Es también un verso de Eliot lo que me sirve de enlace con el desarrollo final al hallar la protagonista el "jardín de rosas" de "Burnt Norton" en un místico turco Füzüli, concretamente en su obra *Leyla y Mecnún*. También de Füzüli utilizo versos, así como frases de Simone Weil, María Zambrano, Platón, Plotino, Heráclito y, por supuesto, Shakespeare. Además me atrevo a recrear algunos episodios de Hamlet, como el del monólogo, el de la locura de Ofelia, es decir la escena de las flores, y el de su muerte. El monólogo de mi personaje quedó, por ejemplo, así:

To be or not to be... Precisamente una de sus frases de aquella noche fue: «El teatro lo es todo y yo no valgo nada; vivo pensando en la muerte día a día», ¿recuerdas? Iniciaba su monólogo: «Vivo pensando en la muerte día a día. ¿Qué es la vida, decidme, qué? ¿Los acontecimientos por los que transcurre nuestra existencia o aquellos que proyecta nuestra mente con tal fuerza que los torna reales? ¿Vivimos en las horas que nos marca el reloj de los hechos – ajenos a nosotros – o en el que marca el de nuestra fantasía? Yo diría que sólo ésta rige nuestras vidas, pues incluso es ella quien determina los acontecimientos que nos afectan, detecta situaciones, personas, incluso atmósferas que permiten que nuestro ser florezca, y cuando esto no se da, consigue que el hombre pueda replegarse en la mente, es decir apartarse de lo que se suele llamar vida, y entregárse a lo que es su verdadera realidad, que, repito, por lo general, está ausente. El punto de intersección entre fantasía y realidad – es decir el momento en que coincidieran – sería acaso el único instante al que se pudiera dar con propiedad el nombre de vida, pero la amenaza de la muerte hace que estos instantes se desvanezcan apenas iniciados, y así, de hecho, lo que somos es muertos que van por el mundo. Yo soy un muerto, y como tal no puedo acercarme a nadie, decir nada a nadie. Somos muertos en un amplio sepulcro que es la tierra. (72)

Y así lo que equivale en el libro a la muerte de Ofelia:

Surgiste de la calle San Nicolás muy repeinado, el rostro marmóreo. Avancé hacia ti y te saludé. Respondiste a mi saludo con fría cortesía y seguiste tu camino: era el final. Entré en el café, me tomé una ginebra, y luego eché a andar. Me metí en el Marceliano, después en el León Roch; vagué por las callejuelas de por allí: Zapatería, Mercaderes, San Agustín, Dormitalería... Me detuve un instante en la Plaza San José bajo los castaños, contemplando los cuatro chorros de la fuentecilla, pero algo me empujaba a seguir. Las imágenes apenas se reflejaban en mi interior, el portal gótico de la catedral, frente a la calle de Redín, y, ya en el Redín mismo, la caseta ante la que solían situarse los cordeleros, la fuente, las acacias, todo pasaba delante de mis ojos de modo fantasmal. Llegué a la puerta de Francia, a la muralla y continué hasta encontrarme en el bosquecillo de Tejera. Me sentí amparada por los chopos entre los que habíamos corrido, ahora con las hojas doradas y algunos ya con las ramas desnudas. Más allá se deslizaba el débil caudal del río aletargado por un tenue vaho. A su orilla misma me dejé caer. Notaba que la neblina ascendía desde el margen y se extendía sobre mi cuerpo. Un leve viento depositó sobre mí algunas hojas secas. De pronto sentí que no estaba en el mundo, que mi cuerpo era un mero vehículo de tiempo; sentí que podía permanecer de aquel modo indefinidamente, estando y no siendo, viendo el cielo entre los árboles: un infinito abismo y no claridad como otras veces, una distancia interminable. Ni por un momento pensé entonces en morir. Sencillamente, era como si hubiera dejado de ser a la orilla del Arga. (139–140)

Este vaivén de textos y de ideas, no sólo considerando todas las versiones que escribí sino dentro de la última y definitiva, llevó mi atrevimiento, ya casi al final, a insertar poesía. En un momento dado me di cuenta de que antes del elogio del amor platónico mi protagonista tenía que vivir una aventura erótica. No queriendo incurrir en un texto realista acudí a la poesía y utilicé, reescribiéndolos, restos de un extenso poema inédito del que ya había extraído la parte erótica del libro *Eros*. Son lo que llamo en la novela "tres fragmentos de una prosa poética extraña" (que figuran en páginas 186 y 187). Pero esto no me bastaba, de modo que mezclé en el relato imágenes procedentes de otro libro totalmente erótico, *Creciente fértil*. Así del poema de *Creciente fértil* que dice:

Del regio firmamento emulemos los astros;
describa yo una rueda mirífica de fuego
y que mi cabellera, ciñéndose a mis pies,
en ígneos destellos, cuidosa, los envuelva.
Cuando el cenit alcance, con precisión de rayo,
como lanza candente clavarás tu fulgor.
Y en la cópula viva, áureos, victoriosos,
por la órbita insomne seguiremos en giros,
movidos por el pulso de nuestro propio ardor. (50)

En este poema me baso para escribir el fragmento en que Alma y el joven de la aventura están mirando un libro de reproducciones de Van Gogh,

Al llegar a la página de la Noche estrellada, él pasó su brazo por mi espalda y me estrechó el hombro. Yo le enlacé por la cintura. Lo que se produjo entonces no sabría describirlo, se puso a besarme de modo que no sé cómo puede aguantarlo un ser humano. Cuando tomaba aliento decía mi nombre. Sin darnos cuenta estábamos desnudos y unidos en una danza agitada y velocísima en la que yo me sentía continuamente en el aire, en un salto; saltábamos los dos en bloque, sin distinción ninguna entre ambos cuerpos. Y él gritaba. Y seguía repitiendo mi nombre sin cesar. Me acariciaba, adecuaba su cabeza a mi cuello, se adentraba en mi oído, me hacía dar vueltas, alejaba de vez en cuando su torso para mirarme sin que por ello se detuviera un instante aquel quedar suspendido en el espacio por momentos. Yo sentía que en

mi boca se prensaba uva dulce, en mi pecho rompía el mar bañado
por la luna y el resto de mi cuerpo se transformaba en una rosa
incandescente y devorante cuyas llamas ascendían por mi espalda
prendiéndome entera, y toda yo en llamas, y él y yo en llamas,
ascendíamos como si fuéramos un astro. (202)

Lanzada a esta técnica incluí luego dos poemas sin modificación, "Rembrandt,
Rijksmuseum", del cuaderno *Esbozos* y "Flores de Grazalema", de *Vivir*.

También es curioso el fenómeno inverso: algunos poemas se habían adelantado a
la novela aportando ideas, por ejemplo, el titulado "Espejismo", que data de 1977,
de *Libro de alienaciones*. Este me proporcionó la confusión de imágenes de Alma
y Lobo, tan importante que de hecho fue lo que decidió el nombre de la
protagonista, que careció de él casi hasta el final. Igualmente escribí – éste en el
año 1981 – un poema que en realidad es como el emblema de la novela. Se titula
"A un muchacho que imaginó ser Hamlet", y se encuentra en el libro *Vivir*. Dice
así:

Ahora que se esboza la caricia
de los frágiles dedos de los árboles
en el canoso invierno,
tu dorada cabeza correr entre los troncos
aún se me figura,
y las candentes lágrimas que iluminan tu rostro,
y la mancha de sangre que dio color al labio,
y yo corro a tu lado
pues deseo arroparte con el manto de sueño
que ya la nieve teje,
pero tú, que a perpetua distancia me condenas... (*Vivir*, 52)

Me doy cuenta de que a pesar de todo lo dicho apenas he hablado de mi poesía.
Tiene una explicación. "Un poema", dice Holan, "es un don". Un poema, por lo
tanto, es o no es. La prosa, en cambio, está más cerca de la angustia de lo que
pugna por llegar a ser. En el caso concreto de esta novela mía, *Los caballos del
sueño*, la prosa se ha movido durante una larga etapa entre el ser y el no ser, y han
sido tantos años y ha sucedido eso hasta tal punto que aún concluida sintiéndola

yo como un ente autónomo, todavía me persigue y sigue replanteándome el hamletiano dilema vinculándolo a la escritura.

Clara Janés
Madrid

1. *Los caballos del sueño* (Barcelona: Anagrama, 1989).

2. Véase Clara Janés, *Antología personal (1959–1979)* (Madrid: Rialp, 1979); *Eros* (Madrid: Hiperión, 1981); *Vivir* (Madrid: Hiperión, 1983); *Kampa* (Madrid: Hiperión, 1986); *Lapidario* (Madrid: Hiperión, 1988); *Creciente fértil* (Madrid: Hiperión, 1989).

3. "Tentativa de encuentro" [1963, 1972] *Rey Lagarto*, I, 2 (1989). Véase la segunda parte, titulada "Tentativa de olvido" [1972] *Doce relatos de mujeres* (Madrid: Alianza, 1982) pp.21–34. Clara Janés prepara un tercer capítulo que, junto a los dos anteriores, podría constituir una próxima novela.

Going Places? The Subversion of Linearity in Tina Díaz's *Transición*

Biruté Ciplijauskaité, in her typological study of first-person narratives, *La novela femenina contemporánea (1970–1985)*,[1] isolates several concerns which contemporary European women authors appear to share. Among these is a re-evaluation of the conventions by which we order time:

> [Con la nueva novela] se introduce también una diferente percepción del tiempo; en vez de una exposición lineal, dentro de cánones racionalmente establecidos, se va hacia la sugerencia casi poética o mística y la repetición cíclica.[2]

This desire to "anular el tiempo lineal"[3] presumably responds to the association, underlined by various theorists, between linear time and the phallic order, the Law, and the realm of the symbolic, in which women only participate as bystanders or as honorary men.[4] The impulse to find an expression of time which undermines this order, and which perhaps also corresponds more closely to the authentic experience of women,[5] while laudable, poses certain practical problems. A novel which forsakes chronological linearity and structures itself solely around "la sugerencia casi poética o mística y la repetición cíclica", violating as it does the conventions of realistic presentation which are a clear part of the genre, will probably seem a rather disordered affair, and may well be rejected by the "average" reader who finds her question, "What happens next?" perpetually ignored. So, is this preoccupation with finding an artistic alternative to linear time the preserve of an elite, who write "experimental" novels not intended to reach a wider audience? Or is it possible to detect an undermining of linear chronology – and hence an undermining of the phallic order – even in novels which appear to depend on linearity and to accept the overt political and social manifestations of patriarchy? Obviously, I believe it is possible, and I propose in this paper to examine one such novel in order to tease out the ways in which the primacy of linear time is subverted. Although discovering unexpected subversion is delight enough in itself, I also hope that this examination will provide a clue to the meaning of the novel.

Tina Díaz's first novel was published in December 1989 by Planeta.[6] It is made up of two intertwined narratives, one which is narrated mainly in the present tense and takes place during August 1988 or 1989 (henceforth, Narrative A); the other (Narrative B), is a memory narrative told mainly in the past tenses and set between summer and Christmas of 1980. It is not, on the face of it, a novel which promises much in the way of a subversive interpretation. The narrator/protagonist of the two narratives is a woman in her forties, mother of two daughters, wife then ex-wife of a UCD minister, daughter of a discreet minister under Franco, a member by birth of the privileged, monied classes. Her world is one of servants, house-visits by masseuses and beauty therapists, seemingly endless shopping-as-therapy, dinners in expensive restaurants with important people, a luxurious house in central Madrid and a villa near San Sebastián. Her identity is inextricably tied to her husband, to such an extent that when he becomes involved with another woman and shows signs of leaving the narrator, she attempts suicide. This emotional dependence on a man continues into Narrative A, when she is involved with Pablo, and is exhibited by all the female characters in the novel: Regina, the narrator's best friend, becomes an alcoholic when her marriage ends, the narrator's mother "nunca tuvo otra vida que mi padre" (137); the narrator sees her daughters, now married, "hacer las cosas que por Él yo hice, organizar las cenas... terminan ellas sus estudios lentamente" (65). The narrator's view of women in general, conditioned by the insecurity born of dependence, is one of mistrust and dislike: "temían las mujeres a las mujeres sin hombres, y eran ellas en realidad quienes iban expulsando de los círculos sociales a esas mujeres recientemente libres, recientemente necesitadas de apoyo" (107); "cómo podían las mujeres mistificar los hechos, echarles a los hombres culpas de las cosas..." (146); "las mujeres eran malvadas, amargaban los amores de las otras mujeres dando consejos, contando chismes, puñaladitas..." (147).

If the novel is apparently lacking in any intention to subvert the order of gender politics, it would also seem to accept linearity as an organizing principle. The very title of the novel is an early indication of this. "Transición" is defined by the *Diccionario de la Real Academia Española* as "acción y efecto de pasar de un modo de ser o estar a otro distinto"; that is, a movement from one state to a subsequent one. That is certainly the sense in which the term is used to define the period in Spanish history from 1975–1981, a period which marked the passage from dictatorship to democracy. Since the Spanish political transition serves as the background for the memory narrative (Narrative B), it is logical to assume that the relationship between Narratives A and B will also be one in which the focus is on the passage from a previous state to a subsequent one, that is, an inherently linear relationship. This assumption is strengthened by the fact that although the two narratives interrupt each other, each narrative maintains an internally coherent linear chronology (e.g., if Narrative B breaks off in August 1980, it begins in September of the same year, and not in June or in 1956, etc.). However, the novel simultaneously rejects linearity through what the narrator herself says about past, present and future. She insists, first, on the need to remember, on the impossibility of forgetting: "siento yo mi ausencia de pasión por el alcohol o por cualquier cosa capaz de trastocar la memoria como una goma grande y blanca que barriese, que borrase todo lo que perturba, lo que trastoca, los tiempos del antes y del ahora" (18). Although the memories are painful, they cannot be denied or forgotten because they are inexorably intertwined with the present, to such an extent that the past and the present are indistinguishable: "Yo evitaba anoche cualquier referencia al mar de Ategorrieta sintiendo el pasado que es mi presente..." (44); "en el antes que es ahora..." (26). This is made manifest on the afternoon in which the narrator relates her Narration B to Pablo: the act of telling in the present the events of the past nullifies for her the temporal distance between them: "El tiempo no ha existido en esta tarde" (42). Not only are the present and the past fused, but the past also projects into and merges with the future: "el horror del pasado se volvía futuro, el único futuro posible" (121). Significantly, this attitude towards time, which runs like an undercurrent through the text, does not apply to the male characters of the novel. When Él falls in love with Ella, he is in fact able to erase the past, or at least he creates that impression, by insisting that Ella is the "Amor de su vida". The narrator understands what this means: "El pasado no existía ya, acababa Él de nacer con Ella" (105). Likewise, there is a marked contrast between the attitude of Pablo and that of the narrator when they go to Ategorrieta together (he, in the hope that she will begin to forget, she in order to remember). She feels a sense of peace when she enters the family villa:

> Está en esta casa todo el tiempo, que es el pasado y el presente, están las amas con ropas escocesas y la muerte y está Él, nada es anacrónico aquí, ni está tan lejos aquí el otoño de la transición en el que... bajaba hasta la sucia playa de Gros pensando en morir, andando entre los pesados trailers de la carretera de esta villa que me devuleve todo el tiempo entero que agrupa los tiempos de mi vida... (74)

Pablo, on the other hand, impatient and unsympathetic, simply says, "No me gusta tu infancia".

What I have outlined above is sufficient indication that it would not be fanciful to suggest that the novel is really about a tension between the "accepted" linear view of chronology and a non-linear view which undermines the authority of the former. I propose now to examine in some detail three loci of this tension: the overall structure of the novel, the transitions between Narratives A and B, and the verb systems in operation.

I. Structure

The structure of the novel – a memory monologue inscribed within a contemporary monologue – is a common enough device in first-person narrative fiction. Usually, the time-lapse between the world of the "narrating self" (here, Narrative A) and the world of the "experiencing self" (Narrative B) is highly significant in that it provides the narrating self with sufficient distance to enable her to take up a more or less critical stance with regard to the experiencing self. Dorrit Cohn[7] identifies various possible stances of the narrating self vis-à-vis the experiencing self, including dissonant self-narration, in which a "lucid narrator [turns] back on a past self steeped in ignorance, confusion and delusion"; consonant self-narration, in which the "unobtrusive narrator... identifies with his earlier incarnation", and several "mixed" types of narration, including the type so cleverly exploited by some picaresque novels in which the narrating self misunderstands the experiencing self. It is important to note that in Cohn's typologies, all forms of self-narration in which the narrating self is obtrusive in the text are implicitly linear: the narrating self *looks back* on the experiencing self with a more or less critical eye, and judges the experiencing self from the perspective of the narrating self. Ciplijauskaité also identifies this inherent linearity in self-narrated texts as a feature of many modern women-authored novels:

> la novela de memorias... no es un sencillo recordar, reconstituir los años juveniles, más bien se trata de juzgar la vida pasada con criterios de la vida actual con el propósito de establecer metas para el futuro... la novela entera es un lento descifrar y crecer hacia una meta ideal.[8]

Thus, women novelists searching for their own voice have, according to Ciplijauskaité, forsaken "la memoria como crónica" for "la memoria analítica", which gives them access to themselves, to their former selves, so that they might arrive at a more complete understanding of who they are and how they have become so: "Para saber quién soy debo saber quién he sido y cómo he llegado al estado actual."[9] In other words, in these novels, called by Ciplijauskaité "de concienciación", the subject of enunciation, the narrating self, is supposed to be the sum total of all or of key past experiences, and the analysis that takes place presupposes that there has been a progression, imbued with meaning, if not from one experience to the next, then from the past in general to the present.

In Tina Díaz's novel, the present is not expected to shed light on the past, nor is the past expected to explain the present: thus, although the novel does not reject linear chronology out of hand, it effectively nullifies its significance. It is difficult to examine what isn't in the text, but the lack of reinterpretation of the past in this novel can, I think, be demonstrated by two key moments in the text when the author resolutely turns her back on the opportunity to re-evaluate narrative B from the perspective of A. The first of these occurs relatively early in the text, when the narrator of A, upset by the serious illness of Regina and plagued, in this susceptible psychological state, by the memories which constitute narrative B, decides to relate narrative B to her lover, Pablo. In the page and a half which constitutes this episode, the narrator begins by announcing: "Mira – le digo –, necesito contarte, estoy mal estos días, quiero contarte, nunca te he contado..." However, what is next described is not the narration of these events, but the *process* of narration:

> son mis palabras un río desbocado del silencio de tanto tiempo de la especie de doble vida que he llevado con él [Pablo]... mis palabras fluyen mientras caminamos por el centro de la Castellana con el sol de las tres de la tarde cayendo como plomo sobre nuestras cabezas, abrasados por el calor, contándole la verdad sin atropellos. (41)

When she has finished the narration – which the reader has not been allowed to overhear – the only interpretation is Pablo's exclamation, "¡Cuánto has sufrido, amor mío!".

The second opportunity to provide a structure for reinterpretation occurs when the narrator describes her psychiatrist's suggestion that she should try to talk to Él about the things that are troubling her:

> Mi psiquíatra de ahora, de después del fallido intento de suicidio, opinaba sin embargo que debía hablar con Él, interesarme por sus cosas, hablar con Él de las cosas que hacían peligrar nuestro matrimonio, *cómo explicarle*, conseguía mi psiquíatra hacerme sonreír... [emphasis mine]. (61)

In other words, the plausible excuse for framing the remembered narrative of relating the story to a psychiatrist (or possibly, even to her husband) is here rejected, as is the opportunity for retrospective interpretation.

The overt rejection of an opportunity to interpret Narrative B, to learn from past mistakes, to re-write the past, is echoed throughout the text by the narrator's refusal to judge her marriage to Él, as well as by her refusal to draw comparisons between the way she is now and the way she was then. We discover in passing that she now works in her father's office, but this fact is not given any particular importance: the narrator of A is in no sense a newly independent woman looking back on the way she used to be. There appears to have been no learning process, no progress from one state (that of dependence on her husband) to another (that of recognition of the need to be emotionally independent, for example). Irritating though it may be for the modern reader to be confronted by a woman who refuses to close the door on painful memories in order to pick herself up, make a new start, realise her potential, who even refuses to analyse what went wrong the first time in order to avoid it happening the second, it is also illuminating and even fundamentally honest to present a text in which linear time confers no cognitive advantage. Perhaps the notion of progressing to an understanding of ourselves is misleading, when the claims of the emotions and relationships of the past, as we shall now see, are inescapable in the present.

II. Transitions between A and B

Another piece of evidence which indicates a desire to undermine conventions of chronological linearity is found in the way in which Narrative A is made to alternate with Narrative B. As was stated previously, the two narratives maintain internally a predominantly chronological structure, yet the shifts of attention from A to B tend not to conform to any linear impulse. The motives which prompt the movement from one narrative strand to the other fall within two broad categories.

First, there is occasionally an overt link between the present and the past through memory, that is, when the narrator specifically announces that what is about to follow is the result of an effort of recollection. These transitions are usually triggered by words such as "memoria", "recordar", etc., and are not used very frequently. An example of this technique occurs when the narrator visits Regina at the beginning of the novel, and then goes into a bar by herself and begins to remember:

> Sentada sola en una mesa del fondo, de espaldas a la puerta, reclusa de esa memoria que no quiere ser perturbada y recordar el día que fuimos a Galgary... (18)

What follows is a fairly long memory monologue of the summer of 1980 in Dublin. There is no obvious or logical link between the present and the specific event about to be narrated, and the text makes it clear that the events of Dublin are the result of a specific effort to remember by the narrator.

The second, and more prolific, type of transition is the link provided by associative memories. The most famous example of this technique in world literature is probably the madeleines at the beginning of Proust's *A la recherche du temps perdu*, in which a specific thing in the present serves as the catalyst to unlocking a myriad of memories. In Tina Díaz's novel, there are associative triggers which move the narrative from the present to the past (as in Proust's novel), as well as from the past to the present. An example of the former occurs on page 137, when the narrator has spread out on the library floor all the gifts that were given to her ex-husband when he was a minister and which he left behind when he went to live with his new wife. Among these are some pieces of pottery from Manises, and this is the trigger for the narrator's memories of a trip to Valencia with her female friends.

There are associative triggers which are repeated throughout the novel and which consequently take on the air of a refrain. The two most notable of these both relate present-day Madrid to the narrator's suicide attempt: the trajectory uphill from Claudio Coello to María de Molina in Madrid recalls the climb over the dunes to the Mar de Gros in Ategorrieta, and the heavy traffic in the August heat of Madrid recalls the narrator's resolve to kill herself, in 1980, "sorteando los trailers pesados" of the village near San Sebastián.

Finally, there are associative triggers which are purely linguistic, as evidenced by the following sequence in which the word "puñaladita" serves as the trigger from one narrative to the other. The narrator, recounting the events of B, says

> [Él] me había hecho tanto daño, alentándolo Ella con su dulzura natural, sin decirle jamás ninguna puñaladita de las que yo le hubiera dicho.

Immediately after this reflection we are immersed in Narrative A:

> Llega Pablo a la terraza de la Castellana, está llena la Castellana de paseantes... La conversación de unas mujeres sentadas en una mesa cercana. Las puñaladitas hablando de los hombres.

After the narrator and Pablo leave the terraza on the Castellana, he tells her unexpectedly that he has seen her ex-husband:

> — Lo he visto hace poco – confiesa Pablo — En Lucio, estaba cenando, parecía satisfecho de la vida.
> Una puñaladita, un puñal. (90–93)

With these final words, the narrator returns us to Narrative B, to her relation with Él when they were married.

This brief overview of the ways in which the novel moves from one narrative to the other exemplifies the way in which the tension between linearity and non-linearity functions. The two narratives are inscribed within a linear framework in that each narrative resumes more or less at the point it broke off. However, access to the memory narrative B from Narrative A is unpredictable and uncontrollable. The narrator of A is surrounded by things which give rise to the memories constituting Narrative B, and it is the randomness and ubiquitousness of these associations that make us realise the impossibility of "exorcising" or eradicating the past. Pablo's suggestion that she sell her house in Madrid in order to sever the associations with Él that it has for her is revealed for the facile and superficial suggestion that it is: what good would it do to get rid of her house when merely walking the streets of Madrid or when a chance word or phrase can trigger such painful memories? Thus, if in the overall structure of the novel we can detect a desire to reject the primacy of a linear view of time in which the past conditions the present or the present illuminates the past, the transitions between the two narratives reinforce the corollary that both past and present are integral elements of the same narrative. Although two events may be separated from each other by years, although they may occupy sequential points on a time line, they can be, through memory and language, simultaneous in the experience of a subject.

III. The Verb System

The subversion of linear time, that is, the intentional blurring of conventional demarcations between present and past, is also conveyed by specific recourses of language, especially the manipulation of the verb system. As has been stated, the two narratives in the novel are related in two distinct verb tenses: Narrative A is narrated in the present or present perfect; Narrative B in the past tenses or the past perfect. This more or less strict correspondence of verb tense to narrative would tend to reinforce the inherent chronological sequence of the two narratives, and hence, to reinforce a linear view of time in which present and past cannot exist simultaneously. However, Tina Díaz uses various devices to undermine this division. First, the division of tenses is itself ambiguous if we concentrate on aspect rather than tense. It is usually assumed that there are two verbal aspects, perfective and imperfective, and that the difference between the two resides in the "actitud del sujeto hablante frente a la acción expresada por el verbo".[10] We can isolate three key moments in reporting any action: the moment of speaking (MS), the moment of focusing on the action (MF), and the moment of the action (MA). The coincidence or lack of same of the moment of speaking with either the moment of action or the moment of focus will determine present or non-present tense, as illustrated:

Present tense	Past tense
MS	MS
⎯⎯⎯⎯+⎯⎯⎯⎯	⎯⎯⎯⎯+⎯⎯⎯+⎯⎯
MF	MF/
MA	MA

Aspect, on the other hand, is determined by simultaneity or not of the MF with the MA:

Imperfective	Perfective
MF	MF
⎯⎯⎯⎯+⎯⎯⎯⎯	⎯⎯⎯+⎯⎯+⎯⎯
MA	MA

It should be noted that as the moment of focusing and the moment of action must coincide in the present tense, this is always imperfective.

The simultaneity of the moment of focusing upon the action and the moment of the action itself results in the sense of greater immediacy that the imperfect has in Spanish vis-à-vis the preterite, that is, it gives the impression that "el sujeto puede, en cierto sentido, 'colocarse' en la corriente de la acción."[11] The preterite, on the other hand, enables the speaker to "[colocarse] fuera de la corriente de la acción y [adoptar] la actitud del espectador que 'mira' la acción desde un punto posterior a su término."[12] It is not surprising to find that the preterite tense is scarcely used in Narrative B, and that the predominant tenses are either the imperfect or the pluperfect.

The first effect of this choice of tense for Narrative B is to insist on the habitual and on the durative aspects of the actions described:

> **Habitual:** Estaba Él a mi vuelta en el despacho, parado frente al ventanal, mirando al infinito con el gesto deprimido y adusto que ya era permanente en Él.
> — ¿Qué tal – me *decía* distraídamente –, qué tal? (188)
> **Durative:** Regina se mantenía sobria, les daba conversación a mis hijas totalmente inmersa en una condición de persona amiga de la familia que tiene que paliar una situación desesperada. Esperando

la vuelta y a las niñas que habían salido a hacer las últimas
compras, *desayunábamos* en el comedor del hotel, *hablábamos*
Regina y yo... (22)

The second effect of the predominance of the imperfect in Narrative B is to create
an aspectual equivalence with Narrative A. In other words, since the present tense
is imperfective in aspect, the habitual and durative aspects of the actions of
Narrative A are also stressed:

> **Habitual:** Para ver a Regina no es necesario subir a su casa.
> Regina baja a ese bar durante toda la mañana, baja de su casa al
> bar para beber ginebra y del bar vuelve a subir. (9–10)
> **Durative:** Atravesamos el tráfico, se hace largo el camino hasta
> casa. Regina lleva la cabeza inclinada hacia atrás... (11)

The insistence in both narratives on the reiterative, durative aspect of the verb
serves to undermine the linear concept of time implicit in the notion of present/
non-present tenses. In other words, while it is true that Narrative B is anterior to
Narrative A by virtue of the use of past rather than present tense forms for B, it is
also true that the actions within Narrative B as well as the actions within Narrative
A are viewed as endlessly repetitive and that actions in both narratives are
conceived of in their durative rather than their terminative aspect. Thus, the
sequentiality of the two narratives is logically undermined: it can be assumed that
at some point the actions of B – habitual and durative – meet and even override
the actions of A, also habitual and durative. The reach of B, then, extends into the
territory of A, and A reaches back to B.

A further obfuscation of the temporal significance of verb tenses is found in
Díaz's use of the pluperfect *había* plus past participle. Most linguistic analyses
agree that the fundamental meaning of this tense is that it is "the past of the past",
that is, it states the anteriority of one situation or action to another which is in the
past. However, in the following sequence, this seems not to be the case:

Sí que la vuelta de Galgary fue tranquila y sombría, y la llegada a
Dublín la recordaría después como un capítulo extraño de mi vida
cuando, frente al hotel Shelbourne, algo antes de llegar a casa,
había parado el chófer obligado por un aviso de bomba que había
agrupado gente en los bordes del parque... Dentro de la limousine
parada *esperábamos*, claxones *sonaban*, *esperábamos* dentro del
coche a que aquello se pasase, en segunda fila delante de las
escaleras del Shelbourne, y entonces los *habíamos visto*, en las
escaleras del Shelbourne, adornada con oros que relucían en el
atardecer, vestida de largo como una jaca enjaezada, espléndida,
dorada su piel... *rodeados* por su escolta y otra de hombres fuertes,
rubicundos, menos *lacerante* sin embargo *en ese momento* la
visión de ellos dos juntos que el fantasma de ellos dos de todo el
tiempo anterior, ...menos *lacerante* la realidad de ellos dos allí...
rodeados de escoltas, unos escalones detrás José y Maika, la
secretaria de él, medio escondidos por el resplandor de Ellos. José,
Maika *ahora* de su brazo esperaban divertidos a que se
restableciese el tráfico interrumpido por el aviso de bomba, como
una anécdota más del divertido viaje, haciendo comentarios
sonrientes, rodeados por más escoltas de los que solía llevar, hasta
que Regina *había bajado* del coche, corrido hacia ellos, abofeteado
a José.
    "¡Eres un infame!", *gritaba*.
    La *habían inmovilizado* los escoltas, mis hijas *habían saltado*
desde el coche a sacarla de allí... [emphasis mine]. (23–24)

In this passage, the use of the pluperfect ("habíamos visto", "había bajado", etc.)
is ambiguous. What is the point of reference in the past to which the pluperfect
situations are anterior? Is it to the "recordaría después" or the "antes de llegar a
casa" of several lines earlier? In that case, the intrusion of the imperfect
("esperábamos", etc.) seems odd. On the other hand, the logic of the narrative
precludes the possibility of the pluperfect situation occurring anterior to the
imperfect of "esperábamos, sonaban": seeing the illicit couples cannot occur
before waiting in the car, and so on. Rather, this is a classic example of one action
(waiting in the car, etc.) serving as background action for another (seeing the
illicit couples) which interrupts it: in this case, all grammars would call for the
preterite and not the pluperfect for the interrupting action. Likewise, the preterite
would normally be indicated for the subsequent actions in the pluperfect: "había
bajado, habían inmovilizado", and so on. The use of the pluperfect is unexpected

in these cases, yet this is a stylistic device which occurs regularly throughout the novel. The cumulative effect is to confuse the time references which are built into Spanish verb morphology: "habían inmovilizado", for example, is both anterior to some deictic centre in the past by virtue of its morphology, and subsequent to other actions in the past by virtue of the logic of the action. Furthermore, the habitual use of the pluperfect where a preterite would be more usual indicates, I believe, a fleeing from the perfective aspect inherent in the preterite, that is, a rejection of the view of the past as something completed, that can be viewed from a subsequent perspective as a finished whole. This is reinforced by the use of non-finite forms – for example the past particple ("rodeados"), the present particple ("lacerante"), the gerund and the infinitive – in which both tense and aspect are neutralized, as well as by the confused use of temporal adjectives: in this case, "en ese momento" (which should indicate a preterite in this context) and "ahora" (which should indicate a present in nearly all contexts).

It would seem, then, that the novel's refusal to view present and non-present as mutually exclusive is echoed not only in its structure but also in its language. Once again we can detect a tension between linear chronology in the choice of verb tense for one narrative or the other, and a desire to undermine the authority of that view through the confusion of the time references usually associated with Spanish verb morphology.

Conclusion

I have attempted in this paper to demonstrate some of the ways in which a novel which appears to work within a linear view of time also subverts this. In *Transición*, the link between linear time and novelistic presentation has been maintained mainly through the vinculation of the action in identifiable historical periods and through the internal linear presentation of the two narratives. The retention of this link has meant that readability has not been sacrificed: our average reader's question, "What happens next?" is satisfied, although it may well be a case of delayed gratification. Yet despite these links, the novel both explicitly and implicitly sets out to display an alternative view of chronology, one which disallows the compartmentalization of events into "then" and "now". These two views of time – linear and non-linear – are associated in the novel with gender. The public sphere of action of the Spanish Transition is a male domain, and it is only the male characters in the novel who forget their past lives in order to succeed in the present: men change their political spots in this novel as readily as they change their wives. Living for these men is a linear process in which the present can only be arrived at by finishing the past, by "moving on" from one state to the next. They exhibit the discontinuous view of time which Claudine Hermann and Beatrice Didier characterize as masculine, in which events or epochs can be boxed off, sealed up, and conjured away.[13] The female characters, on the other hand, especially the narrator, are unable or unwilling to let go of the past, however painful. For them, it is not possible to posit a disjunction between past and present, but rather the two dimensions seem to exist simultaneously and coterminously in an individual's experience – and it is through experience, ultimately, that we measure the world.

It would be erroneous, however, to leave you with the impression that the novel prescribes one view of time and proscribes the other, for this is a novel without heroes, heroines or (happy) endings. Rather, the main characters occupy an uneasy space between linearity and non-linearity, as does the text itself. The men, although quick to shed the skins of their past lives, undermine their own efforts by stepping into second marriages and new political institutions that are virtually indistinguishable from the old ones. The women all "carry on", at least on the surface – after all, what choice is there? Yet they at least are aware that they are living a double life:

> Tanto tiempo pasado explicando, repitiendo mientras otros pensamientos nos ocupan doblemente al tiempo que explicamos lo inútil, conversaciones superpuestas, el pensamiento por distinto sitio que el verbo. La doble vida... Mientras nadie escucha sino las voces de adentro, habitadas por los seres indestructibles, más vivos que los que te cuentan: "He comprado...". (113)

I think it is at this uneasy juncture between linearity and non-linearity, between the desire to break with the past in order to live in the present and the impossibility of doing so, between surface readability and the language and structures which undermine it, and possibly even between the notions of "masculine" and "feminine" organization of the world, that we find the true *transición* of the novel.

Jean Mackenzie
Wolverhampton Polytechnic

1. Biruté Ciplijauskaité, *La novela femenina contemporánea (1970–1985): hacia una tipología de la narración en primera persona* (Barcelona: Anthropos, 1988).

2. Ciplijauskaité, p.17.

3. Ciplijauskaité, p.39.

4. See, for example, Xavier Gauthier, "Is There Such a Thing as Women's Writing?" in Marks and de Courtivron, *New French Feminisms* (University of Massachusetts Press, 1980) p.162.

5. See Claudine Hermann, "Women in Space and Time", in Marks and de Courtivron, pp.168–173.

6. Tina Díaz Azcona, *Transición* (Barcelona: Planeta, 1989). All references are to this edition.

7. Dorrit Cohn, *Transparent Minds: Narrative Modes for Presenting Consciousness in Fiction* (Princeton University Press, 1978) pp.145–161.

8. Ciplijauskaité, p.39.

9. Ciplijauskaité, p.34.

10. J. Slawormirski, "La posición del aspecto en el sistema verbal español," *Revista española de lingüística*, 13 (1983) p.96.

11. Slawormirski, p.96.

12. Slawormirski, p.96.

13. See Claudine Hermann in Marks and de Courtivron, pp.168–173; Ciplijauskaité, pp.37–38.

Engendering the Political Novel: Gioconda Belli's *La mujer habitada*

Gioconda Belli, the Nicaraguan writer known for her volumes of poetry and her commitment to the Sandinista political organization, published *La mujer habitada* in 1988.[1] Belli's anti-Somoza activities led to exile before the liberation of her native Nicaragua took place in 1979. Of the time spent outside, she says in an interview with Margaret Randall: "exile dried me up as a poet. I went for a long time without writing anything because I needed my roots...".[2] (149). The novel does represent a change in genre from her usual literary activity, and appeared in a Basque press. *La mujer habitada*'s subject matter is not easy to incorporate into creative writing (although the attempt has often been made), and includes a gendered perspective in the least traditional area of women's writing: that of armed revolutionary action. I initially had problems with the process by which Lavinia acquires political awareness, then makes the commitment which determines her fate in the novel, but putting these considerations aside for the moment, I will look at how Gioconda Belli has combined the sense of a woman writing with the denunciation of political conditions, before deciding whether she has done so effectively.

La mujer habitada is the story of a 23 year old woman from the bourgeois class of Faguas, involved in carrying out her own "feminist" revolution by moving into her own house and not marrying, in addition to working as an architect. The influences in her life have been her Aunt Inés and her grandfather, one for her kindness and respect for her niece's needs, the other for his love of literature and the opportunities it offers for "adventure". Still, she has been deeply hurt by her parents' indifference, their inability to relinquish some of their activities, typical of a comfortable social position, in order to nurture their only daughter. This woman, named Lavinia, is thus a typical privileged young person from an impoverished country, although she has acquired sensitivity from her aunt and from literary creativity (her grandfather's stories). Although the two coordinates are somewhat traditional (feminine tenderness, masculine cultural knowledge), this very combination will result in the revolutionary actions of the novel.

Lavinia meets another architect at work and falls in love with him, finding out later that he is involved in the Movement against the dictatorship. Although her bourgeois education leads her to reject or distance herself from such activities of the "other society", her love and the aforementioned dispositions lead her to gradually accept the principles of the revolution and to join it.

The *roman à thèse* or ideological novel is defined by Susan Suleiman in *Authoritarian Fictions* as "a novelistic genre that proclaims its own status as both overtly ideological and as fictional", and she adds that its "problematic mode of existence is due precisely to the combination of – or more exactly, to the friction between – those two modes of discourse."[3] In further clarifications, Suleiman refers to this writing's realistic mode and primarily didactic intentions at the service of a certain doctrine. (7) As this critic observes, the combination of creativity and ideology does not always mesh, and as a result the 'literary' is subsumed by the political. There are any number of failed novels of protest in Latin America; if we were to include observation of poetry of protest, the examples would increase. Yet Belli's *La mujer habitada*, in my opinion, is precisely a successful *roman à thèse* because it includes poetic elements that both provide interludes from the strictly political discourse and activity while facilitating the insertion of mythical, historical, indigenous motifs that fortify the main plot by framing it in a context of continuity (inheritance) and endowing it with an epic quality.

It is not coincidental that the vehicle for the interlinking of ideology and fiction is the voice of a woman, Itzá. Itzá speaks from within the orange tree that flowers beside Lavinia's house, yet she is not just the tree itself nor is she a spirit arisen from the unrecorded indigenous past of Central America; neither is she a muse or source of inspiration, which would be too external a role, and too linked to the sphere of the aesthetic. She is simply a force or entity which has remained in existence for centuries and which derives its strength from her identity as a whole, including her awareness of what women's contribution to social conditions is and should be. She embodies the essence of the feminine in the meaning this term has for many today: strength, maternal potential, self-awareness and confidence, sensuality unbound.

As the novel progresses, there is a double transformation: Itzá's intimacy with Lavinia increases, and the poetic motifs which she incarnates branch out to other sections/characters of the book in insistent yet unobtrusive ways. The reader too passes from proximity to the flesh-and-blood Lavinia (increasingly immersed in clandestine activity) to greater proximity with Itzá, as the latter continues to reveal memories of her experience as a woman warrior resisting the Spanish invasion. In this sense, the protagonist appears to both grow within herself and to grow into the historical female voice that constantly accompanies her, at times seeming to be her unconscious, at times her companion or guardian, reminiscent of the *nahual*. The encouragement is silent, but in that very space occupied by a voice which emerges from the past, there is a numinous sense of the ability to interpret, predict, even alter the human protagonist's life. However, the voice in counterpoint is not that of an omnipotent deity. She is interposed, not controlling, but rather functioning through suggestion, or better yet, by instinct. Important also is the temporal articulation of Lavinia's world: Itzá comes forth from the past yet simultaneously faces the future. She subtly interweaves her reality with the protagonist's, such as when Lavinia is drawing building plans and later realizes she has sketched bows and arrows. In contrast, the narrative from the viewpoint of the young architect is more limited, predictable, perhaps even superficial or artificial at some points. This is not unusual: it is the product of her upbringing and the society she lives in, that yearns to fully enter the capitalist economy. It is thus symptomatic that the human protagonist's expression is occasionally uninspired. Moreover, it often shows the self-consciousness of metadiscourse as her political sensitivity grows.

The aforementioned fusion of the two female identities is completed with Lavinia's death, which serves to underline the strength of love and the loss of that self-consciousness of purpose, and leads to the creation of a collective ideal of natural, rightful existence. In death, Itzá–Lavinia is joined by Felipe, the divisions separating the two sexes having been nullified or at least reduced by the attention to other political responsibilities.

That Itzá occupies a tree gives rise to a series of themes, such as reproduction or creation, the unfettered giving of one's body (fruit or flesh) for another's sustenance or pleasure, the ability to resist the passing of years, to remain rooted in the earth while pointing upward toward ideals. The latter is of course a symbolism of womanhood from the pre-patriarchal period, when the Goddess was Mother Earth, giver of life (and not Eve, seductress of Adam). Paula Gunn Allen, native American writer, affirms: "The mortal body is a tree; ... it is truth and myth because it has so many potential conditions... Healing the self means honoring and recognizing the body, ... cherishing its multitudinous forms and seasons, its unfailing ability to know and be, to grow and wither, to love and die, to mutate, to change...".[4] Allen then asks: "What can we do to be politically useful, spiritually mature attendants in this great transformation we are privileged to participate in? ... Our Mother, in her form known as Sophia, was long ago said to be a tree, the great tree of life..." (57). The answer, for many indigenous peoples, is clearly to be found in the wise, polysemic tree that unites the lower and upper worlds.

Starhawk portrays the tree of life in the modern world with a drawing in her article, "Power, Authority and Mystery: Ecofeminism and earth-based spirituality."[5] In *La mujer habitada* the sense of branching or growing in a direction (Lavinia's experience) is accompanied by the fixing or rooting of her convictions in her choice of action, and by a rhythm that might best be described as a flowing of vital fluids: words, cyclical blood, nourishing juice, water in various forms, and that other life flow that designates sacrifice. Thus the significance in the main character's conscious political commitment is precisely at the start of the rainy season and the culmination of the novel is at Christmas, the moment of Epiphany, or better, the birth of a new era.

The lyrical tone of the novel also stems from the love between Lavinia/Felipe and Itzá/Yarince, and in turn from the erotic nature of each relationship. Lavinia's acceptance of her desire is described by the omniscient narrator:

> Se hundió en el pecho de Felipe, se dejó ir con él en la marea de calor que emanaba de su vientre, ahogándose en las olas sobreponiéndose unas a otras, las ostras, moluscos, anturios, palmeras, los pasadizos subterráneos cediendo, el movimiento del cuerpo de Felipe, el de ella, arqueándose, tensándose y los ruidos, los jaguares, hasta el pico de la ola, el arco soltando las flechas, las flores abriéndose y cerrándose. (39)

Lavinia may unwittingly become involved with participants in the revolution, but she is convinced of its correctness by that same love, which does not blind her to one man's physical attraction but instead opens her heart to a series of persons and ideas that she is predisposed to love. This inclination is first put to the test when she helps heal the seriously wounded Sebastián, brought to her house by Felipe. But it is Flor, a woman whose name is also nature (translated by Itzá as Xotchitl, the name of her best friend), whom she turns to for information concerning the Movement. Flor, who shares her knowledge of love and war, becomes Lavinia's friend and serves as her role model, while Itzá binds Lavinia's personal and political commitment to her own:

> Hoy vino un hombre. Entró con la mujer... Se amaron desaforadamente cual si se hubiesen contenido mucho tiempo. Fue como volver a vivirlo. Vivir otra vez la hoguera de Yarince atravesándome el recuerdo, las ramas, las hojas, la carne tierna de las naranjas. Se midieron como guerreros antes del combate... Se amaron como nos amábamos Yarince y yo cuando él regresaba de largas exploraciones de muchas lunas. Una y otra vez hasta quedar agotados, extensos, quietos en aquel mullido petate. El emana vibraciones fuertes. Lo rodea un halo de cosas ocultas. Es alto y blanco como los españoles. Ahora sé, sin embargo, que ni ella, ni él lo son. Me pregunto qué raza será esta, mezcla de invasores y nahuas.

¿Serán quizás de las mujeres de nuestras tribus arrastradas a la promiscuidad y la servidumbre? ¿Serán hijos del terror de las violaciones, de la lujuria inagotable de los conquistadores? ¿A quién pertenecerán sus corazones, el aliento de sus pechos?

Sólo sé que se aman como animales sanos, sin cotonas, ni inhibiciones. Así amaba nuestra gente antes que el dios extraño de los españoles prohibiera los placeres del amor. (40)

Lavinia's love is couched between the ancient woman and the modern, both *guerrilleras*, both warriors in the physical sense as well as the spiritual.

The protagonist approaches mythical/heroic proportions herself through her resemblance to the prototype of the Warrior Queen. These are women who are double figures, both historical and based on beliefs in the Great Goddess of matriarchal times. In her book, Antonia Fraser notes that such women tend to be widows, are of noble lineage, and have extraordinary sexual appetites (the latter characteristic is naturally the one of greatest mythical contribution, appropriate to the post-matriarchal periods during which these women became legendary).[6] Lavinia is not a widow in that she has not been married, but she enters armed combat after the death of her lover. She is not noble, as there is no nobility in Latin America, but her family is considered to be aristocratic and as high on the social hierarchy as is possible. And she does not have an excessive or distorted sexual drive – just a healthy erotic sensuality (perhaps not so acceptable, it is true, in the society that surrounds her). The fact that the main character does not conform exactly to the facets of the Warrior Queen does not contradict my affirmation that she belongs to this prototype. Rather, it suggests that Gioconda Belli utilizes the figure with an intent to rewrite or write out the negative connotations it came to acquire under patriarchy. Perhaps too this realistic version of the woman warrior explains the survival of Lavinia's bourgeois characteristics some time after she decides to join the resistance movement. She is not simply an idealistic follower of others' desires, but rather struggles with her own position and right to change her behavior. It is a confrontation between natural features and acquired ones, birthright and political awareness. Interestingly enough, Lavinia's struggle with herself, her continued participation in elite social circles in order to serve the information-gathering needs of the revolutionary cause, offers the readers a chance to observe the world she is fast rejecting. The flatness, fore-shortened perspective, and intranscendent activities of friends such as Sara, who is absorbed in acting out the role of the perfect wife, further strengthen the protagonist's convictions both for herself and for the reader.

The novel takes on greater momentum after the death of Felipe, shot not in combat but by a frightened taxi-driver when he tried to confiscate the vehicle for guerrilla use. (Ironically, these men frequently support the liberation movement.) At this point the threads of the plot become more tightly woven, as the woman who once complained about feeling like the ever-awaiting Penelope prepares for the imminent moment when she too will go forth. Here her professional knowledge and training as an architect manifest their depth and accuracy, underlining the contribution she has made to the Movement. Her intimate knowledge of a house and the household members – she has designed the mansion for General Vela – enables the *guerrilleros* to launch a successful attack upon this vital member of the repressive forces of order in Faguas. Lavinia is also successful in her task because she uses her feminine attributes in a way that are not flattering to women but which are precisely those which military and other such minds perceive as "appropriate" to her sex. The sexuality deliberately exploited by the female architect succeeds in camouflaging any suspicion that she might be able to think, except to design living quarters (of course), even though the blueprints include an intricately structured room for the display of an arms collection. The narrator points out more than once that the design was inspired by a similar room belonging to Patty Hearst.

In spite of the sensitivity to the protagonist's situation, at times the dialogue between characters is somewhat forced, as the other ideological project of Belli, that of feminism, guides it. For example, on one occasion Lavinia discusses *machismo* with Sebastian, the *compañero* whose wound had first brought the movement into her life. The aspects of the problem as discussed by the two may admittedly be of importance, but as novelistic material they lose force and border on the dangerously propagandistic prose of many political novels. (I will return to this shortly).

However, if we ask whether Gioconda Belli has achieved a successful political novel, my own answer would be yes. The intricacies of political organization, the motivation and results are portrayed convincingly, interwoven with the personal, daily affairs of the participants. And there is a didactic achievement in that no doubt remains as to right and wrong. There is no idealistic resolution of personal matters, as first Felipe then Lavinia meet with death. Lavinia's death is heroic in the true sense of the word: in the end, she uses all her strength, physical and mental, to carry out her commitment and essentially is responsible for the success of the mission. Her death, a sacrifice she accepts for her *compañeros'* sake, has two aspects. One is her bourgeois background: both she and Pablito, the other *guerrillero* who is killed, are from this class. This may symbolize the disappearance of this social group in a true revolution. Secondly, the fatal few seconds during which she struggles with the idea of killing a man, even General Vela, known for his tortures of peasants and revolutionaries, indicate she is respectful of life. Moreover, she is being observed by the general's son, a boy who dreams of flying, and whom she once told flying military planes meant killing, that there were other ways to travel skyward. The loyalty to those words, not fear of her own death nor of carrying out the role in armed combat she has so recently assumed, is what causes her to hesitate, giving the general she has discovered in the hiding place she herself designed, time to fire. That doubt, brief and justified as it is, results in her death. That it may be the result of inexperience in such situations is possible, but it is also the most profound portrayal of what a woman faces in causing another's death; the role is not willingly assumed by one who, as she had recently realized, would have wanted a child. Like Itzá, she denies herself and is denied the role of life-giver. The depth of this sacrifice is testified to by all of Belli's poetry, for female fertility is one of its primary motifs.

To the question of whether the novel is a successful example of woman's writing, I would also answer yes. Aside from the self-conscious interest in presenting women's issues, there is the aforementioned poeticity, an interrelating of motifs, which is perhaps more effective in the structuring of a woman's perspective. An example is Itzá's name. She recalls: "La partera me lavó, me purificó implorando a Chalchiuhtlicue, madre y hermana de los dioses y en esa misma ceremonia, me llamaron Itzá, gota de rocío. Me dieron mi nombre de adulta, sin esperar que

llegara mi tiempo de escogerlo, porque temían el futuro." (10) Later, in dreams
Lavinia sees herself flying: "El vuelo sobre inmensas flores: heliotropos,
gladiolas, helechos gigantescos. Gotas de rocío. Magníficas, enormes gotas de
rocío donde el sol se quebraba abriendo caleidoscopios prodigiosos." (58) The
feminine follows the threads of spinning and weaving images – Itzá herself says
"El destino teje sus redes" (307) – and permeates discursive structures. When Itzá
says that Lavinia "Está en el vértice del verdor de la vida," (307) she is weaving
the protagonist into an intelligence that emerges from nature. As Paula Gunn
Allen explains in *The Sacred Hoop: Recovering the Feminine in the American
Indian Tradition*: "Many non-Indians believe that human beings possess the only
form of intelligence in phenomenal existence... The more abstractionist and less
intellectually vain Indian sees human intelligence as arising out of the very nature
of being, which is of necessity intelligent in and of itself."[7]

The feminine also flows throughout the aqueous elements used to characterize
Faguas and its inhabitants; Lavinia especially is nurtured by fertile nature and the
watchful orange tree. The land which sustains it is indigenous, its existence and
manner of expression a lesson for the invaders of both then and now. It is thus
truly a tree of life for her and for Central America.

Whether or not we are convinced by Lavinia Alarcón's commitment to a cause
that contradicts her entire social upbringing, she *does* go through with her
decision, she does ultimately give her life without questioning. She is not the first
example of a literary Latin American woman who participates in combat – we
may cite Claribel Alegría's *No me agarran viva* among others – although she is
one of the few who has played a major role in a work of fiction. There are
elements in the novel which can be traced to experiences of the *sandinista* Nora
Astorga, whose use of "feminine wiles" and knowledge of architecture led to the
capture and death of General "Perro" Pérez Vega. Also, Leticia Herrera
participated in a successful assault on the home of a wealthy Somocista at
Christmastime, from which important *sandinista* demands were met.[8] Belli
participated in preparations for that assault.

Lavinia symbolizes the new woman of Latin America which Belli hopes to see, who is perhaps not so new, as Itzá has revealed, since before the advent of Christianity, it is believed, women had occupied radically different positions in society. She also symbolizes America's passage through a period of darkness and gradual growth toward new/renewed beliefs. The slow emergence of the warrior woman from oblivion may be likened to the early accounts of Amazons in the New World. From Columbus through Cortés, Fathers Carvajal and Acuña, Fernández de Oviedo and other chroniclers, the women who participated in armed resistance against the Spanish invaders were called Amazons. To modern day male novelists such as Gastão Cruls of Brazil and Demeterio Aguilera Malta of Ecuador, the figure of the Amazon had multiple connotations and posed problems for those who would explain her existence. But Aguilera Malta turns her into a virtual muse who seduces by her dangerous beauty alone. *La mujer habitada* is a woman's answer to the spiritualization or disarming of the woman warrior. It means foregoing the deformation of sexuality or body, for Amazons were frequently said, through erroneous etymology of their name, to remove a breast in order to combat and were thought to limit their sexual encounters to one period during the year. Instead, her answer has a firm grounding in reality (Starhawk's sketch identifies this foundation or lower level as the economy) whence branching out in diverse directions takes place. From the perspective of the natural and complete development of the figure of Lavinia Alarcón as the sensual, lifeloving woman warrior, *La mujer habitada* is a successful novel. It is the story of a woman, what makes her physically a woman, and what constitutes her internally. In essence, it is the expression in fictional prose of what Gioconda Belli has portrayed in her poetry: the model of strength that is strength precisely because it has its roots in the feminine. Recall the poem "Metamorfosis":

> La enredadera
> se me está saliendo
> por las orejas.
>
> Mis ojos se han convertido
> en pistilos movibles
> y mi boca está repleta
> de flores moradas.

(...)
Me repasan mis dedos
y su contacto es abono
para mis ramas que crecen
(...)
Mi boca llena de flores moraditas
ha cuajado mi cuerpo
y estoy enredadera,
metamorfoseada,
espinosa,
sola,
hecha naturaleza.

In the feminine lie creativity and the ability to coherently apply that creativity to a political goal. As Gioconda Belli herself has said: "Yo al sandinismo le debo lo que soy...".[9] And it is creativity because it is based on the life force, giving birth and nurturing, growing and changing, responding to stimuli. In the context of woman's life-giving potential, any actions of the revolutionaries which cause death are not to be interpreted as violent aggression but as resistance or as unnatural acts imposed upon those carrying them out. And this may be what is Belli's ultimate message: that conditions such as those in Latin America (the fictional Faguas, Central America, Nicaragua, or anywhere) which lead a woman such as Lavinia to her commitment and finally to her death, are hardly living conditions: they are destructive and unjust.

The cohesive nature of the novel even stems in part from the previously mentioned self-consciousness as metafiction and within this, of the attention given to literature as a factor for shaping human existence. Lavinia acquires a love for adventure and nature from the stories she is told and reads; at the beginning of her relationship with Felipe, she is aware of her role as a woman waiting for her lover to arrive home, through the story of Penelope (*not* designated as the story of the male character, Ulysses), and rebels against it. She also rebels against literary models that are inappropriate to her Central American experience: "Sería mejor aceptar de una vez que no podía dejar que el romanticismo la envolviera. Es verdad que a ella también le gustaba soñar. Lo hacía desde niña, desde Julio

Verne... ¿Quién no soñaba con un mundo mejor? Era lógico que le atrayera [sic] la idea de imaginarse «compañera», verse envuelta en conspiraciones, heroína romántica de alguna novela; verse rodeada por esos seres de miradas transparentes y profundas, serenidad de árboles". She then adds, "Pero nada tenía eso que ver con ... su realidad de niña rica, arquitecta de lujo con pretensiones de independencia y cuarto propio tipo Virginia Woolf." (123) And her relationship to the tree, other than a source of physical and mental nourishment (she drinks the juice of its fruit, and contemplates its leaves), recalls for her the "dichoso árbol, apenas sensitivo" of Rubén Darío. These literary references combine to signify a collective, lyrical vision, the result of centuries of struggle.

I find the communication between Itzá and Lavinia, the spiritual and the physical essences of woman, the most successful aspect of *La mujer habitada*. Their relationship, its force and intimacy, renders traditional feminist discourse superfluous, their context makes it appear somewhat self-centered. But Belli's commitment to feminism is not to be questioned, for in the survival of Lavinia and her indigenous heritage of resistance, along with that of Felipe (from the popular class), there is no doubt as to the *thesis* of the novel. Good will, must, triumph over evil. That individuals perish in the struggle to achieve this end is not a sign of failure but rather to be read as the text of commitment. If, paradoxically, feminist declarations become obtrusive, this may be one of the truly revolutionary aspects of *La mujer habitada*; or it may be seen as the author's lesson for readers who are not Third World residents. For white Euro-American feminist critics/ theoreticians may not find themselves vindicated in this novel. If I am not convinced that Felipe was as *machista* as Lavinia laments, nor that at first she was as liberated or revolutionary as she wanted to be, this may be part of the author's plan.

My final evaluation of Gioconda Belli's *La mujer habitada*, includes the sincerity of its belief in woman's capacity to play a valid role in creating a new, more just society of peace. Lavinia twice observes, "Las mujeres entrarán a la historia por necesidad" (343, 367). Is this not appropriate? Are not women's rights something more than theory? Are they not something that we care enough for to take enormous risks to guarantee them? On a global level, from the broadest perspective of peace and the concrete one of ecofeminism, can we afford to separate natural rights from the natural, political context? Can we all echo these lines from another poem by Gioconda Belli?

Amo a las mujeres desde su piel que es la mía.
A la que se rebela y forcejea con la pluma y la voz
    desenvainadas,
a la que se levanta de noche a ver a su hijo que llora,
a la que llora por un niño que se ha dormido para siempre,
a la que lucha enardecida en las montañas,
a la que trabaja – mal pagada – en la ciudad,
a la que gorda y contenta canta cuando echa tortillas
    en la pancita caliente del comal,
a la que camina con el peso de un ser en su vientre
    enorme y fecundo.
A todas amo y me felicito por ser de su especie...

Kathleen N. March
University of Maine

1. All references are to Gioconda Belli, *La mujer habitada* (Tafalla: Txalaparta, 1990); *Amor insurrecto* (Barcelona: Editorial Amarantos, 1986).

2. Margaret Randall, *Risking a Somersault in the Air. Conversations with Nicaraguan Writers* (San Francisco: Solidarity Publications, 1984) p.149.

3. Susan Rubin Suleiman, *Authoritarian Fictions. The Ideological Novel As a Literary Genre* (New York: Columbia UP, 1983) p.2.

4. Paula Gunn Allen, "The Woman I Love Is a Planet; The Planet I Love Is a Tree", in *Reweaving the World. The Emergence of Ecofeminism*, eds. Irene Diamon and Gloria Feman Orenstein (San Francisco: Sierra Club Books, 1990) pp.52–57, pp.56–57.

5. Starhawk "Power, Authority, and Mystery: Ecofeminism and Earth-Based Spirituality", in *Reweaving the World*, pp.73–86.

6. Antonia Fraser, *The Warrior Queens. The Legends and Lives of the Women who have led their nations in war* (New York: Random House, 1988).

7. Paula Gunn Allen, *The Sacred Hoop: Recovering the Feminine in the American Indian Tradition* (Boston: Beacon Press, 1986) p.60.

8. Margaret Randall, *Sandino's Daughters. Testimonies of Nicaraguan Women in Struggle* (Vancouver: New Star Books, 1981).

9. Clara Murguialday, *Nicaragua, revolución y feminismo (1977–89)* (Madrid: Editorial Revolucion, 1990) p.245.

Expression and Silence in the Poetry of Juana de Ibarbourou and Idea Vilariño

> La muger ser mucho parlera, regla general es dello: que non es
> muger que non quisiese siempre fablar e ser escuchada ...
> ella bien ama e quema de fuego de amor en sí de dentro, más
> encúbrelo, porque si lo demostrase, luego piensa que sería poco
> presçiada.
>
> Arcipreste de Talavera

> La mujer y la pera, la que calla es buena.
>
> Spanish proverb[1]

At the beginning of the more recent debate over women and language, in the mid-seventies, Shoshana Felman notices in an article on Balzac's short story "Adieu" (1830) what has often been corroborated in feminist criticism of male writing:

> It is... striking that the dichotomy Reason/Madness, as well as
> Speech/Silence, exactly coincides in this text with the dichotomy
> Men/Women. Women as such are associated both with madness
> and with silence, whereas men are identified with prerogatives of
> discourse and of reason.[2]

The article, which also reviews two important texts that address the issue of female expression, concludes that "The challenge facing the woman today is nothing less than to 're-invent' language, to *re-learn how to speak*".[3]

Whether Felman's suggested challenge is likely to materialize, or whether it is bound to remain utopian, the issue of women's relationship with a language which has been an important device to define the social role of gender is still an important source of debate.[4]

The authors I have chosen to comment on here, the Uruguayan women Juana de Ibarbourou (1892–1979) and Idea Vilariño (born 1920), have no explicit feminist goal, but in some of their poems they address, possibly unconsciously, the question of expression and silence. What follows was inspired by the discovery that in some of their poems of heterosexual love the poets sometimes request that their lovers should speak or express certain feelings nonverbally, and at other times they demand restraint. Similarly, they either speak or remain silent themselves. I shall consider this dialectic choice of either expression or silence in relation to the issue of a woman's capacity to communicate with men as well as in the light of the common prejudice that dictates that the word within the boundaries of reason, truth and control is a male privilege. And so my aim is to search in specific texts for a female voice to reply to my epigraphs and to Balzac's male characters as regards expression and silence not only by women themselves, but also by men according to women. Whilst I will refrain from producing categorical answers, I would like to explore the possibilities of dual readings of the texts in question: a positive interpretation, where the woman is depicted triumphantly, and a negative reading, where the poems are seen to represent female suppression. Since there is a certain degree of stylistic consistency in the texts chosen I discuss only one poem by each poet in some detail, and then move more quickly through the others. I start with Ibarbourou.

Juana de Ibarbourou

The first poem, "El fuerte lazo", is about neither silence nor speech proper; it is about eliciting tears from the lover. Juana de Ibarbourou must be the most popular female poet in Uruguayan literature, and one of the most famous literary women in Latin America. She was hailed "Juana de América" in 1929 and during her lifetime she received several official titles from different Latin American governments; some of her writings are still often used as school texts in Uruguay and perhaps also elsewhere in the continent.

El Fuerte Lazo

> Crecí
> Para ti.
> Tálame. Mi acacia
> Implora a tus manos su golpe de gracia.

> Florí
> Para ti.
> Córtame. Mi lirio
> Al nacer dudaba ser flor o ser cirio.

> Fluí
> Para ti.
> Bébeme. El cristal
> Envidia lo claro de mi manantial.

> Alas di.
> Por ti.
> Cázame. Falena,
> Rodeo tu llama de impaciencia llena.

> Por ti sufriré.
> ¡Bendito sea el daño que tu amor me dé!
> ¡Bendita sea el hacha, bendita la red,
> Y loadas sean tijeras y sed!

> Sangre del costado
> Manaré, mi amado.

¿Qué broche más bello, qué joya más grata,
Que por ti una llaga color escarlata?

En vez de abalorios para mis cabellos,
Siete espinas largas hundiré entre ellos,
Y en vez de zarcillos pondré en mis orejas
Como dos rubíes dos ascuas bermejas.

Me verás reír
Viéndome sufrir.

Y tú llorarás
Y entonces... ¡más mío que nunca serás![5]

This poem immediately strikes for its formal structure, notably in its use of repetition, a feature which gives a tone of insistence to the message. The repetition is most notable in the first four stanzas, which reiterate the same structure: verb, complement of purpose or cause, single imperative verb, closing statement. Each of these four stanzas begins with a verb in the preterite, a tense that conveys finality. Each first line tells of a completed event in a way which strengthens the importance of the offering that is made to the lover in the second line through "Para ti" in the first three stanzas and, more finally, "Por ti" in the fourth. The poet is summarizing in each case a long process (growing, flowering, flowing, developing wings) and stressing only the final result of that process. Such a summary in itself is a symbol of the complete surrender by the poet to the lover: the gift is both simple and exhaustive, and no details of the processes of growing, etc., are given. The implication is that the poet has lived all her life with the sole goal of giving herself to the lover. No hesitation or distracting descriptions seem necessary.

The fifth stanza expresses what she is determined to do next. The tone of finality of the simple future tense (as opposed to the "ir a"/ "going to" future) resembles that of the preterite in the opening lines of stanzas one to four. Furthermore, just as these first stanzas convey a definite past, which corresponds to the first half of the poem, the term "sufriré" signals a change to the future which dominates the second half. From now on there are no more preterites; instead, the dominant tense is the future: "manaré", "hundiré", "pondré", "llorarás", "serás". The poem, then, falls into two halves: one of preparation and another of projected consummation.

The rest of the fifth stanza reiterates the message of the first four in different terms: its celebratory tone is conveyed by the exclamation "¡Bendito!" and by the exclamation marks which are used here for the first time. The second line expresses the poet's devotion in general terms, "¡Bendito sea el daño que tu amor me dé!", whilst the other two lines refer to the tools that are used typically to carry out the requests of the previous section: the axe, the net, the shears, and the lover's thirst. This stanza then summarizes the content of the poem so far.

Stanzas six and seven convey happiness in terms normally associated with suffering, which recalls traditional poetic images that describe love through paradoxes: thus an injury ("llaga") becomes a jewel ("broche", "joya"), and the poet's love is so intense that it resembles pain. In a reference to the highest symbol of suffering in Western culture, Christ, she is prepared to wear a crown of thorns instead of glass beads on her hair, and the core of the poem so far is succintly summarized in the two highlighted lines of stanza eight: "Me verás reír / Viéndome sufrir".

Up to this point the poem appears to convey a rather disturbing impression of masochism, but as we read on we encounter a twist in the tale: "Y tú llorarás / Y entonces...¡más mío que nunca serás!" These last two lines suggest that the aim of the poet was to move the lover into tears, into a situation of despair and weakness. We could read this in two ways. Negatively, it might mean that the woman wants to play a maternal role of control over the lover, which adds to the undesirable connotations of masochism already indicated. But there is a more positive reading, which I prefer, namely that the woman poet is trying to undermine the traditional coldness of the man, who does not typically show tears. This reading places the poet in a position of strength.

"El fuerte lazo" is therefore demanding the nonverbal expression of feelings from the lover. The woman poet is presented as working, suffering, in order to attain her goal: "Me verás reír/ Viéndome sufrir". The poem, then, is a show of strength, I suggest. Before exhausting this interpretation (and dealing with any problems that it might seem to leave unattended) it is useful to consider the next poem by Ibarbourou, where the poet is more explicit about her request for speech from her lover, "Suprema ofrenda". Her route to this speech is even more disturbing, if taken literally.

Suprema Ofrenda

¿Tienes sed, amante? Morderé una vena
De éstas que me azulan el puño como una
Ramazón de luna,
Y una copa llena
De vino tendrás.
Y en la copa plena
Tu sed calmarás.
Y yo he de azuzarte:
—Bebe, amante, bebe,
Pues vaso como éste ya nunca hallarás.

Bebe, bebe, bebe... Y me he de quedar blanca,
Como mármol limpio, como yeso nuevo.
Mientras a tus labios traspaso esta viva
Corriente ardorosa que en las venas llevo.

Y tan blanca, tan blanca seré,
Que acaso, embriagado, después me dirás:
—¡Agua del camino que apagó mi sed:
En qué fría piedra contenida estás!

The poem begins with an address to the lover, "¿Tienes sed, amante?", and goes on to offer him the poet's blood, in a description which again recalls Christ, in this case the Eucharist. The woman presents her body as a vessel of life, which echoes traditional associations with motherhood and menstruation. As in the previous poem, the recurrent use of simple tenses (especially the future) stresses the poet's determination. The outcome of the poem is a fantasy where the man, in exchange for the help provided by the poet, finally speaks: "—¡Agua del camino que apagó mi sed: / En qué fría piedra contenida estás".

Reading it literally, the poem is even more disturbingly masochistic than the previous one, as this time not only does the poet die for the man, but also she is not even recognized as a person by the lover (he addresses the water and speaks of a stony vessel). Still, once again a positive reading can be attempted.

I said above that the outcome of the poem was a fantasy: the man speaking to the dead woman who has turned into a stony vessel. In fact, the whole of the poem, as all of the ones by Ibarbourou discussed here (and many in the collection that contains them) is doubly fantastic. This is so firstly, because the descriptions involved are not realistic in terms of verisimilitude; secondly, because they draw on well-established literary sources, perhaps the most notable here being that of the agonizing anaemic female beloved of Romanticism. It is important to read Ibarbourou, then, within the tradition where she belongs. (I make this rather obvious statement in anticipation of the work of the other poet to be discussed below, who writes within a very mundane version of contemporary realism.)

But we can still consider the statement being made seriously. The situation depicted in this poem brings to mind Georges Bataille's explanation for eroticism, which is in summary as follows. Bataille says that humans are "discontinous beings" in the sense that they are existentially separate from all others ("Between one being and another, there is a gulf, a discontinuity. This gulf exists, for instance, between you, listening to me, and me, speaking to you. We are attempting to communicate, but no communication between us can abolish our fundamental difference. If you die, it is not my death. You and I are *discontinuous beings*").[6] Bataille sees eroticism as a means to break away from our individual "discontinuity" and to return to the "continuity" to which we belonged before birth, and whose only and inevitable alternative is death. (He also sees eroticism as intrinsically linked to death.) The only way for two people to achieve, fleetingly, a feeling of continuity, is through orgasm.

I would like to press this line of argument further and say that in an even more explicit way, giving one's life for another is the ultimate form of continuity, and I propose that what Ibarbourou is hinting at in these two poems is precisely such a (positive) situation. In fact, the situation can be further illustrated by a fascinating and poignant case of real life, namely the story of a young couple of Californians which was reported in the newspapers a few years ago. A 14-year-old girl was suffering from a degenerative heart disease that would lead her inexorably to death. On hearing the news, her perfectly healthy 15-year-old boyfriend said to his family that he would die in order to give the girl his heart. Astonishingly, the boy died of a brain haemorrhage, the cause of which was unknown, and his heart was given to his girlfriend to save her life.[7]

If we accept the continuity argument as grounds for a positive interpretation of these poems, the issue of masochism becomes less problematic. Still, it would be helpful to deal with that too. The crucial point is that masochism is generally *only* a fantasy, and to a good extent a perfectly understandable one. Several women have spoken of having fantasies of domination which they would never wish to happen in reality. Simone de Beauvoir put it succinctly:

> We have seen that usually the young girl accepts *in imagination* the domination of a demigod, a hero, a male; but this is still no more than a narcissistic game. It in no way disposes her to submit in reality to the carnal exercise of such authority ... It is a mistake to seek in fantasies the key to concrete reality; for fantasies are created and cherished as fantasies.[8]

In fact, the distinction between fantasy and reality remains clear even in more overtly and serious masochistic practices which can be seen as having the role of bringing the individual to a state where he or she is no longer in charge of his/her destiny, a kind of release from life's responsibilities. Indeed, the sadomasochistic game has very clear rules for stopping if the pain becomes out of hand; that is, if it becomes *real* pain.[9] Seen in this light, masochism loses much of its negative aura. In any case, in "Suprema ofrenda" any impression of masochism is further toned down, as in the previous poem, by the achievement of the woman's goal of getting the man to speak.

Ibarbourou does not always demand expression from her lover, however. In the poem that gives its title to the collection which contains all four of the poems I am discussing, the request is for silence:

Las Lenguas de Diamante

Bajo la luna llena, que es una oblea de cobre,
Vagamos taciturnos en un éxtasis vago,
Como sombras delgadas que se deslizan sobre
Las arenas de bronce de la orilla del lago.

Silencio en nuestros labios una rosa ha florido
¡Oh, si a mi amante vencen tentaciones de hablar!
La corola, deshecha, como un pájaro herido,
Caerá, rompiendo el suave misterio sublunar.

¡Oh dioses, que no hable! ¡Con la venda más fuerte
Que tengáis en las manos, su acento sofocad!
¡Y si es preciso, el manto de piedra de la muerte
Para formar la venda de su boca, rasgad!

Yo no quiero que hable. Yo no quiero que hable
Sobre el silencio éste, ¡qué ofensa la palabra!
¡Oh lengua de ceniza! ¡Oh lengua miserable,
No intentes que ahora el sello de mis labios te abra!

Baja la luna-cobre, taciturnos amantes,
Con los ojos gimamos, con los ojos hablemos,
Serán nuestras pupilas dos lenguas de diamantes
Movidas por la magia de diálogos supremos.

This poem describes two lovers walking by a lake in silence, under a full moon. The setting is ethereal and stylized; and as before, it is also fantastic. The imagery is romantic and has some *modernista* touches ("éxtasis vagos"; "dioses"; "corola"; "diálogos supremos"), which are predictable in a collection published in

1919. The interesting thing in this text is that the poet is prepared for the lover to die rather than let him undermine the intense feeling of peace and community with nature which she is experiencing (we are reminded of the traditional association between woman and nature, also recalled by Simone de Beauvoir: "It is when she speaks of moors and gardens that the woman novelist will reveal her experience and her dreams to us more intimately").[10] Thus "Las lenguas de diamante" overturns tradition by describing a fantasy where the woman imposes silence on the man.

The feeling conveyed is also that the situation being described is not unlike that of erotic bliss. The lover is explicitly referred to as "mi amante" (in Spanish, a term often more sexually loaded than its alternative "amado"), and the atmosphere is one of "éxtasis vago". One is reminded of what Simone de Beauvoir also says of women and love-making: "Sex pleasure in woman, as I have said, is a kind of magic spell; it demands complete abandon; if words or movements oppose the magic of caresses, the spell is broken".[11] To this, de Beauvoir opposes the traditional male ways with words:

> But she is hurt even more by words that run counter to the amalgamation in which for a moment she has firmly believed. [The male request for post-coital commentary] horrifies many women because it reduces erotic pleasure to an immanent and separately felt sensation. "Was it enough? You want more? Was it good?" – the very fact of asking such questions emphasizes the separation, changes the act of love into a mechanical operation directed by the male. And that is, indeed, why he asks them. (417–418)

In "Las lenguas de diamante" we see quite the opposite situation: there a woman poet takes a positive stand to lead the lover not only to her own pleasure but to a common experience of extasis ("gimamos... hablemos... serán nuestras pupilas..."). In the next and final poem by Ibarbourou it is the poet who has the last word:

Rebelde

Caronte: yo seré un escándalo en tu barca.
Mientras las otras sombras recen, giman o lloren,
Y bajo tus miradas de siniestro patriarca
Las tímidas y tristes, en bajo acento, oren,

Yo iré como una alondra cantando por el río
Y llevaré a tu barca mi perfume salvaje,
E irradiaré en las ondas del arroyo sombrío
Como una azul linterna que alumbrara en el viaje.

Por más que tú no quieras, por más guiños siniestros
Que me hagan tus dos ojos, en el terror maestros,
Caronte, yo en tu barca seré como un escándalo.

Y extenuada de sombra, de valor y de frío,
Cuando quieras dejarme a la orilla del río
Me bajarán tus brazos cual conquista de vándalo.

Here, the woman poet strongly challenges death. She refuses to keep silent and obey Charon's request to behave on his boat towards Hades. In fact, the poet is not merely speaking, but rather, openly challenges the rules of darkness and sobriety of the context through song, light and "escándalo". It is appropriate that Charon is referred to as "siniestro patriarca", since the poet's behaviour fits rather nicely the description which a robust denouncer of patriarchal discourse, namely Hélène Cixous, makes of female language:

> Listen to a woman speak at a public gathering ... She doesn't "speak", she throws her trembling body forward; she lets go of herself, she flies; all of her passes into her voice, and it's with her body that she vitally supports the "logic" of her speech. Her flesh speaks true. She lays herself bare. In fact, she physically materializes what she is thinking; she signifies it with her body.[12]

In summary, therefore, Juana de Ibarbourou appears to achieve her goals of getting her lover to recognize her, or to be silent when she thinks it most appropriate; she also manages to express herself in fullness in the face of death,

thus defying attempts to suppress her voice as tradition would demand. I propose
that, like Cixous's Medusa, Ibarbourou laughs at my epigraphs, but does so
without having to relinquish highly powerful and dramatic images of the
continuity of love. This positive situation does not quite obtain in the work of the
next poet to be discussed.

Idea Vilariño

The next three poems come from a best-seller of Uruguayan poetry, Idea
Vilariño's *Poemas de amor*, first published in 1957 and dedicated to Juan Carlos
Onetti.

Sabes

Sabés
dijiste
nunca
fui tan feliz como esta noche.
Nunca. Y me lo dijiste
en el mismo momento
en que yo decidía no decirte
sabés
seguramente me engaño
pero creo
pero ésta me parece
la noche más hermosa de mi vida.[13]

The language in this first poem is extremely simple and colloquial, and therefore
uses the "voseo" typical of the region. Although, or perhaps because it is in free
verse, the poem leads the reader to make pauses or to move at a particular speed
more by means of the layout than by punctuation. "Sabés" is highly economical
on punctuation, and indeed many of Vilariño poems consist of a single sentence
where the only punctuation marks are the capital letter of the first word and the
full stop at the end.

The poem describes one particular moment during a meeting with the lover: the moment when the man expresses his happiness at being with the poet, which he classes as the greatest in his life. The rest of the poem is about the poet's own response to the lover, which is in essence the same although it is qualified and, unlike the lover's, was probably never uttered.

The poem works on account of its rhythm: it flows gently from line to line, and although it lacks commas, we get the feeling of where to pause. This is achieved through a layout which is based on units of sense and intonation. The first three lines work as three separate units of sense which if written in prose would need commas: "Sabés, dijiste, nunca". The message is only completed in the fourth line, after the highlighting isolated presence of the "nunca", and reinforced by the second "nunca" of line 5 which makes up the sentence following the declaration by the lover. From now on each line seems to form a clear sense unit: "Y me lo dijiste / en el mismo momento / en que yo decidía no decirte / sabés / seguramente me engaño / pero creo / pero ésta me parece / la noche más hermosa de mi vida".

This telegraphic style which has little recourse to punctuation gives the impression of how the poet perceived and felt the event at the time: made up of separate units of experience, as if her powers of abstraction were numbed by her emotions. We get the sense of her sensing the vibrant solidity of the message as she dwells on each sense unit: "sabés / dijiste / nunca / me sentí tan feliz como esta noche. / Nunca. Y me lo dijiste / en el mismo momento / en que yo decidía no decirte / sabés / seguramente me engaño ..."

Reading the poem in the way the layout invites us to do, we relive the experience step by step: we first hear the lover's voice, we weigh the first two words "sabés" and "nunca", then the statement, then the repetition of "nunca". Then we take the words of the poet with the same gradualness as she thought them: one by one, weighing her own words with pleasure and care to say just the necessary terms for the simple message. Her caution, expressed in the three warning phrases "seguramente me engaño / pero creo / pero ésta me parece" which account for a large section of the poem, is reinforced by the perception that she probably never uttered the message but rather waited to write in down later.

"Sabés" recalls "El fuerte lazo" where Ibarbourou wishes to see her lover cry: here too the woman seems moved by the words of emotion from the man, and this experience inspires the poem. Thus at the heart of this poem there is also the celebration of a man's "unmanly" expression of feeling. That in the second half the poet appears to withhold her own declaration, as if knowing that such a statement should be issued with caution, and our impression that she never uttered the words to the man, gives us an insight into the material that poems are made of: quiet recollection after the event. The poem, as it is written, colloquially and simply, is a clear example of that Wordsworthian re-construction of experience.

"Sabés" can also be read in the light of the cultural stigma that says that a woman's tongue is quick, that what she says is not what she feels and that her words should be taken lightly – as implied by my epigraphs.[14] "Sabés" is in this light an illustration of a woman's struggle to withhold her feelings and her words. Negatively put, it represents male suppresion and thus, unlike Ibarbourou's "Rebelde", contradicts Cixous's description of female speech. Ironically, it corroborates the epigraph by the Arcipreste regarding women's covering of their real emotions. Moreover, it also indicates that the only space for this woman to express her feelings is the freedom of poetry. The next two poems are further illustrations of this condition.

Seis

Entonces
todo se vino
y cuando vino
y
me quedé inmóvil
tú
tú te quedaste inmóvil
lo dejaste saltar
quejándote seis veces.
Seis.
Y no sabés qué hermoso.

This is another disarmingly simple poem, where the poet rejoices in her lover's experience of orgasm, an experience which is devoid of words. The poet's positive assessment of the man's reaction is consistent with Ibarbourou's rejection of words in "Las lenguas de diamante", and with Simone de Beauvoir's description of post-coital female experience. In fact, here we have a man who does not behave as Beauvoir says men behave, but rather as she would like them to behave. The poet's position is one of celebration of the man's unorthodox behaviour, and the poem stresses the mutual quality of the experience in the middle lines "me quedé inmóvil / tú / tú te quedaste inmóvil". However, once again the fact that Vilariño turns to poetry may be seen as a consequence of cultural suppression of female expression. (This impression may be further corroborated if this reaction of the man is seen as exceptional, and thus strong enough to inspire the poem.) The issue of expression suppressed is also clear in the final poem to be considered briefly.

Yo Quisiera

Yo quisiera llorando
decírtelo
mostrarte
y que tú me entendieras
o decirte se fue
el verano se fue
o decirte
no te amo
y que tú me entendieras.

This poem is about a woman's inability to convey to a man a sense of dissatisfaction. The poem's message of failure is indicated in several ways, firstly by the choice of the subjunctive in the title and first line, which stresses that it may never be actually delivered. Also in the subjunctive is the phrase pertaining to the addressee's response, "Y que tú me entendieras", which appears at significant points in the poem, in the middle (l.5) and in the last line (l.10). Moreover, the words of the poet are tangled with tears: "Yo quisiera llorando / decírtelo", a language which though perhaps salutarily female in quality ("she signifies... with her body", as Cixous says), it is presented by the poet as pragmatically inappropriate. In brief, and as in the other poems, the woman is consciously unable to use direct language to express herself; the poem quite clearly results from self-imposed silence. Unlike Ibarbourou, Vilariño conveys a suppressed voice, which could only find expression in poetry.

Conclusion

We could sum up the circumstances of silence and expression in these poems by considering three main questions: i) when do these two women poets want silence, either from the lovers or from themselves? ii) when do they want nonverbal expression? and iii) when do they want words?

It seems as if silence is expected in moments of extasis, as when the poet feels a part of nature in "Las lenguas de diamante", which can be seen as equivalent to the moments after love-making. If the man speaks in those circumstances, he punctuates the lovers' separateness, and summons their discontinuity, as Bataille says. Instead, the poets welcome nonverbal expression during orgasm, as in "Seis", and they are prepared to fight and sacrifice for the lover's tears, as in "El fuerte lazo". They want words as a token of recognition from the lover, as in "Suprema ofrenda", and when the words describe feeling, as in "Sabés", although Vilariño feels that she herself should remain silent. Ibarbourou suffers no such restraint and she uses language, and not merely words, to challenge death in "Rebelde", thereby imposing her own will till the end. Women would use words to dispel love, as in "Yo quisiera" where the aim is to summon discontinuity; but even then, Vilariño's speech fails to materialize and remains tangled with tears.

The general impression is that although most of the poems discussed can be read negatively or positively, Ibarbourou manages to convey a happier message of self-realization in love than Vilariño, and this is consistent with the general tone of each collection. *Las lenguas de diamante* celebrates joyful times for the poet and her husband, as Ibarbourou says in the book's dedication to him ("la mayor parte de estas poesías, que datan de la dulce época de nuestro noviazgo, son y serán actuales, porque es perdurable el sentimiento que las ha inspirado"). Vilariño's collection, on the other hand, conveys a more woeful mood which has often been noted by critics: one famous contemporary reader of an early edition which did not contain either "Sabés" or "Seis" noted that the book "trata de la soledad del amor, no del amor mismo, que siempre falta a la cita",[15] and a recent article speaks of "estos desolados poemas del desamor".[16] Although in the light of my commentaries to the first two poems by Vilariño studied here such an assessment is plainly inexact, it is true that many of the poems in the collection refer to situations where the poet is not contented.

This last point bears on the difference between the two poets as regards verisimilitude, which was mentioned above. Although in each case the woman is writing about a love affair with a particular man, Ibarbourou has an evident recourse to fantasy and intertextuality, which is absent in the transparent realism of Vilariño. Furthermore, the difference between the two poets is nicely engraved in their style, through the use of highly wrought forms by Ibarbourou and of free verse by Vilariño. It is clear that Ibarbourou's poems do not simply describe what happened to her, but that her experience has been stylized in an artificial, literary way. On the other hand, we get the impression that Vilariño is dealing with concrete and more ambiguous experience, and from the above analysis of her poems we must conclude that she speaks in poetry what she has chosen not to say in real life. In both cases, therefore, poetry represents a space for self-expression, either where experience is decorated or where silence is broken.

Gustavo San Román
University of St Andrews

1. "La pera calla cuando no cruje por estar muy madura", is the gloss provided by Juana de Campos & Ana Barella, *Diccionario de refranes* (Madrid: Anejo XXX del Boletín de la Real Academia Española, 1975) p.309.

2. Shoshana Felman, "Women and Madness: the Critical Phallacy", in *The Feminist Reader; Essays in Gender and the Politics of Literary Criticism*, eds. Catherine Belsey and Jane Moore (London: MacMillan, 1989) p.145. This article first appeared in *Diacritics*, 5 (1975) pp.2–10.

3. Ibid., p.153.

4. See the Introduction to the anthology cited in note 2, especially pp.13–20.

5. Juana de Ibarbourou, *Las lenguas de diamante*, 5th edition (Montevideo: Biblioteca Artigas 1963) p.20; the other poems to be discussed also come from this edition, p.122, p.7, p.15 respectively.

6. George Bataille, *Eroticism*, translated by Mary Dalwood (London: Marion Boyars, 1987) p.12.

7. "Heartfelt donation", *The Guardian*, 8 January 1986, p.8. After complications, the girl died in March 1989 (see *Los Angeles Times*, 8 March 1989, p.3)

8. Simone de Beauvoir, *The Second Sex* (Penguin, 1987) p.419. More recently, Cristina Peri Rossi has insisted on that difference: "Los juegos eróticos de Amo-esclavo tienen el mismo valor que las representaciones teatrales: los actores pueden ser excelentes, el público se identifica y emociona, pero una vez terminada la obra cada cual recupera su propia identidad. Del mismo modo, la mujer independiente, culta y eficaz a quien le gusta que su amante simule una violación, en ningún caso *desea* ser violada: el simulacro cumple la función de aumentar su excitación justamente porque no es verdad, justamente porque él sabe, y ella también, que cuenta con su asentimiento" See Cristina Peri Rossi, *Fantasías eróticas* (Madrid: Ediciones Temas de Hoy, 1991) p.143.

9. A male masochist told me about these rules. The sexologist John Bancroft suggests that masochism involves at least three factors: the "abrogation of responsibility" I have indicated; guilt over sexual pleasure ("This could well account for the sexually arousing effects of fantasies of sexual dominance in the adolescent girl"), and the fact that during sexual arousal the threshold for pain is increased. See his *Human Sexuality and its Problems* (Edinburgh: Churchill Livingstone, 1983) pp.183–184.

10. *The Second Sex*, p.719. Having quoted this very sentence from de Beauvoir, Annis Pratt, in her Jungian study of *Archetypal Patterns in Women's Fiction*, (Brighton: Harvester Press, 1982) goes on to assert that "The 'experience' and 'dreams' that are revealed in this recurrent archetypal pattern in women's fiction are of a sense of oneness with the cosmos as well as of a place to one side of civilization" (p.17). The association man/culture v. woman/nature has however often been criticized by feminists; see, for example, Paulina Palmer, *Contemporary Women's Fiction. Narrative Practice and Feminist Theory* (London: Harvester Wheatsheaf, 1989) pp.24–25.

11. *The Second Sex*, p.417

12. Hélène Cixous, "The laugh of the Medusa", in *A Reader in Feminist Knowledge*, edited by Sneja Gunew (London: Routledge 1991) p.226.

13. Idea Vilariño, *Poemas de amor*, 10th edition (Montevideo: Arca, 1988) p.66; the next three poems are also from this edition, pp.69 and 48 respectively.

14. A more modern illustration of this traditional position is a poem by D.H. Lawrence called "To women, as far as I'm concerned", where he says "The feelings I don't have I don't have. / The feelings I don't have I won't say I have. / The feelings you say you have you don't have", D.H. Lawrence, *The complete poems* (Penguin, 1977) p.501.

15. Emir Rodríguez Monegal, *Literatura uruguaya del medio siglo* (Montevideo: Alfa, 1966) p.172.

16. *Diccionario de literatura uruguaya*, Vol.3, ed. A. Oreggioni (Montevideo: Arca, 1991) p.375.

Julie Sopetrán and Jorge Guillén: Poetry of Harmony?

Julie Sopetrán was born in Mohernando, Guadalajara. She has lived in California for ten years and now works as a cultural journalist in Madrid. To date she has published six books of poetry: *Amorismos, Un Siglo en Atherton, Polvo luminoso, Silvas de mi Selva en Ocaso, Los Dioses y el Anfora* and *En Hita hoy es otoño y se oye el mar.*[1] I shall be referring to two of her works: *Silvas de mi Selva en Ocaso* (1985)[2] and *Los Dioses y el Anfora* (1987).[3] For the second of these Julie Sopetrán was awarded the IV Premio Carmen Conde de Poesía de Mujeres.

Although Jorge Guillén needs no introduction, the basis for a comparison of his work with that of Julie Sopetrán does demand some preliminary clarification, despite the fact that its justification will become clear in the course of this essay. Originally it was the tone of their poetry which struck me. Both poets seem possessed of a spiritual tranquillity and happiness in the world which is curious to the extent that their tranquillity is apparently achieved with a sense of ease or naturalness, even, in Guillén's case, without effort. Any turmoil and trauma, present in the work of each at different stages, is expressed as functioning within, as opposed to against, an essentially ordered universe. This sense of cosmic wellbeing is accompanied by an unshakeable confidence in the expressivity of language. The similarity in Guillén's and Sopetrán's attitudes is further strengthened by the fact that, although the language each poet uses has religious overtones, they both prefer to place their faith in the creative power of poetry rather than in religious or political dogma.

My task here is to clarify the nature of the poetic voice of each writer, pointing out the similarities between them whilst, at the same time, suggesting that the imperatives behind their poetic utterances differ quite substantially. This difference of imperative, I shall suggest, is largely due to the gendered standpoint of each poet. Concern with one's place in the world must necessarily involve an assessment of one's gender status and, consciously or not, the poets acknowledge this.

Catherine MacKinnon's definition of gendered perspective is precisely pertinent to the comparison of poetic voice that follows in this essay:

> The perspective from a male standpoint enforces woman's definition, encircles her body, cicumlocutes her speech, and describes her life. The male perspective is systemic and hegemonic. The content of the signification "woman" is the content of women's lives. Each sex has its role, but their stakes and power are not equal. If the sexes are unequal, and perspective participates in situation, there is no ungendered reality or ungendered perspective. And they are connected. In this context, objectivity – the nonsituated, universal standpoint, whether claimed or aspired to – is a denial of the existence or potency of sex inequality that tacitly participates in constructing reality from the dominant point of view. Objectivity, as the epistemological stance of which objectification is the social process, creates the reality it apprehends by defining as knowledge the reality it creates through its way of apprehending it. Sexual metaphors for knowing are no coincidence. The solipsism of this approach does not undercut its sincerity, but it is interest that precedes method.[4]

I shall be looking at how each poet exemplifies this notion of "interest that precedes method" in their portrayal of harmony.

Guillén's opening comment to his essay "Lenguaje suficiente. Gabriel Miró" is "Una obra literaria se define tanto por la actitud del escritor ante el mundo como por su manera de sentir y entender el lenguaje."[5]

Both Guillén and Sopetrán have a positive attitude to the world and both see Art as a supreme act of communion with a world which is essentially ordered and harmonious. This "fe de vida",[6] to use Guillén's dictum, is felt rather than sought, "Todo arranca de aquella intuición primordial. Una conciencia amanece en una conexión de armonía."[7]

Sopetrán, too, posits feeling as a testament to truth,

> ...siento en mis manos
> el palpitar divino
> en comunión humana. (S.27)

These are not religious poets in any ordinary sense; however, the assumed "concordancia del ser con el ser" (C.449), common to their "actitud... ante el mundo", does make a vessel of the person of the poet. Sopetrán's poetic persona is even transformed into an amphora,

> Me transformé en un ánfora
> que no es cáliz, ni copa, ni vaso, ni vasija...
> es un espacio lleno derramándose en suelo
> de museo perdido
> donde sólo los dioses de vez en cuando entran
> a guardar en sus huecos
> las monstruosas máscaras. (D.40)

I shall be returning to the amphora image, since in this respect her poetry differs from Guillén's, however, for the moment, I simply want to signal the similarity between Sopetrán's image and Guillén's tendency to see himself as a medium for the expression of creation,

> La realidad me inventa,
> Soy su leyenda. ¡Salve! (C.19)

and,

> Y sin decir su perfección me colma. (C.126)

Both poets are overflowing, filled and overwhelmed by creation.

Poetry is, for Sopetrán, a copy of reality, but not in any negative Platonic way because,

> Todo es copia: hasta el Alma
> que pareciera liberada en forma
> y oculta en fantasía.
> Ella es copia sagrada
> y aún más fotografía,
> de esa Suprema Luz que nos hermana
> en tiempo, espacio y vida. (S.48)

Art is not divorced from life; Art is the fruit of life, its sensuous culmination and simultaneously a life-giver,

> y mis versos racimos
> y manzana madura la palabra.
> . . . .
> Todo parado en fruto,
> estático el momento
> y la ansiedad del corazón saciado. (S.28–29)

With her urge to inclusion, Sopetrán conflates different strata of creation, or as she sees it, Nature. *Nature moves towards Art.* God is a painter, the landworker is a telluric artist and the poet adds to the landscape through God the artist, the copyist, rather than God the Creator,

Pintor de las eternas soledades,
constante innovador
que pintas el alma en los marrones claros,
con tu estilo amorista
añades la palabra
a estas silvas en selva de mi ocaso. (S.25)

Guillén, however, feels naturally inclined towards an expression of reality,

porque sí, porque es mi sino
propender con fervor al universo. (C.127)

For him human creation, Art, lends itself to the purposiveness of Nature; *Art moves towards Nature*,

Una tranquilidad
De afirmación constante
Guía a todos los seres,
Que entre tantos enlaces
Universales, presos
En la jornada eterna,
Bajo el sol quieren ser
Y a su querer se entregan. (C.25)

Both poets are dealing in different ways with an idea of harmony, and both are testifying to a natural and poetic process of communion. Their attitude is not one of pseudo-religious submission. It is simply that, given their basic faith in the order of the world, neither poet is unduly concerned with _who_ they are. As part of creation, of its "esencial compañía", what concerns them most of all is their *place* in the world and the realisation of their pre-designated potential for plenitude. Language, like Identity, is unproblematic, being concerned as it is with the fullness of its own realisation. Its expressive potential is undoubted and unquestioned and, for Guillén as for Sopetrán, Art contributes to and even completes reality, "El contorno distingue y realza lo que es."[8]

Forma como una fuerza en su apogeo,
En el fulgor de su dominio justo. (C.389)

and so, "La poesía no es un ornamento que se superpone a la existencia sino su culminación."[9] For Guillén, poetry is an act of inclusion that answers an urge to integrate himself in reality. This is a conscious intellectual task,

Quiero mi ser, mi ser
íntegro. (C.73)

"Es la tarea humana. Hay que mantener y acrecer este privilegio de ser entre los seres participando de su plenitud."[10] Sopetrán's artistic act is beyond her Self. It has its own autonomous existence. Nature itself is an artistic act, or rather a continuing process of creation and the poet involves herself in that act. On the one hand painting brushes are converted trees that wanted to live beauty,

Son árboles plantados a destiempo
que crecieron rebeldes
tan sólo por vivir de su hermosura. (S.16)

And on the other hand trees are depicted as the painting brushes that describe a landscape,

Son cedros resaltando
lo agradable y lo bello.

Son acacias buscando blanco y rosa.
Son robles duros describiendo estepas. (S.16)

Their destiny is circular. Their existence is an act of communion, the metaphor describes a transformation already present in Nature in which the poet participates.

So, whereas for Guillén his poetic act of inclusion into nature is an intellectual task, for Sopetrán this movement towards plenitude, this culmination of existence, is brought about through a loving communion with Nature, inside Nature. The poet's relationship with the world is the sentimental relationship of lovers, one of mutual adoration and affirmation. Sopetrán is visited one night by the rain,

> Mi amiga lluvia y yo
> nos pasamos la noche hablando de la tierra
> y de los cuerpos,
> lo hermoso que es tocarlos,
> sin romperlos... (D.26)

Aurora de Albornoz, in her introduction to *Silvas*, reminds us of the sensorial basis of the poetic image in modern Spanish poetry. She places Sopetrán firmly in the same tradition of poets who,

> percibieron el misterioso hilo que les unía a las cosas – árbol, flor
> o nube...; intuyeron que cada cosa tiene un alma; que cada cosa –
> agua o brizna de hierba – posee un lenguaje de secretos signos... es
> preciso agudizar todos los *sentidos* porque son los sentidos el
> camino que lleva al *sentimiento*.[11]

Of course, Guillén privileges sensory perception, particularly sight and touch, in poetry which is for him a literal task of incarnation, the task of the poetic symbol,

> El espíritu llega a ser forma encarnada misteriosamente, con algo
> irreductible al intelecto en estas bodas que funden idea y música.[12]

For neither poet does communion or contact signify a loss of identity. A sense of distinction and differentiation is maintained precisely through the sensorial contact which sets up that communion. Fusion and its annihilating potential is anathema because both poets believe so firmly in the concrete existence of things. Their harmony is the harmony of substance, of materiality,

> Irreductibles, pero
> Largos, anchos, profundos
> Enigmas – en sus masas
> Yo los toco, los uso
>
> Hacia mi compañía
> La habitación converge. (C.21)

This is quite straightforward for Guillén, but from this point on Sopetrán and Guillén part company (not to labour the metaphor). For the second part of this essay I shall be attempting to describe Sopetrán's worldview and the implications of this for her artistic production. For it is in perspective that Sopetrán differs from Guillén.

Silvas de mi Selva en Ocaso is concerned with the nature of artistic production and *Los Dioses y el Anfora* is concerned with the poet's experience of the world. We have already seen how Sopetrán draws the natural world into a global concept of Art, how Nature itself is a continuous creative act. We could say that Sopetrán is humanising "things" so that, in her poetic images those "things", in the aforementioned poem "Pinceles" for instance, can become an active part of the creative act; both the trees and the transformed brushes initiate and complete, respectively, the creative act,

> Son álamos gigantes
> definiendo la gama
> del impacto que logran los matices. (S.16)

In "Lienzo", a lake, the raw material of Nature, is the artist's canvas onto which the spirit is drawn,

> y en la tela de cáñamo y de charca
> emborrono mi espíritu (S.15)

This is of course a conceit. The painter actually paints on a canvas which is not the lake, and the canvas offered to the Maker is not the lake. However, this poem about the copy of nature that is nature and so also art testifies to something else. The poem itself is neither the canvas of the artist nor the canvas of nature. The poetic function is one of distinction: the poetic voice is one that seeks to revere communion and at the same time site a place for the poet,

> espero a que florezca el firmamento
> para mostrar al Hacedor mi sarga. (S.15)

The poet's cloth, "sarga", or canvas, voices definition or form, conjoining things in the material world by becoming a vessel for the vision of such communion, being at once the line that distinguishes one substance fron another and the line or surface of contact; the double purpose of the profile,

> Siguiendo van mis pasos
> esa luz que reposa en el perfil,
> polvo de un fondo en flor
> proyectándose en formas. (S.22)

The poet acts as an intermediary therefore between a hidden light or essence of being in reality and language,

> El Sol detrás de todos los adornos
> y un retoque de flechas, luz y sombra,
> pulsando la aureola de cada sustantivo. (S.22)

and she captures the vision of the very process of union and communion at work in the world,

> ¡Qué momento divino
> el de la sombra en luz
> que luz de sombra imprime! (S.23)

If the poem fails to do this it becomes like the oil painting that obstructs vision because of the weightiness and inappropriateness of its expression, its langauge, becoming an,

> ...ilusión sin perfume
> en verdinegra muerte de gramáticas. (S.37)

lacking in light, lacking in reality.

If we turn to *Los Dioses y el Anfora* we see the poetic persona achieving a similar visionary status. *Los Dioses y el Anfora* can be seen as an oneiric trajectory towards the plenitude of Being not simply for the poet but also for the world as a sentient entity.

Dream, for Sopetrán, is the light in a world of darkness. Dream accesses her to the hidden world, the world that affirms her through a sense of correspondence to a world of sentient things,

> El canto de la lluvia
> tocaba con la yema de sus dedos mi nebuloso aliento.
> . . . .
> Pude tocar, por fin, las cenizas iluminadas de los besos
> que en el sueño sonámbulo
> caían cada noche a cada cosa como niebla. (D.14)

Sopetrán inhabits an intensely contradictory world, "mi locura" (D.13) as she calls it, engaging with the "loca armonía" (D.25) of the world. She is nebulous, the dream is also nebulous and yet dream throws her into an intensely physical, corporeal, material world of sensation,

> Caían, sí, a mi cuerpo – cenicero de dioses –
> y así me fui quemando en la caricia
> lenta y pulcra
> de la luz de una vela. (D.14)

Sopetrán perceives the things of the world as naturally sentient. This is their natural or true state although the "bodies" of the world normally feign sleep, "los angulosos cuerpos de mi cuarto fingían dormir" (D.14).

Paradoxically the poetic persona is both silenced by and affirmed by the sentience of things,

> ¡Cuántas cosas callaban mi existencia,
> me miraban atónitas
> ....! (D.14)

> Y no fue nada fácil desnudarse,
> dejar que miraran los árboles
> mis pechos. (D.15)

A mixture of shame and pleasure is associated with her first moments of contact with essence, with the gods. The shame is all hers, the gods of things know only pleasure,

> y sonrió la fuente al verme igual,
> igual que ella desnuda, transparente,
> bajo la intensa luz de las miradas...
> ¡Qué gozo!
> Ver mi sombra sin ropa rodeándome
> renovándome el ser y la vergüenza. (D.16)

However, the light of the poetic persona's new sense of vision soon wipes away all inhibition and fear,

> Todo mi cuarto despedía luces:
> las arañas con sus hilos verdes
> y sus dedos de plata,
> destejían el miedo de mis ojos. (D.19)

She is transported to a place where she has cosmic proportion through what comes to be expressed as her sexual union with Nature,[13]

> Mis raíces se hundían en el barro,
> mis brazos se marchaban a la orilla
> . . . .
> Y era aquella honda marcada, casi ola:
> sexo habitando la ilusión del alba...
> Y aquel golpe de fuego, casi astro,
> transportaba mi sangre al universo... (D.17).

Sopetrán expresses the heightened perception of her oneiric world through sexual imagery,

> El agua de la noche
> – lluvia de nube rosa para llenar mis cántaros sin asas. (D.25)

and

> nos fundimos de barro hasta perder la forma,
> tocamos el pulso de la tierra. (D.27)

From the union of the poetic persona with the elements of nature comes the material of human creation, "barro", both physical and spiritual. From this "barro" comes a renewed Self, a receptacle of life,

> Soy urna, baúl, tarro...
> orza esperando manos que me alcen
> como cáliz para saciar los símbolos de vida. (D.28)

The physical elements of the world show the poet that the senses of the world lead to a correspondent spiritual reality,

> Nieves de esa montaña que me señala sendas
> por donde el tiempo jamás escaló altura;
> lámpara, ánfora,
> emitiendo belleza desde siempre. (D.19–20)

Approaching an earthly centre, overwhelmed by Nature she reaches Art,

> Se me cubrió de tierra la mirada
> y en los dibujos griegos
> donde la idea se transforma en arte,
> me vi escrita en el nombre
> de aquel eterno libro de las luces. (D.20)

At this moment Sopetrán is ejected out of her human world and enters the nether regions of myth,

> y las cuatro paredes de mi cuarto
> se rompieron,
> dejándome en el aire los caminos. (D.20)

Surviving the abyss, "las cavidades de la nada" (D.21), with gothic resilience, holding on to "la pequeña y temblorosa llama de una vela" (D.22), this glimpsed eternal essence, the poetic persona is rewarded by the gift of mythical sight; her "cántaro" is transformed into an amphora,[14]

> Mi ánfora
> siempre perdida en transparencias,
> siempre en los fondos,
> estática como templo,
> se llenó de palabras y me sació con el numen sagrado
> de aquellas ambrosías
> con que el alma degusta la belleza. (D.31)

After this artistic purgatory, she is ready to experience the wisdom of the gods. Principally, this mythical knowledge of "el puro contacto de la esencia y la sangre" (D.41), experienced through dream, "Te conocí en un sueño." (D.41), is imparted by Athene, the goddess of wisdom,

> Era una diosa virgen y guerrera
> salida de las nubes
> con ojos de lechuza y telúrico aspecto,
> la que me sacó de los infiernos
> retornándome a mis campos de olivares y búhos,
> donde cantan las fuentes y posan los estanques las estrellas
> sabiendo que en la fuerza de los símbolos
> se recrea la vida. (D.39)

Athene's contact transfigures,

> Toqué el barro cocido
> y una metamorfosis se me enlazó en el tacto
> sacudiéndome el cuerpo
> . . . .
> Me transformé en un ánfora
> que no es cáliz, ni copa, ni vaso, ni vasija...
> es un espacio lleno derramándose en suelo
> de museo perdido
> donde sólo los dioses de vez en cuando entran. (D.39–40)

Although Nature, the sentient things of the world, have been left behind, Sopetrán's experience of the gods, her artistic world, is still intensely physical. Still art and nature are one and the same; for the things of the spirit are experienced in sensual terms too,

> Anduve mis llanuras, escalé mis montañas,
> nadé mis lagos vivos,
> vi arder el corazón, los pulmones vibrar,
> la garganta reír,
> el óvulo cantar su-ser-mujer en libertad de diosa. (D.46)

Although inhabiting a world beyond the physical "más allá del todo" (D.48), the poet perceives this mythical and artistic realm through her senses and as a woman.

It is significant that in order to experience her "ser-mujer", Sopetrán has to gain the freedom and perspective of a goddess. If woman has largely been the object of art rather than the artist, it is logical that the gendered female poetic persona should have to go through a process of transformation before reaching her plenitude of being as the creative subject. Sopetrán conflates the notions of nature and art as she also conflates the subject and object of art, thus sustaining a feminine poetic voice that has itself as the focus of art. By doing so she retains her faith in the harmony of the world, vindicates her place as a poet who contributes to the the world by leading it towards art, and defines her gendered self as both nature and art and as the subject and object of art.

Sopetrán claims to do this beyond the "objectivity" of MacKinnon's "systemic and hegemonic male perspective".[15] This is why her metamorphosis is portrayed in physical terms, "sacudiéndome el cuerpo" (D.39), her transformation begins with her gendered female body; this is why she enters a world of chaos which sweeps away the world as she knew it, a world of chaos which will prove to be the realm of the gods,[16]

> Los mares encendidos golpeaban las calles.
> vomitaban petróleo,
> saqueaban el planeta
> y barrían con sus lenguas de espuma
> la acumulada farsa de la historia.
> . . . .
> . . . .
> Todo se ahogaba con su hez y con su hambre.
> El lodo, la saliva, el sudor y las lágrimas
> me llovían el cuerpo.
> La tierra se movía. El agua ardía en furia... (D.37–38)

It is also why her amphora refuses its linguistic definitions, so definitely not a chalice, cup, glass or vessel, but rather is its fluid function, its essence, "es un espacio lleno derramándose" (D.40), the space, or rather place, it creates with its shape where only the divine enter. Through the amphora, Sopetrán symbolically creates and envelops her own self-defining space.

Guillén needs no intermediate world or site from which to perceive the harmony of the world and his place in it. Guillén as a gendered male poetic persona already speaks reality. His "yo" already speaks objectivity which as MacKinnon has told us "creates the reality it apprehends by defining as knowledge the reality it creates through its way of apprehending it."[17]

Sopetrán, however needs to filter her experience through dream and myth, "El sueño es una experiencia de dioses." (D.33). Sopetrán speaks myth, so that she can speak herself as artifact, myth and creator. It is no accident that Athene, the goddess of knowledge, acts as her guide,

> sabiendo que en la fuerza de los símbolos
> se recrea la vida. (D.39)

Athene teaches her to envelop hidden essence whereas Guillén simply and incisively penetrates essence.

It seems to be then a gendered perspective which differentiates Guillén and Sopetrán; gender which colours their vision and gender which tunes their poetic voice. For both poets use elemental, sensual imagery to describe their experience of reality and of art. And, as poets, both act as intermediaries for the expression of and completion of Nature in Art. This crucial difference is symbolized in the fact that Guillén is not an amphora.

Helen Wing
University of Hull

1. Julie Sopetrán, *Amorismos* (Barcelona: Ediciones Rondas, 1984), *Un siglo en Atherton* (Barcelona: Ediciones Rondas, 1984), *Polvo Luminoso* (Guadalajara: Colección Gacela, 1984), *Silvas de mi Selva en Ocaso* (Madrid: Torremozas, 1985), *Los Dioses y el Anfora* (Madrid: Torremozas, 1987). Julita González Barba (Julie Sopetrán), *En Hita hoy es otoño y se oye el mar* (Guadalajara: Colección Avena Loca, 1990).

2. References to Julie Sopetrán's *Selvas de mi Selva en Ocaso* (Madrid: Torremozas, 1985) are to page numbers; and for economy of space the relevant number, preceded by the initial S, is put in brackets after each citation in the text.

3. References to Julie Sopetrán's *Los Dioses y el Anfora* (Madrid: Torremozas, 1987) are to page numbers; the relevant number, preceded by the initial D, is put in brackets after each citation in the text.

4. Catherine A. MacKinnon, "Feminism, Marxism, Method and the State: Toward Feminist Jurisprudence." *Signs* (Summer 1983) pp.636–637.

5. Jorge Guillén, "Lenguaje suficiente. Gabriel Miró", in *Lenguaje y Poesía* (Madrid: Alianza, 1969) p.145.

6. References to Guillén's poems are to the page numbers of *Cántico* (Barcelona: Seix Barral, 1983); the relevant number, preceded by the initial C, is put in brackets after each citation in the text.

7. Jorge Guillén, *El argumento de la obra* (Barcelona: Ocnos, 1969) p.49.

8. ibid. p.54.

9. Jorge Guillén, "Lenguaje suficiente. Gabriel Miró", p.146.

10. Jorge Guillén, *El argumento de la obra*, p.49.

11. Aurora de Albornoz, "Palabras ante unas palabras" in Julie Sopetrán, *Silvas de mi Selva en Ocaso* (Madrid: Torremozas, 1985) pp.9–10.

12. Jorge Guillén, "Lenguaje de poema, una generación", *Lenguaje y Poesía*, p.187.

13. One is reminded here, putting aside the gender implications, of Neruda's *Veinte poemas de amor y una canción desesperada*.

14. Note here the Romantic element in Sopetrán's gothic experience.

15. Catherine A. MacKinnon, op.cit., p.636.

16. Sopetrán's surrealistic dreamworld is reminiscent of Alberti's *Sobre los ángeles* except that it is not accompanied by the disintegration of self but rather by a heightened sense of the physical self as the witness of cosmic phenomena and as the guardian of poetry,

> Sin apenas agitar los brazos,
> mi cuerpo subía, subía como grulla hacia la altura,

gravitaba por auroras boreales,
pasaba por esos orbes aislados,
crepitaba la lava
. . . .
. . . .
Tuve miedo a comprobar la nada
o a saber que lo es todo esta materia de mi grito
en no se sabe qué lugar vertido. (D.36)

17. Catherine A. MacKinnon, op.cit., p.636.

Poesía femenina en Cuba

En los abundosos estudios, investigaciones, ponencias, antologías, tesis, y otras conjuras por el estilo, sobre las particularidades de la literatura cubana escrita en – dentro, con, durante, por, ante – el período revolucionario cubano que se abrió en 1959, uno de los temas hasta ahora bastante olvidado es el llamado discurso femenino. Por ello, todavía es un terreno sin desbrozar aquel donde se precisen los detalles peculiares de las relaciones entre la ideología revolucionaria – y los cambios sociales de Cuba – y la creación literaria de la mujer a través de este período, con sus especificidades como fenómeno artístico concreto. Su mayor interés radica, a mi modo de ver, en que dentro de estas relaciones se agudizan los conflictos, las contradicciones, el afán de ruptura, la necesidad de transformación ética y estética y la toma de conciencia de la propia responsabilidad como individuo y ser social, que han marcado todo el movimiento literario cubano en la Revolución.

La discriminación de la mujer ha sido, en primera instancia, un mal destilado del vasallaje económico. Y sus rémoras provienen de la incapacidad de renovación de una conciencia domada a lo largo de los siglos. En Cuba, mejor que pintar los remanentes subjetivos del machismo con la clásica imagen del troglodita que hala a su mujer por el cabello para meterla en la cueva, o con otra – a tono con la exacerbada explotación del auge industrial – donde los billetes del patrón se acumulan sobre la epalda de una esposa "fregona", valdría más en el caso de la mujer cubana – aportadora por igual de los bienes familiares, obrera, profesional, cumplidora de tareas extras y que cubre con un esfuerzo adicional la retaguardia hogareña – a manera de simbólica sátira de esas supervivencias del pasado, representar el instante donde la compañera, agotada, le acomoda a su compañero las criollas "chancletas". ¡Y ni hablar de aquellas que tengan inquietudes creativas! El tiempo de la creación quedaría para una improbable tercera jornada de trabajo, en último renglón después de las labores domésticas, sociales y de "trabajo" propiamente dicho. Y todavía, después de esto, quedan algunos "ingenuos" que se asombran de la poca cantidad, en verdad, de narradoras, si se compara – hago una cuenta cuantitativa y no cualitativa – con la abultada lista de narradores.

La vieja aristocracia de los varones se insertó en Cuba dentro de un orden económico subdesarrollado y se asentó sobre peculiaridades que caracterizaron la antigua sociedad cubana. Desde la llegada de los conquistadores españoles hasta el cambio revolucionario de 1959, la población femenina se ubicaba mayoritariamente en las zonas rurales donde dominaban – y subsisten aún hoy – hábitos patriarcales y costumbres de la severa tradición hispánica. Junto a esto, la neocolonización norteamericana con la avalancha propagandística acerca de la "eficacia" del ama de casa y la imposición de cánones consumistas a favor de un mercado de la moda, incrementó los tabúes acerca de la inferioridad física y mental de la mujer para su eliminación competitiva como probable fuerza de trabajo en un ambiente de creciente desempleo. Un proletariado femenino casi inexistente, abundancia de sirvientas y prostitutas en las zonas urbanas y una burguesía inculta y de ingrato gusto, eran el propicio caldo de cultivo para los prejuicios de raíz católica, acuñados desde la etapa colonial española, que se sumaban con explosividad a los patrones de conducta tribales y mitos heredados de la emigración negra esclava. Así se conformó un modelo inconmovible que permeó todas las capas sociales, tanto en la creación de una mentalidad masculina prepotente y subestimadora de la condición femenina, como en una proyección sumisa y pasiva de esta, mientras se inculcaba bien, desde la infancia, que *la carrera de la mujer es el matrimonio*. Toda vulneración de este axioma trascendía penosamente sobre su imagen pública y privada. Por cierto, los hombres tampoco escapaban a los daños inmanentes a la exasperación tropical del machismo que actuaba compulsivamente sobre el complejo de "hombría" y los obligaba a su demostración constante, lo cual los colocaba tanto en situación de victimarios como de secretas víctimas.

Estas realidades de la población cubana antes del año 1959 promovieron un tipo de comportamiento entre los sexos de aguda influencia y peso en la organización práctica de la vida y muy difícil de superar aún cuando se erradiquen las causas que le han dado lugar. Ha subsistido, sobre todo, en el plano de la relación familiar o íntima de la pareja, en los prejuicios acerca de la virginidad o en la diferente apreciación de la infidelidad conyugal, en la distribución de las tareas domésticas, en la educación de los niños y, también, en algunos planos de la vida laboral, profesional, política, social, incluso de proyección masiva de divulgación. Hasta hace apenas muy poco tiempo, los noticieros cinematográficos recurrían de manera reiterada al *close-up* de las espaldas femeninas como casi único recurso expresivo para la emisión de mensajes tales como la alegría del verano, la belleza de las playas o la hospitalidad cubana.

Como fenómeno, lo anterior no se circunscribe a un ámbito específico ni tiene vínculo directo aparente con el grado de formación, origen, profesión o región; esta problemática se matiza según esas coordenadas, mas como realidad concreta corta longitudinalmente a la sociedad cubana actual. Ni los decretos, ni las buenas leyes bastan por sí solas. El propio hecho de su resistencia a desaparecer debe ser motivo constante de la crítica serena y del arrinconamiento a las filigranas de una moral retrógrada todavía coleante.

En Cuba no pudiera hablarse de un cuerpo literario de temática femenina, ni en el pasado, ni en el presente, aunque sí se puede calar en la idiosincrasia de la mujer a través de los textos escritos por nuestras poetisas, narradoras, dramaturgas, ensayistas, periodistas; y condensar algunas precisiones acerca de las particularidades de la literatura escrita por mujeres desde los siglos pasados hasta hoy y sus aportes en cuanto a excepcionalidad, por ejemplo, de la voz poética, rigor formal, penetración singular del mundo. Y, por qué no, hacer un balance en cuanto a su amplia presencia cuantitativa dentro del panorama literario cubano. Las cifras, es cierto, no dicen mucho cuando se trata de una historiación estética, mas sirven como indicios de consolidación de la labor realizada por la mujer

cubana como escritora y, en especial, como poetisa. La larga nómina de autoras
que ha influido de manera incisiva en el acontecer de la cultura cubana vale,
aunque más no fuera, para cerrar la boca de aquellos que todavía se escudan en su
supuesta minoría para dejar ausentes sus nombres de antologías, encuentros,
lecturas, diccionarios. A principios de este siglo se publicó un texto que reunía,
bajo el sonoro título de *Florilegio de escritoras cubanas*, más de un centenar de
mujeres dadas en ejercer el solitario oficio de la poesía.[1] Se anda ya por los
umbrales del siglo XXI y sospecho que si me empeñase en recoger *todos* los
nombres de poetisas que han surgido en los últimos treinta años, aquellas con uno,
dos o más libros en su haber, presentes en antologías y recopilaciones, con
premios y menciones en concursos, miembros de talleres literarios, publicadas
apenas aquí y allá en revistas y periódicos, o mejor aún, totalmente inéditas y que
han ido dando a conocer su obra en debates y lecturas, casi podría repetirse la
hazaña de reunir una legión semejante y dar a la luz un segundo tomo de
Florilegio.

El desarrollo de la poesía escrita en Cuba por mujeres – y toda esta perífrasis para
mencionar a las poetisas, tiene un sustento de discriminación que ha llegado hasta
afectar el uso correcto de la lengua – no pudiera hacerse si se perdiera de vista el
devenir de la cultura cubana, de su intelectualidad, de los establecimientos
profesionales referidos a la creación, y de la sociedad en su conjunto, como
sistema de interrelaciones y complejidades tanto en las ideas, como de la
psicología cotidiana y lo concreto material que se manifiesta también en
problemas paraliterarios como las editoriales, la divulgación, el apoyo
institucional.

Desde los primeros años de la república mediatizada, en las iniciales décadas de
este siglo, la poesía cubana alcanzó un notable grado de madurez y originalidad,
en buena medida gracias a su elevado sentido del papel que le correspondía como
expresión de la cubanía y del reflejo de esencias, en respuesta al peligro de
contaminación neocolonizadora y la presencia de apócrifas proposiciones
artísticas. En todo ese largo proceso que fue desde el Posmodernismo – como se
le llama en América al tiempo transicional entre nuestro llamado Modernismo
finisecular y la Vanguardia – hasta la irrupción de los ismos más recientes, la

poesía escrita por las mujeres en Cuba ha tenido sus figuras excepcionales, así como sus figurantes, de igual forma que fue sucediendo con la poesía escrita por los hombres, los poetas, en el estricto sentido del vocablo.

Quiero apuntar ahora, aunque peque de perogrulladas, que la valoración de la mujer escritora como parte con idénticos derechos del conjunto de la cultura, no implica que se desconozca en su creación las peculiaridades propias de su experiencia singular como mujer. Estoy objetando la segregación en los fenómenos paralelos al acto mismo de crear, es decir, a la delimitación paternalista de carácter discriminatorio que se ejerce, por ejemplo, en muchas historias literarias que han usado el acápite confinatorio de "las poetisas" para resumir en pocas líneas su estudio – diera la impresión de que sus autores quieren salir aprisa de asunto tan "enojoso y trivial" – y enjuiciar dentro de un mismo saco a todas aquellas que, a su leal saber y entender, no alcanzaban las tallas masculinas para ser presentadas en los epígrafes que definían la tendencia de una época o un movimiento literario dado.

Una de las condenas actuales a las reivindicaciones de la mujer carga la mano sobre la probable *automarginación*, pero, como ya es aceptado en otros temas, para que exista una actitud de "automarginación", como de "autocensura", ¿no es lógico que se produjese primero una *marginación*? Las poetisas no pidieron andar en capítulo aparte, aunque así se les encuentra en muchos textos y antologías en minúsculos capitulillos de consuelo y como fuera de la corriente del tiempo y de la estética.

La respuesta de muchas mujeres intelectuales fue, como es bien sabido, poner "tienda aparte" y crear revistas, editoriales e instituciones femeninas, por igual forma que se hace todavía necesario proponer coloquios, encuentros y conferencias que estudien el tema para así reparar el silencio y el desconocimiento de tantos años. También trajo como resultado que autoras de poco aliento o francamente mediocres eran de esa manera nombradas para hacer bulto, en tanto las escritoras de calibre se veían sometidas a la colectivización emparejadora del término de "poetisas" que se terminaría convirtiendo, por esa razón, en algo casi bochornoso o insultante, ya que muchas creadoras se ofendían – y aún se ofenden

– de verse llamadas así, por estimar esa palabra alusiva a lo menos estimable de la producción poética, nominación que de hecho representaba un sinónimo de la emoción domesticada, del lirismo de "ama de casa". Por todo ello, este sustantivo en correcto español, que como toda palabra del lenguaje en uso porta determinada carga positiva o peyorativa extra, recibida de determinados contextos históricos, fue rechazado con mucha virulencia por las mujeres dedicadas al ejercicio poético. Estimo que si se analiza este asunto con calma y objetividad, no puede aceptarse que el término de *poetisas* tenga nada de vergonzoso en sí, ni en lo estético ni por ninguna otra razón, y, por el contrario, es una tarea de todos despojarlo del matiz de subestimación y reponerlo en el legítimo lugar que le corresponde por su significado y su belleza sonora. ¡Poetisas sí!

Cierto es que después del período romántico, mucha de la poesía escrita por autoras femeninas en Cuba era portadora de un lenguaje caduco, de sentimentalidad petrificada, de quejas casi exclusivamente amorosas, y que no se interesaba en romper con los patrones que seguían definiendo lo "clásico femenino" como lo había entendido un pensamiento de estirpe señorial que aspiraba a reducir la imagen cultural de la mujer a una esclava de la pasión amorosa tradicional, sin derecho alguno a abordar otros temas, ni incluso otros géneros como no fuesen el diario, la epístola y la composición lírica. Lo que no se suele decir es que también abundaban entonces los "poetisos" – me tomo la licencia de usar por última vez el sustantivo con el antiguo signo negativo – que comercializaban un verso facilista y de mala imitación romántica.

Casi cincuenta años atrás, Camila Henríquez Ureña dictaba una conferencia sobre la mujer en la cultura, cuyas ideas mantienen una vigencia y frescura que sobresaltan por su lucidez y fina percepción:

> Si estamos de acuerdo en que *cultura* es el esfuerzo consciente mediante el cual la naturaleza moral o intelectual del ser humano se refina e ilustra con un propósito de mejoramiento colectivo, no es posible decir que existiera antes del siglo XIX una *cultura femenina*... La llegada de la mujer, de la mitad de la humanidad a la libertad y a la cultura es una de las mayores revoluciones de

nuestra época de revoluciones. Y es un hecho indiscutible e indestructible.

Y más adelante añade:

La inferioridad mental de la mujer ha sido principalmente falta de libertad. Y la libertad no se conquista de pronto: es obra prolongada, conquista cotidiana.[2]

Esta "obra prolongada" ha alcanzado sus triunfos: en Cuba, después del cambio social de 1959, ya la mujer participa activamente en el colectivo social y no es excluida como voz pública, erradicando así para siempre los falsos conceptos que colocaban la condición de la mujer como ajena de manera "natural" a los procesos históricos e ideológicos.

Pero la novedad de estos cambios no ha encontrado una infraestructura que elimine por completo los patrones culturales impuestos en el pasado y el reconocimiento espontáneo de la práctica intelectual de la mujer. Incluso algunas de nuestras autoras hablan todavía de sí mismas como fenómenos aislados y no como parte dialéctica de un sistema donde la mujer ya tiene su voz destacada, como conjunto, dentro de la literatura cubana.

No todo son espinas, ni las excepciones desmienten las anteriores afirmaciones, mas crecientes cambios permiten vaticinar que en la literatura se generará un replanteamiento del papel de la mujer, de manera semejante a lo que ya existe en otras esferas de la cultura como la danza y las artes plásticas.

En el desarrollo del género poético cubano, y dentro de los avatares generales estilísticos y temáticos, la proyección consciente o no entre las poetisas de su condición femenina − que la mayoría reconoce como rasgo esencial, aún cuando rechacen la diferenciación discriminatoria entre Poesía con Pe mayúscula y "poesía femenina" − ha permitido una captación excepcional de la realidad, una revelación del mundo *distinta*, con tonos y matices innovadores, surgidos con toda seguridad del legítimo afán de imponer su perspectiva en un entorno donde todavía los rezagos sexistas del pasado pesan en distintas esferas de la sociedad.

Participar en la elaboración de la historia es también intervenir en la *elaboración de la cultura*. La lucha por la asimilación de estas ideas, por la repercusión en la práctica, y por la eliminación completa de prejuicios, son el meollo de la relación entre la verdadera posición que ocupa la mujer en una sociedad específica y la obra literaria que surge dentro de estos contextos.

Sin que este camino haya resultado – ni resulte – fácil, no obstante ya se habla otro lenguaje dentro del terreno social, y de hecho ha cambiado también el lenguaje poético. La poesía escrita por mujeres nacidas a partir de 1940 y que han recibido como experiencia capital el fenómeno de la Revolución, es penetrante, lúcida y crítica como suma total, y en muchos aspectos con una asimilación más madura, honesta y profesional que muchos de los colegas varones profusamente publicados. Aventuro el criterio que quizás la poca atención de antologadores y críticos – fuese por las razones que fuese – y la inevitable decantación que ello fue propiciando, haya favorecido que no prosperara entre las poetisas la mala versificación – rimada o libre –, los temas de ocasión, la poemalia oportunista, el regodeo pastoril, la chabacanería, el falso cubanismo, como sí ha ocurrido entre las camadas abundantes de poetas que atestan los listados, donde la indiferenciada presencia de todos afectó durante un buen período de tiempo la pulcritud de la proyección poética cubana.

Las esencias de un período literario sólo se alcanzan como resultado de muchas cabezas pensando y de la acumulación gradual de una crítica honesta y profunda, mas ya a estas alturas es un suceso evidente que la cualidad relevante de la intelectualidad cubana es la voluntad común de revelar, con sus medios expresivos singulares, el fragor de la sociedad contemporánea desde el detalle personal hasta la vastedad épica, es decir, la presencia constante de la realidad, aún cuando la motivación del acto creador sea una interpretación del universo íntimo, un desbroce de la memoria o una elaborada información sobre el suceder del exterior. Las dos tendencias tradicionales de la poesía cubana, la de preocupación social y la lírica de aristas filosóficas, comparecen en la actualidad en una síntesis superior en las poetisas herederas del rigor del idioma de una Dulce María Loynaz, de la pasión deslenguada de una Gertrùdis Gómez de Avellaneda y de la inquietud por el destino del ser humano de una Mirta Aguirre.

En la actualidad, todavía viven – y publican – algunas de las más importantes poetisas que fundaron una obra ya madura antes de 1959; entre ellas, Dulce María Loynaz, Carilda Oliver Labra y Fina García Marruz, son tres nombres decisivos en el desarrollo de la poesía cubana del siglo XX. Junto a estas autoras, ya se pueden distinguir algunas poetisas de talento entre las promociones literarias que empezaron a publicar después de esa fecha.

Aunque no me gusten las clasificatorias, el grupo de poetisas que publica por primera vez después del cambio revolucionario de 1959, integra lo que pudiera llamarse la "Quinta Generación" de este siglo, con las diversas promociones que lo conforman; junto a ella, se hace visible ya la presencia de una nueva generación con las muy jóvenes nacidas en los años sesenta y setenta. Lo esencial para una primaria descripción del signo general que organiza su fisonomía generacional es que han escrito y publicado su obra dentro del contexto histórico que significa el triunfo y el desarrollo de una revolución socialista. Sus vivencias generacionales son prácticamente las mismas que las de los hombres: el propio suceso revolucionario que provocó su inmediata incorporación a todas las tareas de la sociedad, ha proporcionado a la mujer un plano de igualdad en cuanto a experiencia vital, a asimilación de los conceptos de la nueva sociedad, y, de hecho, a recibir motivaciones semejantes. La poesía escrita por mujeres en la Revolución se ocupa de los mismos grandes temas – los tradicionales y los nuevos – por la razón de participar al mismo nivel en los acontecimientos sociales capitales. Ello no quiere decir, ni mucho menos, que su *condición de mujer* no trascienda dentro del acto creador como parte de sus esencias. Todo lo contrario. Si bien en el proceso literario anterior, la mujer asumía de forma natural la norma impuesta por una perspectiva masculina predominante, el mismo hecho de ruptura de los códigos sociales propició el desencadenamiento de una nueva óptica donde la mujer ha empezado a buscar – a tientas, con sus altas y sus bajas – su propio discurso.

Los tópicos que a lo largo del desarrollo de la poesía escrita por mujeres, en distintas épocas y lugares, se han reproducido con mayor o menor variedad, es decir, el amor, la maternidad, el dolor elegíaco, la fe religiosa, la familia, el hogar, la naturaleza, cobran nuevos sentidos a la luz del complejo marco de referencias y de vivencias de una sociedad en plena transformación. En la mayoría de las obras de las poetisas cubanas se manifiestan cambios en el tratamiento de estos asuntos junto al surgimiento de tópicos novedosos. Cabe hablar, pues, de manera general, de una actitud desprejuiciada hacia las relaciones sexuales, un desenfado en el abordaje de los temas amorosos, pérdida de la autocensura ante situaciones escabrosas, visión crítica de las relaciones familiares – con cierta dosis de compasión bien entendida hacia las mujeres del "pasado" – tono irónico acerca de la pareja, protesta ante los rezagos de la moral pequeño-burguesa y machista, erradicación de posturas sumisas, pudorosas, ñoñas suplicantes o pasivas, rechazo explícito a mantenerse dentro de roles secundarios, autorreconocimiento de su posición en el mundo, lucidez analítica ante otras figuras femeninas – famosas o mujeres del común – pérdida de la falsa solemnidad ante el fenómeno de la maternidad, nostalgia ante determinados detalles del pasado inmediato, registro periodístico de la realidad, refutación de los artificios vigentes ante el tratamiento de algunos temas, todo ello con un discurso concientemente desmistificador de los códigos patriarcales y exaltadores de "lo eterno femenino".

La promoción inicial, según las edades, no comenzó a publicar al mismo tiempo. Algunas vieron editados sus primeros poemas desde los tiempos inaugurales de la Revolución, con la aparición de polémicas editoriales como "El Puente", otras presentaron sus primeros libros en concursos literarios organizados por distintas instituciones culturales, desde finales de los años sesenta, otras apenas han comenzado a publicar en fechas muy recientes.

Cinco poetisas encabezan esta primera promoción: Georgina Herrera, Nancy Morejón, Lina de Feria, Milagros González y Minerva Salado. Cada una de estas autoras tiene un estilo muy definido, con un énfasis en la comunicación, incluso en el caso de la más críptica de las cinco, Lina de Feria. El desafío de enfrentar la nueva realidad desde la perspectiva de la mujer como ente social que concibe el acto creador bajo novedosos códigos, entre ellos el de la igualdad entre los sexos, permitió una inicial lucidez desenfadada en el plano de los contenidos que abrió el camino para un renovación del discurso poético escrito por las mujeres en Cuba. Las poetisas expresaban – concientes o no – una imagen distinta de sí mismas, de quienes les rodeaban, de los contextos concretos, a partir de experiencias que rompían por completo con los esquemas del pasado, sin abandonar del todo tampoco eso que los estudiosos gustan de llamar la tradición, y que es la vertebración de una voz esencial que surge con el nacimiento de nuestra literatura y continúa hasta hoy. Las contradicciones entre los patrones impuestos en la antigua sociedad y los diversos procesos del cambio revolucionario que han llevado tanto a hombres como mujeres a asumir conductas a veces extremas, y de hecho una determinada conciencia, están presentes por primera vez en los asuntos de la poesía de esta promoción. La mujer participa como miembro pleno de la sociedad en los acontecimientos políticos, en los debates ideológicos, en las tareas y situaciones que ha exigido la construcción de un mundo nuevo: los trabajos agrícolas voluntarios, la alfabetización, la defensa militar, la adopción de nuevos oficios necesarios a la economía, el replanteamiento de la responsabilidad de la pareja. Todo ello traía consigo una reconsideración de la propia perspectiva de las creadoras. Llama la atención que, aunque atravesaron en su etapa formativa por el momento más prosaico de la llamada poesía coloquial, no cayeron en sus excesos y mantuvieron un rigor formal dentro de un amplio registro temático, cuyo rasgo más evidente es, al igual que en el resto de sus colegas, el intento de una definición humanista dentro de una cotidianidad múltiple y cambiante. Un análisis de los recursos expresivos muestra, en algunas, madurez y dominio de la lengua, mientras en otras la sencillez pudiera ser resultado (y lo es) como poca elaboración del lenguaje.

La segunda promoción, cuyos nacimientos se enmarcan alrededor de los años finales de la década del cuarenta y principios de la siguiente, es la más fecunda hasta ahora en cuanto a eclosión numérica; pero, sin embargo, las circunstancias de la época rompieron el equilibrio entre espontaneidad y compromiso, y la poesía – en general – perdió en frescura y originalidad. La segunda promoción se caracteriza por dar sus pasos iniciales en una etapa de agudas definiciones, que se manifestó dentro de lo literario en una repetición de motivos, en un énfasis por encontrar y mostrar a toda costa una identidad – social, nacional – en detrimento de las revelaciones individuales, y de cierto desconcierto en cuanto a la resolución estética. Todos estos problemas surgieron al sedimentarse la emoción de los primeros años, al elevarse el rechazo a la simplicidad de la peor poesía conversacional y a la exigencias de adaptación de la conciencia creadora ante una realidad compleja y polémica. Estos conflictos actuaron sobre la intelectualidad como conjunto, pero marcaron de manera singular a los escritores en formación. Excilia Saldaña, Albis Torres, Mirta Yáñez, Yolanda Ulloa y Enid Vian, entre otras, ganaron concursos, publicaron, y se dieron a conocer a través de diferentes vías, a pesar de que los años setenta – período en que escriben sus primeras obras – no fueron muy propicios al desarrollo literario y en particular las poetisas no aparecían con frecuencia en las antologías ni en los distintos eventos literarios.

La tercera promoción de las nacidas en la primera mitad de los años cincuenta ha conformado un grupo numeroso, aguerrido, y que ha sabido buscarse su lugar. Con sus matices personales muy definidos, comienzan a hacer escuchar sus voces con más énfasis al final de la década del setenta y, junto con otros poetas y narradores, rompieron lanzas contra el facilismo – formal y de contenido – de esos tiempos. Las más conocidas son Soleida Ríos, Reina María Rodríguez, Raisa White, Lourdes González, Cira Andrés, Marilyn Bobes y Chelly Lima.

Esta generación de poetisas nacidas entre 1940 y 1955 no se reconoce por sus propias integrantes como homogénea y hay una buena parte de verdad en ello que se manifiesta en la diferente proyección pública de unas y otras, en distintas afinidades electivas, tanto de influencias como en la forma de asumir las tareas generacionales, mas la circunstancia objetiva ineludible del corto período de coetaneidad que están obligadas a compartir con las determinantes contextuales que actúan sobre el acto creador, quiéranlo o no, confirman muchos puntos de contacto en las esencias que serán a la larga, cuando el decantamiento del tiempo se imponga, lo relevante perdurable de una generación o promoción literaria. Como tendencia generacional, su discurso poético se encamina hacia una mayor elaboración formal, sin dejar a un lado las ganancias de la etapa del coloquialismo. En unas se nota una inclinación hacia una lírica sin concesiones a falsos patrones de definición ideológica; en otras, una búsqueda de interpretación ética del mundo; en otras, una convicción no explícita de que la cubanía no se sostiene en la palma o en la tojosa, sino en una profundidad conceptual que reevalúe la realidad desde la óptica auténtica de la poesía. En este sentido, con sus altibajos, la obra de las poetisas que empezaron a escribir en tiempos difíciles de confrontación política, mantiene una postura profesional, rigurosa, coherente, y que ya empieza a rendir sus resultados. Muchos de los nombres de poetas surgidos en esa etapa han transitado, felizmente y con una rapidez tal que superó las más aventuradas expectativas, hacia el olvido; sin embargo, casi la totalidad de los nombres de las autoras que comenzaron tesoneramente a hacerse su lugar en antologías y textos, continúan en plena vigencia, en producción y, generalmente, en ascenso. Con los años ochenta se ha notado un nuevo florecimiento del fenómeno poético en Cuba, no sólo en los más jóvenes autores que sostuvieron desde el inicio una voluntad de estilo, sino en muchos otros que, extraviados momentáneamente sus caminos, han recobrado la exigencia verbal y el interés por penetrar con profundidad la realidad.

El espacio formativo de estas poetisas, donde se amalgamaban las canciones del filin, la explosión inicial de la Nueva Trova con los Beatles; la muerte del Che y la guerra en Viet Nam; el movimiento de la llamada contracultura y los *hippies*; el arte psicodélico y las protestas de Mayo en París; el aprendizaje y la práctica del materialismo; los sucesos de Playa Girón, la Alfabetización y la confirmación de vivir en una sociedad que empezó por eliminar los sustentos básicos de los prejuicios hacia la mujer, son los épicos, resplandecientes y angustiosos años sesenta. En esos mismos años estaban naciendo las nuevas poetisas que ahora ya han comenzado a publicar. Elena Tamargo, Damaris Calderón, Odette Alonso y Wendy Guerra tienen ya libros y premios en su historial.

Larga tradición de poesía escrita por mujeres, por *poetisas*, como es y debe ser dicho, que llega hasta hoy cuando ya se ha erradicado para siempre la casi exclusiva opción de reproducir el falso esquema de "lo eterno femenino" o aceptar el punto de vista "masculino". En la afirmación individual como creadora, y también como partícipe de una transformación social poderosa, las poetisas aceptan su responsabilidad, con no pocos contratiempos, de intelectuales y de mujeres. El mundo que compartimos es uno y múltiple, en tanto la sensibilidad sigue siendo única, y en esa singularidad que se mueve dentro de la unidad toma vuelo el talento cuando es sincero.

Quisiera, pues, hacer mías unas ideas que expresa Fina García Marruz en su hermoso ensayo sobre la poesía:

> No se debiera tener una poética. En la poética personal debieran entrar todas las otras poéticas posibles. Que el sinsonte y el "divino doctor" no se recelen mutuamente. Que el arte directo no excluya el viejo preciosismo. La naturaleza crea el ala para el vuelo pero, después, la decora. El realismo verdadero debiera abarcar el sueño y el no-sueño, lo que tiene un fin y lo que no tiene ninguno, el cacharro doméstico y la Vía Láctea.[3]

En la poesía de las poetisas cubanas tiene, efectivamente, cabida un cacharro doméstico que ha recuperado su dignidad y una Vía Láctea, un universo por conquistar.

Mirta Yáñez
La Habana

Notas:

1. Antonio González Cerquera, *Florilegio de escritoras cubanas*. recopilado por González Cerquera (La Habana: La moderna poesía, 1910–1919), 3 vols.

2. Camila Henríquez Ureña, "La mujer y la cultura", (conferencia leída en la Sociedad Lyceum en el acto de propaganda por el Congreso Nacional Femenino el 9 de marzo de 1939), en *Estudios y conferencias* (La Habana: Letras Cubanas, 1982).

3. Fina García Marruz, "Hablar de la poesía", en *Hablar de la poesía* (La Habana: Letras Cubanas, 1986).

El oficio de escribir (a modo de conclusión)

En un mes de las brujas nos reunimos en la Universidad Nacional de Colombia, en Bogotá, para pensar en el oficio de escribir, la tarea mágica que a tantas mujeres ha convertido en seres prohibidos. El encuentro se había planeado desde hacía meses y varias veces habíamos pospuesto la fecha, por razones supuestamente ajenas a mi voluntad. Creo, sin embargo, que yo también era parte de las dilaciones, o por lo menos las aceptaba con alivio. Mi resistencia a hablar del oficio de escribir ha persistido con extraños disfraces y aplazamientos. Para una trabajadora exacta y sin tregua, como yo, estas huídas son transparentes: me resisto a la identidad impuesta de escritora y me resisto a mi propio discurso sobre la escritura. ¿Por qué no escribir, en lugar de hablar de lo poco (porque siempre es poco) escrito?

Es cierto, sin embargo, que esta identidad que se me adjudica no es gratuita, a pesar de que me doy cuenta de no tener una obra pública, coherente y clasificable según criterios académicos, estéticos o editoriales. Me siento un camaleón de la palabra, que cambia de color y tal vez no tiene uno propio. Pero aún así soy un animal consistente. Siempre he vivido con/de las palabras, como lectora, estudiante y profesora de idiomas y de literatura, editora, traductora, conferencista, periodista, crítica literaria, poeta. He comido de mi manejo de la lengua aunque los escritos que más me representan son los que sólo me han alimentado metafóricamente. Mi obsesión es irremediable e inútil, como la del camaleón, que sospecho se engaña a sí mismo más de lo que logra engañar al otro.

Si considero resbaladiza mi identidad de escritora, me identifico sin embargo plenamente como lectora. Lectora traidora, desde antes de ir al colegio y de saber leer, cuando me aprendía de memoria los cuentos que me leían y los repetía línea por línea, señalando las palabras con el dedo índice como si tradujera signos. Luego, esa gracia infantil se convirtió en maldición, para mí y para todos los que me rodeaban, cuando devoraba colecciones completas y las palabras ajenas eran mi refugio, mis ecos, mis referencias secretas, sin verbalizaciones compartidas. Leía sola y mi mundo se dilataba, desarticulado, lleno de esas telarañas que se apoyan en la vida y que no son la vida.

De las arrolladoras palabras ajenas creí aprender que todo está ya escrito y que solo hay que buscarlo para encontrarlo. Aún me persigue esta labor de exploración en la que me he pasado la vida. Reconstruirla es un peligroso trabajo de autoevaluación y de acribillamiento, cuando años y décadas después amigos y estudiantes me recuerdan por los libros que yo leía, que en algún momento me obsesionaron y obligué a compartir como pesadillas, y ahora desearía olvidar. Pero el pasado también está hecho de letra leída, deslizada, coyuntural, y nadie se escapa de su historia. Compartir y divulgar es también el eje de la enseñanza de la literatura, esa transmisión que los obsesivos del libro hacemos en clase, entre amigos, entre editores, en los comentarios que a veces escribimos. Queremos que otros lean lo que nos gusta, incluso tratamos de obligar a que les guste lo mismo. El placer de leer desencadena una serie de diálogos que incluye a muchas más personas, fuera de un autor y de un lector esquemáticos. Los mundos imaginarios de ambos están poblados de voces que entran en esa misma enorme y silenciosa conversación, que como un iceberg apenas muestra unos cristales. En las profundidades se producen los naufragios.

Si la lectura está en la raíz de todos los desastres, su producto es un monstruo mítico. Todas las decisiones vitales de un lector están supeditadas a su obsesión. De ahí salen periodistas, editores, profesores de lengua y literatura, coleccionistas de diccionarios, amistades con las que se puede leer y escribir pero nunca hablar, parejas hechas de libros y no de cuerpos. Cuando ese monstruo comienza a tragar y a vomitar, la lectura que comenzó como traición termina en robo: todos los excesos están permitidos, no hay ética, no hay paz. El mundo se mide por palabras y se roba tiempo, ideas, cualquier cosa, para leer y escribir.

Si ese ser maldito, traidor y ladrón, es además una mujer, el desastre es total. Para leer y escribir hay que estar en contacto con el caos y con el cosmos, pero sólo se puede plasmar en soledad, con la libertad que da el candado por dentro de la puerta. Y si hay algo negado a la mujer es su soledad y su espacio. La mujer debe ser desprendida y estar siempre disponible. Por eso no escribe, sólo habla y usa sus palabras como imán. Siempre rodeada, lo regala todo, administra y promueve las escrituras ajenas. Revisa, corrige, arma plataformas para que otros despeguen, devuelve multiplicada la imagen del que se le acerca. Su oralidad la ahoga y obliga a que los que la rodean se conviertan en esponjas. Sabe que la vida es más que el lenguaje, ese esqueleto que apenas la sostiene, pero se delata, seduce, vende y compra afectos con palabras en trans/misión. Hasta que aprende, muchas veces tarde, a ser rinoceronte y escorpión y caracol para escribir. La defensa de su mínimo espacio ante la invasión se convierte en una pelea que la agota más que la misma escritura. Tiene que explorar nuevos sistemas de vida, porque se considera que la mujer no puede ser feliz escribiendo, no puede ser feliz si está sola, ni siquiera por unas horas, y porque escribir es un acto egoísta, que no se le permite a ese ser supuestamente creado para la entrega indiscriminada. Y la desprendida no logra desprenderse. Paga con silencio su adaptación y su supervivencia.

Pero aun no hablo de mí, de lo que escribo y cómo lo escribo. Y sigo resistiéndome a hacerlo, porque no quiero reemplazar la escritura con el discurso sobre la escritura. Porque sería demasiado fácil aplicarme mi propio discurso crítico, para excusarme, inflarme o justificarme. Además, siempre repito que no hay que creerles a los escritores sino a la escritura, así que de todas formas mi opinión sería inútil. Repito también que la escritura no se hace de café, de nubes, de espuma en la ducha o de descargas eléctricas sino de escurridizas palabras, solas y planas. Y una vez combinadas y convertidas en objeto añadido al mundo, esas palabras son más inteligentes que sus presuntos autores y transmiten voces que ellos o ellas ni siquiera identifican. Así, lo que yo pueda decir sobre mi escritura nadie debe creérmelo, porque yo no puedo saber bien qué hago. Lo sospecho, lo intento, escojo conscientemente, pero lo que escribo es parte de un tejido que yo no controlo. Como cuando cocino que, en la mitad de mis decisiones y combinaciones más creativas y supuestamente autónomas, me hielan y me calientan otros gestos repetidos y recuperados. Por otra parte, lo que escribo, cuando hago poesía y prosa poética, es muy distinto de lo que hago o lo que digo. Puedo hablar por horas con fluidez y sin embargo cuando escribo salen textos de piedra y de silencio, despojados, sin concesiones, en contra de la desmesura que siempre me ha rodeado. Hago lecturas críticas y las escribo, pero a menudo decido que estoy harta de pretensiones de originalidad y primeras personas, y decido dejar el espacio a las voces de los otros. Así, con frecuencia he preferido ser lectora y transmitir, impresas, compilaciones de mis lecturas. Traduzco, porque traducir es también compartir y es la más adecuada combinación de una buena lectura y una buena escritura. Edito porque, como me sucede en la docencia, me gusta ser puente. Escribo artículos sobre literatura, porque en los últimos años he encontrado un discurso crítico contemporáneo en donde me puedo hallar con alguna comodidad, un discurso de autodelación y de apertura, que acoge mis obsesivas metáforas, que se opone a la omnipotencia y a la supuesta objetividad de la crítica de mi época de estudiante, un discurso en fin que se basa en una profunda conciencia de género (masculino/femenino) y de historia. Ahí ubico, o quisiera poder ubicar, mis trabajos sobre la revisión del canon literario o sobre la escritura de la mujer en América Latina y en Colombia.

Como le decía Milena Jesenska a Kafka, creo que dos horas de vida son muchísimo más que dos páginas escritas. Pero escribo porque lo que quiero decir no aprendí a transmitirlo con la danza, ni con el silencio, ni con el gesto, ni siquiera con el amor, y si no lo escribo lo olvidaré y sin memoria me quedaré sin vida, sin esa única vida de azar en contra del azahar, tan vulnerable, tan prescindible. Las palabras me persiguen y aunque sé que no son mías, que no hay discursos propios sino apropiados, que yo no soy la única con acceso a esas combinaciones precisas, si no las escucho me ahogan, me acorralan, me lapidan, y sólo vuelvo a reconocer mi cuerpo si logro despojarme de mis palabras y de mis pieles viejas y, desollada, vuelvo a empezar.

Creo, también, que para mí escribir es una batalla contra la injusticia y contra el caos, contra los silencios impuestos, contra las continuas agresiones que recibimos las mujeres, aunque yo casi pertenezca (me suena irónico después de mi errática escritura de toda la vida) al grupo de las privilegiadas. A veces me han dicho que hay tortura en lo que escribo. En verdad, no podría escribir desde las rosas, los jazmines, las auroras y el amor, aunque los conozca, si he vivido entre el dolor y la violencia. Por otra parte, no creo mucho en una escritura sólo de paz y celebración, sin tensiones ni contradicciones. Escribir no es fácil, porque para llegar hasta la página hay que vencer nuevas barreras cada día, porque es un oficio que se practica sin fin, una carrera sin meta. No es una actividad natural, a la que el cuerpo se entregue como al agua, al sol, al sueño, a la comida, o al amor. Es una decisión, a veces demencial. Un tiempo sin reloj, papeleras que se llenan, letras que bailan, libros que caminan, caras alucinadas. Escribir no es libertad, porque la persona que escribe vive torturada en un espacio de espejos y de aristas, entre lo ya escrito, lo que escribe, lo que quiere escribir, lo que nunca escribirá. No es permanencia, porque su escritura es ajena y no le evitará los desgarros de sus muertes. Es una extraña forma de vivir, una mediación despellejada, que reemplaza mucha vida pero no la oculta ni la ignora.

Y sin embargo, la persona que quiere escribir y no lo hace, vive y muere condenada. Por eso, hablar de la escritura y del oficio de escribir es suicida. Los que hoy queremos seguir viviendo con palabras, debemos ahora, ya, callarnos e irnos a nuestro posible o imposible rincón y escribir, escribir para poder morir en paz.

Montserrat Ordóñez
Universidad de los Andes